Thanks for your help. Elm

Turkish Cypriots who came to England
between 1934 and 1963: 36 interviews

Publisher:	Turkish Cypriot Community Association
Funders:	Heritage Lottery Fund & Turkish Cypriot Community Association
Editor:	Hatice Abdullah
Sub Editor:	Mark Sinker
Interviewees:	Emine Ahmed, Emine Ahmet, Fezile Ahmet, Ibrahim Ahmet, Sadiye Bayram, Kemal Davrandı, Hatice Fetti, Dudu Hakkı, Ali Hassan, Celal Hassan, Hatice Ibrahim, Hulus Ibrahim, Hatice Ismaıl, Nevcivan Jevan, Gülsen Larkins, Şaban Hüseyin Lefkaridi, Hulusi Mahmud Gürçayoğlu, Emine Mehmet, Gökmen Mehmet, Seyit Mehmet, Ibrahim Mustafa (Bili), Hüseyin Hassan Memour, Niazi Osman, Meryem Sherefettin, Mustafa Hüseyin (Shishman), Osman Tahir, Hüseyin Yusuf (Şufdas) (interviewed by Hatice Abdullah)
	Mehmet Ali Bekir, Ibrahim Derviş, Çetin Kaya Mustafa, Süha Faiz, Melek Kazım, Mehmet Mustafa, Reşat (Richard) Niazi, Mehmet Şeref Ali (interviewed by Hatice Abdullah & Yaşar Ismailoğlu)
	Ali Gasbar (interviewed by Yashar Ismailoğlu)
Transcriptions:	Sonay Ozen
Translations:	Hatice Abdullah & Sonay Ozen
Volunteers:	Dr Ayşe Abdullah & Şeniz Mehmet
Designer:	Adrian Ward at Signwave
Cover:	Royal Geographic Society, used with permission
Printer:	Nice and Easy
Distributor:	Turkish Cypriot Community Association
ISBN:	978-0-9552362-1-1 0-9552362-1-5 First published Feburary 2006. Reprinted April 2006.

Departures and Arrivals has been produced as part of the Turkish Cypriot Heritage Project.

Project Managers:	Tahsin Ibrahim & Erim Metto
Acknowledgements:	Bayram Abdullah, Saraç Cankaya, Hulya Cıncık, Geoff Cox, Niyazi Enver, Olivia Gooden, Turkay Hadji-Filippou, Nevci Hassan, Sophie Lewis, Mehmet and Sensal Mehmet, Rahme Mehmet, Kemal Nami, Mehtap Riaz, Dr Victoria de Rijke, Abdulli, Halil, Osman and Rifat Reyman.

628 – 630 Green Lanes,
Haringey,
London,
N8 0SD.

tel. 020 8826 1080

http://www.tcca.org/
info@tcca.org

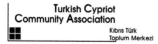

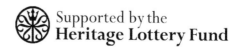

CONTENTS

i. FOREWORD

Turkay Hadji-Filippou
Chairperson, Turkish Cypriot Community Association

Turkish Cypriot Community Association (TCCA) was established in 1976 to serve the Turkish Cypriot community with the provision of information and advice, social care, counselling, social and cultural activities through the needs led projects.

In 1983, Turkish Cypriot Community Association gave the Turkish Cypriot community a voice through publishing the first London based Turkish newspaper *'Toplum Postasi'*, which has developed to become one of the popular community newspaper for the Turkish households in the United Kingdom and Cyprus.

In 1995, Turkish Cypriot Homecare project was developed with the aim to support and enable Turkish Cypriot elderly and disabled to live in their home independently and to prevent them from being admitted into an institution for long term care. The project currently works in collaboration with nine local authorities' social services departments and provides culturally sensitive care services to our elderly and disabled.

Due to the growth and high demand to our services Turkish Cypriot Community Association successfully tendered for and acquired its second premises on Green Lanes, Haringey, which was another major success in the organisation's history. A strong Management Committee, over eighty members of staff and several volunteers from the community implement the organisation's aims and objectives to further develop it to reach to a wider community.

Through monitoring, evaluation and feedback from our members TCCA recognised the need to collect and record the history of Turkish Cypriots in the United Kingdom. The aim was to initiate and develop a project that gave these pioneers an opportunity to voice their experiences and thoughts during their early years in the UK. Not only would this inform and educate others about their social history, it would also allow their stories to live on. In 2003, a fund application was submitted to the Heritage Lottery Fund, which was successful and the work officially began in October 2004. The project consists of 'Departures and Arrivals', a documentary film called 'I Used to Live in Cyprus', a touring exhibition called 'By Invitation Only' and a website www.turkishcypriotheritage.org.

ii. INTRODUCTION

Dr Isfendiyar Tüncer

When I came from Cyprus in September 1953, by Italian Boat to Napoli and from there by train to Calais and by boat to Dover, I had arrived in London to stay for good, and was struck with great disappointment. I was astonished when I saw the cracked tea glasses at Victoria Station. I was embarrassed. As a result of the war, London at the time was in ruins; streets and buildings were in desperate need of repair.

There were hardly any foreigners in the streets of London. The very few Turks here were residing in Islington, and Greek Cypriots were residing in Camden Town. When the Turkish Cypriot population started to increase here in London, they (the Turks) started to spread towards Peckham and Stoke Newington. Every 15 days migrants would arrive from Cyprus. Coming here to London was by invitations sent to those in Cyprus by family, friends or acquaintances in England.

Many of the Turks that came to England came to look for employment as a way to improve their lives. The businessman Irfan Nadir* came in the beginning of 1959-60, saw the future and opened a clothing factory in the East End of London (Wearwell, later Polly Peck). A large group of Turks started to work there. A majority of our community would work in clothing factories for £3 or £4 per week, and at weekends the men would meet in a café in Islington, such as the one run by Halil Basri from Sinde. They would socialise in the cafés, as well as hear and exchange news about Cyprus and fellow countrymen. There wasn't many televisions in the homes of Turks, and news about Cyprus would come through the radio or from those arriving from Cyprus. The English papers would carry the news, as Cyprus was a British Colony.

Unlike the present there wasn't a lot of [Turkish] food in the markets. Cucumbers could be seen in some shop windows. There weren't any Turkish grocery shops. In the early 50s the Greeks had opened grocery shops and cafés in Camden Town, and later in Finsbury Park. Many of our Turks would go to the Greek grocery shops to buy foods imported from Cyprus, such as hellim and olives.

Those [Turks] who had heard that I had come here as a doctor and that I worked in Kings College and Dulwich Hospital would come to explain their problems or

---

* Prominent Turkish Cypriot businessman during the 50s. Ran factories in the East End of London. Father of Asil Nadir, who was founder of Polly Peck.

to get a second opinion, would come [to the hospital] at all hours of the day and night.

Days, months and years passed, and the Turkish population increased and spread towards Haringey, Dalston and Wood Green, and we – a small society of Turks – gradually became, within 50 years of arriving in England, a large strength in British society.

iii. CHRONOLOGY: A SHORT HISTORY OF CYPRUS

Yashar Ismailoğlu

This chronology provides background information to political and economic matters in Cyprus before and after the period covered by the book (1934 – 64). Its purpose is to give an idea of some of the pressures and insecurities for those who chose to leave Cyprus and move to the UK during this time.

For further information on people mentioned, see Key to Major Political Figures on page 237, and for explanations of acronyms and organisations, see the Glossary on page 243.

Cyprus under the British Colonial Administration (1878 – 1960)

A: British Rule until World War Two

1878   Cyprus Convention with Ottoman Empire assigns Cyprus to British occupation and administration.

1881   British Colonial Government establishes two separate boards of Education for each respective community.

1882   British Administration prepares First Cyprus constitution, establishing a Legislative Council consisting of Greeks and Turks, whose decisions the British Governor can override by decree.

1914   Formal British annexation at outset of World War One, in which Ottomans sides with Germany. (British have de facto Sovereignty over Cyprus.)

1915   Britain offers Cyprus to Greece; Greece turns offer down.

1922   Newly established Republic of Turkey under Mustafa Kemal Ataturk defeats Greece after brutal two-year war; enormous population exchange between Greece and Turkey.

1923   Treaty of Lausanne: British annexation of Cyprus recognised by newly established Republic of Turkey; all Turkish claims to the island renounced. Nevertheless, a Turkish Cypriot delegation to Ankara presses for return of island to Turkey.

1925   Cyprus becomes Crown Colony and is administered under a Governor and not a High Commissioner.

1930   Primary education put under direct British control; growth of Greek identity (and later Turkish) begins a split between economic and cultural elites.

1931   Greek Cypriots riots against British with the pledge for Enosis; British Governor suspends Constitution. Legislative Council abolishes Consultive Council appointed by British.

1941   AKEL (Anorthotikon Komma Ergazomenou Laou -Progressive Party of the Working People) formed and claims to be the successor of CCP (Cypriot Communist Party), forced underground in 1931.

1942   KATAK (Kıbrıs Adası Türk Azınlığı Kurumu – Association of the Turkish Minority of the Island of Cyprus) formed.

1943   First Turkish Cypriot trade union formed (prior to this most Turkish and Greek workers were united under PEON: Pankyprios Enotike Omospondia Neoleas – Pancyprian Federation of Labour. Many Turkish and Greek Cypriots fight as British soldiers in North Africa, Italy and Greece: some veterans settle in the UK after the war.

B: The post-War years

1948   Proposals for self-government, excluding self-determination, are rejected by Greek Cypriots. Turkish Cypriots form special committee in response to rising Greek Cypriot demand for Enosis.

1949   First Turkish Cypriot public protest against Enosis in Nicosia; two Turkish Cypriot groups unite, becoming the Turkish National Party. AKEL switches from supporting self-government to support for Enosis.

1950   Makarios III becomes Archbishop and organises a petition for Enosis in churches, signed by an overwhelming majority of the Greek Cypriot population.

1952   Makarios blocks General Grivas's plans for an armed campaign, asks Greece to make UN effort. Turkey and Greece enter NATO.

1954   British move Middle East Forces' joint HQ from Suez to Cyprus; Hopkinson makes "never" statement with regard to self-determination. In July, attempt made to put Cyprus question before the UN, defeated by Anglo-Turkish co-operation. In August, Turkish Cypriots hold mass meeting in Nicosia, formation of 'Cyprus is Turkish Committee' in Ankara, encouraged by PM Menderes.

C: The Struggle against the British

1955   EOKA (National Organisation of Cypriot Fighters) is established in April. Armed violence against British begun by General Grivas and EOKA, which is retaliated. Turkish Cypriot leader Dr Küçük renames National Union Party the 'Cyprus is Turkish' Party. London Conference: Britain invites Greece and Turkey to discuss problems, including Cyprus. Conference ends without agreement.

1956   Negotiations for self-government. Makarios is deported from island. Violence and repression intensify. EOKA targets police. Greek Cypriots and British murdered. Greek Cypriots in police replaced by Turkish

Cypriots; Turkish Cypriots become casualties of EOKA terrorism. Radcliff Plan for self-governance rejected; first official reference to partition.

1957   Bombing kills one Turkish Cypriot, wounding three; Turkish Cypriots retaliate with riots in Nicosia against British forces; seven Turkish Cypriots killed. Trade unions joint appeal for calm. EOKA ceasefire; release of Makarios to Athens. Turkish Cypriot demand for 'taksim' ('partition') between Turkish and Greek sectors; rise of TMT (Türk Mukavemet Teşilatı – Turkish Resistance Organisation). Demand for Turkish army base. New Governor Sir Hugh Foot's pursues new policy of conciliation. In April 1957, in new conditions created by Suez problem, British government accept that 'bases in Cyprus' are acceptable alternative to 'Cyprus as a base', producing relaxed British policy to Cyprus problem. Problem from now on to be solved in conjunction with Greece and Turkey, the latter thoroughly alerted to dangers to Turkish Community of Enosis. Violence renewed in Cyprus by EOKA, which increasingly draws in the Turkish Community when new Governor Foot's plan (for unitary self government) incites Turkish Cypriot riots and a hostile response from the Turkish government. Violence between the Greek and Turkish communities develops into new and deadly forms.

1958   Plan for Cyprus's self-government is postponed, rejected by Turkey owing to sovereignty issue. Turkish Cypriots riot for partition. EOKA end of year-long ceasefire. Turkish Cypriot PIO office bombed, EOKA blamed (it will later be established that Turkish Cypriot extremists are responsible). Macmillan plan involving Greece and Turkey; some implementation begun. EOKA targets and burns Turkish Cypriot villages. Inter-communal ceasefire. Makarios announces he will agree to guaranteed independence.

1959   Greek and Turkish foreign ministers meet in Zurich to draft treaties for independence of Cyprus. Greek Foreign Minister Averoff and Turkish Foreign Minister Zorlu draft basic articles of constitution. Cypriot Greek Leader Makarios and Cypriot Turkish Leader Küçük brought to London to sign without alteration. Treaties provide for guarantee of limited independence, British bases, with Greek and Turkish troops stationed on the island. Makarios and Küçük elected President and Vice-President. Grivas retires to Athens. With some exceptions, Cypriots disarm.

The First Years of the Republic (1960 – 63)

The Zurich Agreement (1959) between Turkey and Greece produced a bi-communal constitutional framework for Cyprus, which recognised the equality of the two 'communities' in many important matters, and a large degree of political and cultural separateness. The President of the Republic would be a Greek, while the Vice-president would be a Turkish Cypriot.

1960   Cyprus – an independent republic – is established 15 August, Makarios president. Initial efforts at governing under new constitution.

1961   Disputes over certain basic articles: separate municipalities, public service and Cypriot army ratio, taxes. Turkish Cyprus vetos tax law and becomes member of Council of Europe.

1962   Failure to agree on separate municipalities; continuing gridlock and terrorism. In April, Turkish Cypriot extremist murders two Turkish Cypriot journalists, Hikmet and Gurkhan, who have advocated intercommunal cooperation. Assassins never found.

1963   Constitutional crisis after court rulings: taxes imposed but cannot be collected; ruling against both sides on municipalities issue. Akritas Plan formed. Makarios submits 13 points for constitutional reform to Küçük to revise the constitution; rejected by Turkey.

Constitutional Breakdown and Intercommunal Conflict (1963 – 67)

A Key period in Cyprus History, with thousands of displaced Turkish Cypriots, most of whom migrate to the UK.

1963   21 December: inter-communal violence explodes. Casualties in first ten days: Turkish Cypriots 136, Greek Cypriots 30. Truce force set up with British troops, Greek and Turkish liaison officers. Ceasefire after Turkish jets buzz Nicosia.

1964   January: London Conference. British/US efforts to create NATO force. Makarios announces abrogation of treaties, then backs away; Turkish Cypriots want partition. Turkish Community Leader Rauf Denktaş is summoned to Ankara, his return to Cyprus barred by Greeks until 1968. NATO plan rejected by Makarios.

February: brutal attacks on Turkish Cypriot civilians in Limassol.

March: UNFICYP established; British troops on island seconded to UN force. National Guard put under command of Greek army general. Some 20,000 Turkish Cypriots flee areas where violence occurs, taking refuge in enclaves; some Turkish villages looted and destroyed.

June: Turkish invasion threatened. Grivas returns to command Greek army contingent; expansion of control to National Guard leads Greek commander to resign. US President Johnson's letter to Inonu of Turkey deters invasion; Acheson Plan for 'double Enosis' proposed and rejected.

August: arms and men imported by both sides. Greek Cypriot attack on and capture of Turkish Cypriot villages in the Tylliria area (Northwest Cyprus) in effort to control coastline, leads to Turkish bombing of Greek Cypriot villages. Ceasefire arranged.

1965   UN mediator Galo Plaza issues controversial report, which is withdrawn.

1966   Talks begin between Turkey and Greece to resolve Cyprus Problem.

1967   Coup d'etat (military coup) in Greece 21 April and extremist colonels obtain power. As a result, General Grivas reinstates power, leads National Guard and attacks Turkish Cypriot villages of Kophinou and Boğaziçi. Turkish ultimatum leads to withdrawal of Greek Troops and Grivas from Cyprus by Junta. Turkish Cypriots also announce 'Provisional Cyprus Administration'.

1971   Grivas infiltrates to Cyprus secretly to establish EOKA-B with pledge for Enosis.

1972   Cyprus–EEC Assoctiation Agreement is signed.

1974   Denktaş's questionable election to Vice Presidency of Republic of Cyprus. Makarios demands withdrawal of Greek Officers. Coup d'etat against Makarios as President of Republic of Cyprus on 15 July and Nicos Samson is declared as president.

17 July: Ecevit as Turkey's prime minister flies to London (Britain also Guarantor) to evaluate crisis in Cyprus.

20 July: Turkey's intervention begins in Cyprus.

23 July: Clafkos Clerides temporarily assumes the duties of the President of the Republic. Failure of Peace talks between Guarantor Powers (Greece, Turkey and Britain) resulting in a second phase Turkish Military invasion on 14 August 1974. 37% of Republic of Cyprus is occupied by Turkey.

22 August: Turkish Cypriots unilaterally declare 'Autonomous Turkish Cypriot Administration'.

iv. THE INTERVIEWEES

Some interviewees when asked their place of origin gave the Turkish or Greek name of the village as it was known or referred to when they lived there, while others gave the name given by the Turkish Cypriot Government after 1974.

Village names are given first in Turkish, English, Greek, then the 'new' Turkish names which were assigned starting in 1959, and increasingly so after 1974.

The first Turkish village name is the 'old' Turkish name for the village or the Turkish spelling of the Greek name, as told to us by the interviewees.

English village names have been taken from Survey of Cyprus Motor Map, eighth edition, prepared originally in the Drawing Office of the Dept. of Lands and Surveys, Cyprus, 1932. Eighth edition redrawn 1965.

Greek village names have been taken from A Visitor's Map of Cyprus compiled and drawn by the Dept. of Lands and Surveys, Kypros (Cyprus), first edition 1986, revised 2004.

'New' Turkish names have been taken from A Bilingual Map of Cyprus, drawn by Assoc. Prof Dr Ata Atun for the Samtay Foundation. October 2004, Nicosia.

EMINE AHMED
Born: 01/12/1939
From: Sinde/Sinda/Sinta/Inönü
Arrived: 1961
Interviewed in: Turkish

EMINE AHMET
Born: 10/11/1938
From: Çatos/Chatos/Kiados/Serdalı
Arrived: 1959
Interviewed in: Turkish

FEZILE AHMET
Born: 21/07/1932
Form: Sinde/Sinda/Sinta/Inönü
Arrived: 1962
Interviewed in: Turkish

IBRAHIM AHMET
Born: 25/11/1930
From: Çatos/Chatos/Kiados/Serdalı
Arrived: 1955
Interviewed in: Turkish

MEHMET ŞEREF ALI
Born: 09/08/1931
From: Lefkoşa/Nicosia/Lefkosia/Lefkoşa
Arrived: 1953
Interviewed in: Turkish

MEHMET ALI BEKIR
Born: 25/03/1940
From: Pirga/Pyrga/Pyrga/Çamlıbey
Arrived: 1960
Interviewed in: Turkish

SADIYE BAYRAM
From: Paramalı/Paramali/Paramali/Çayönü
Arrived: 1956
Interviewed in: Turkish

KEMAL AHMET DAVRANDI
Born: 26/08/1939
From: Kazafana/Kazaphani/Kazafani/Ozanköy
Arrived: 1959
Interviewed in: Turkish

IBRAHIM DERVIŞ
Born: 01/11/1926
From: Vadilli,Lefkosa/Vatili,Nicosia/Vatili, Lefkosia/Vadilli, Lefkosa
Arrived: 1948
Interviewed in: Turkish

SÜHA AND LALAGE FAIZ
Born: 28/12/1926
From: Lefkoşa/Nicosia/Lefkosia/Lefkoşa
Arrived: 1934
Interviewed in: English

HATICE FETTI
Born: 13/12/1930
From: Iskele/Scala/Skala/not indicated on map
Arrived: 1957
Interviewed in: Turkish

ALI GASBAR
Born: 31/10/1939
From: Larnaka/Larnaca/Larnaka/Larnaka
Arrived: 1956
Interviewed in: Turkish

HÜLUSI MAHMUD GÜRÇAYOĞLU
Born: 29/09/1936
From: Dohni/Tokhni/Tochni/Eski Taşkent
Arrived: 1958
Interviewed in: English

DUDU HAKKI
Born: 17/01/1937
From: Lefkara/Lefkara/Lefkara/Lefkara
Arrived: 1960
Interviewed in: Turkish

ALI HASSAN
Born: 01/08/1935
From: Sandallar/not indicated on map/Santalaris/Şehitler
Arrived: 1957
Interviewed in: Turkish

CELAL HASSAN
Born: 01/01/1935
From: Kuruova/Korovia/Koroveia/Kuruova
Arrived: 1955
Interviewed in: English

MUSTAFA HÜSEYIN (SHISHMAN)
Born: April 1934
From: Kaleburnu/Galinoporni/Galinoporni/Kaleburnu
Arrived: 1953
Interviewed in: Turkish

HATICE IBRAHIM
Born: 28/01/1935
From: Mumandali/not indicated on map/Mamountali/Soğucak
Arrived: 1955
Interviewed in: Turkish

HULUS IBRAHIM
Born: 12/04/1931
From: Polemitya/Polemidhia/Polemedia/Binaltı
Arrived: 1958
Interviewed in: English

HATICE ISMAIL
Born: 13/05/1937
From: Köfünye/Kophinou/Kofinou/Geçitkale
Arrived: 1957
Interviewed in: Turkish

NEVCIVAN JEVAN
Born: 31/05/1935
From: Larnaka/Larnaca/Larnaka/Larnaka
Arrived: 1952
Interviewed in: Turkish

MELEK KAZIM
Born: 01/05/1944
From: Larnaka/Larnaca/Larnaka/Larnaka
Arrived: 1953
Interviewed in: Turkish

GÜLSEN LARKINS
Born: 19/09/1937
From: Luricina/Louroudjina/Louroukina/Akıncılar
Arrived: 1959
Interviewed in: English/Turkish

ŞABAN HÜSEYIN LEFKARIDI
Born: 16/03/1924
From: Anafodiya/Anaphotia/Anafotia/Akkor
Arrived: 1955
Interviewed in: Turkish

EMINE MEHMET
From: Anafodiya/Anaphotia/Anafotia/Akkor
Arrived: 1952
Interviewed in: Turkish

GÖKMEN MEHMET
Born: 10/12/1936
From: Lefkoşa/Nicosia/Lefkosia/Lefkoşa
Arrived: 1954
Interviewed in: English

SEYIT MEHMET
Born: 04/12/1923
From: Larnaka/Larnaca/Larnaka/Larnaka
Arrived: 1949
Interviewed in: English

HÜSEYIN HASSAN MEMOUR
Born: 06/02/1929
From: Luricina/Louroudjina/Louroukina/Akıncılar
Arrived: 1958
Interviewed in: English

ÇETIN KAYA MUSTAFA
Born: 18/04/1944
From: Leymosun/Limassol/Lemesos/Limassol
Arrived: 1959
Interviewed in: Turkish

IBRAHIM MUSTAFA (BILI)
Born: 17/02/1943
From: Luricina/Louroudjina/Louroukina/Akıncılar
Arrived: 1961
Interviewed in: English

MEHMET MUSTAFA
From: Leymosun/Limassol/Lemesos/Limasol
Arrived: 1960
Interviewed in: Turkish

REŞAT (RICHARD) NIAZI
Born: 02/12/1940
From: Sarama, Baf/Sarama, Paphos/Sarama, Pafos/Kuşluca, Baf
Arrived: 1958
Interviewed in: English/Turkish

NIAZI OSMAN
Born: 25/05/1920
From: Aytotoro/Ayios Theodhores/Ayios Theodhores/Boğaziçi
Arrived: 1962
Interviewed in: Turkish

MERYEM SHEREFETTIN
Born: 28/02/1932
From: Arsoş/Arsos/Arsos/Yiğitler
Arrived: 1955
Interviewed in: English

OSMAN TAHIR
Born: 12/11/1915
From: Aytotoro/Ayios Theodhores/Ayios Theodhores/Boğaziçi
Arrived: 1960
Interviewed in: Turkish

HÜSEYIN YUSUF (ŞUFDAS)
Born: 06/10/1931
From: Aytotoro/Ayios Theodhores/Ayios Theodhores/Boğaziçi
Arrived: 1949
Interviewed in: Turkish/English

DR ISFENDIYAR TÜNCER (INTRODUCTION)
From: Magosa
Arrived: 1953
Interviewed in: Turkish

1. CYPRUS

MELEK KAZIM: My name is Melek Kazim. I came to England when I was nine years old. I didn't come from a village, I came from a town. From Larnaka. I remember everything, when I think back to before I was nine years old in Larnaka. We use to live in Princess Zehra Street. I even remember that there was a dentist factory opposite. The dentist factory made false teeth.

We went to the sea every day because my grandmother's house was very near the beach. All the children in the neighbourhood would get together and go to the beach every day. At that time I could swim. All the children could swim. We used to go in our swimming costumes. At that time the English were there too.

The English would come and take photos of us. I mean, the children. Yes, I remember all of this. There were some more photos. My life there going to the sea was very beautiful.

Melek Kazim, her mother and brothers, at the latters' Circumcision, Cyprus 1952/53

HULUSI MAHMUD GÜRÇAYOĞLU: My name is Hulusi Mahmud Gürcayoğlu. That is the surname they gave [in Cyprus]. I came from Dohni [now Eski Taşkent]. I was single before I came here. I was a farmer, a shepherd. I left Cyprus because I got so fed up outside behind the sheep doing farming. I was a shepherd, you know. The flock belonged to my family.

That's what I was doing most of the time. Just before I come over I was 20, 21, 22 I was when I come over. I came here in 1958 in April. I had family in Cyprus. Ye, I had a brother as well, my sister was still there. They came here after me. My oldest brother was here already. I had two brothers here.

REŞAT NIAZI: My name is Reşat Niazi. In those days we had English passports, because when I left Cyprus, it was still a British colony. So they wrote the names in English – which is why it is 'N, I, A, Z, I'. 'Reşat' is also spelled differently, but I'm better known as 'Richard'.

I was born 2 December 1940. Actually it's 1942 on my passport. I was born in Paphos, in a village called Sarama. My family moved to Nicosia when I was young. When we moved I was seven.

My father was a British Soldier in World War Two. He went Italy and France, then up to Germany. He was on the Italian front. He was wounded, and when he returned [to Cyprus] he died of his wounds.

KEMAL AHMET DAVRANDI: My name is Kemal Davrandi. I was born 26 August 1939. I used to live in Kazavana in Cyprus. I was unmarried there. My occupation there, beginning in my childhood I went to work with a mechanic for two years. I gave up later.

After that I fell in love with a girl. I loved but was unloved. I sent my mum. She said she had asked for the girl's hand in marriage. It had been given, my mum said. That's what she came and told me. "In any case," I said, "at the end of the day the girl is mine." A neighbour heard about this and went and told the girl's parents. Apparently my mum had not gone to ask for the girl's hand in marriage. I left and went to the seashore, the seashore below our village. I was a waiter for two years at the seashore.

ŞABAN LEFKARIDI: My name is Şaban Hüseyin Lefkaridi. My date of birth, if you look at the truth, wasn't recorded inside – but I use the date that I went into the army with. My age is shown as being 16 March 1924. This is the date that was given for the army. According to *muhtar* of the village, when we went to see him last year, I should be 76. I told him that I was 79 and he said, "Are you trying to make me out as mad? I am 78 and you are at least three years younger than me!" So I should be 75 or 76 years old. I lived in the village, in Anafodiya.

I was married before I came here. We had a one-and-a-half-year-old child. I was married in 1953.

We had a garden over there. We had olive trees, vineyard, that is to say we never worked as a labourer, we had our own business. That was my work. I provided for myself, my mum, my father died when I was little. My brother Mehmet was in Cyprus, who was older than I was.

That year we suffered a lot of loss. We used to cover our vineyards, and our grapes used to go to the market last. That year it became frost-bitten, and shrivelled our grapes totally. The grapes went black and fell underneath. And then after, let's say our garden was sown, shared with my father-in-law, the river came, drowned all of it. The English used to take the rest of it and they used to take it to the army in Egypt. That year they didn't take any, all of them stayed in the field. They weren't sold either. I said, "I should go to London for a couple of years and come back." According to my calculation, I came for three years. I hadn't sold none of my things, I left my houses, my furniture.

HÜSEYIN YUSUF: I am Hüseyin Yusuf Şufdas. There are lots of Hüseyin Yusuf. Hüseyin Şufdas is like a *lakab* [nickname]. Then they know who you are talking about. I lived in Aytotoro, Boğaziçi, whatever you call it, before I came to England.

Hüseyin Yusuf' family, Aytotoro, Cyprus 1950

EMINE AHMED: I came from a village. Its previous name is Sinder. Now it's called Inonu. Magosa district. I was single before I came here. We used to do my father's job. My father used to do farming and we used to help him as well. He used to sow barley, wheat; we had a garden.

HATICE ISMAIL: I lived in Köfünye. I was single before I came here. I used to go to the *Usta*.

ALI GASBAR: I came in June 1956 on a Sunday. I am from the town of Larnaca. I was a policeman in Cyprus. I unavoidably had to desert Cyprus after a situation during the course of duty. Four friends and myself were left forced to escape to England. Along with this reason, finding myself in the Turkish and Greek events, I was forced to come to England.

Since the age of 17 I was a English Policeman (CSC). My father was an English soldier, he was on duty in Germany, Belgium, Egypt and Holland. In 1950 after the army he had been on shift duty in Famagusta Customs. My mother was a housewife. I had three uncles [brothers of his dad] and they were English soldiers.

ALI HASSAN: I was born in Sandal. After finishing primary school, I started tailoring. To learn, of course. I was going in the village, we used go to Perestorun, in the end I came to Famagusta. I learnt tailoring in Famagusta, in fact, I did tailoring for a period of time. I was a policeman for a period of time.

I got married in Cyprus and had a three-month old baby before we came here to London. I got married in 1956

There was no studying to become a policeman at that time – the English government just took us on. The English government in 1956.

Obviously we filled out forms, they recruited us because they needed us. They made us practice inside a few times about how and what we were going to do. After that we started. I was with a gun. I wasn't working in the village, I was working in Famagusta

HATICE IBRAHIM: I am from the Baf side of Cyprus, Mamundali. I came here in the month of March 1955. I was not married before I came here, and I was not working. My life is a little complicated.

From the age of nine till 15, I lived very nicely with a Turkish family, Doctor Adnan. After that, at 15, I started to become shy. I was in Nicosia and I didn't want to go to Baf to my mother. In that period I was unable to go to Baf, as my brother did not allow it. There was a family in a Greek neighbourhood. They took me in as foster parents, because my brother had gone to Adana in Turkey to find my mum's brother. And he handed me over to them, until he found my uncle, and then come back and get me.

My brother found my *Dayı* [her mother's brother] and sent for me. I went to Adana. I was there for three years. I would cry everyday. And of course my mum in Cyprus didn't know. As soon as I was 19, I returned to Cyprus [from Adana]. I wasn't even 19 yet. I returned to Cyprus and three months later they married me to Emine Hanım's brother. We came back from Adana and three months later they married me off. I was married in 1955. I was married towards the end of March. Right in April.

CELAL HASSAN: My mum is from Andronikos, which is called Yeşil Köy now. My dad was from Kuruova, same village. I was born in Kurova. I was single in Cyprus. I was a taxi driver in Cyprus. I used to look after the tourists, take them around, feed them. In the evening I'd come home, when the time to come to meet them, we used to meet them, with my mother.

MEHMET MUSTAFA: I'm from Limassol. My mum's side is Mehmet Rusti, Softa. Mehmet Rustu. My father's side is Durmuşlar. A quarter of Limassol belongs to Softa. He used to have 21 houses and they are still there.

MERYEM SHEREFETTIN: I lived in Arsos in Cyprus before I came here. I was married in 1949. I get engaged, married, you know – it's registry.

MEHMET ŞEREF ALI: I'm from Yeni Cami Mahallesi, from Nicosia. At the age of seven, there was Yeni Cami nursery, I used to go there. I went there for six years. From there to Haydarpaşa, I studied there for two years in Haydarpaşa. The schools were under the control of the English.

I was about 18 years old when I started work. I was working as a carpenter when I was about 18. They used to call it Larda [the place he worked] at that time. I started carpentry there.

NIAZI OSMAN: My present address is Enfield. I am actually from Yeni Boğaziçi in Cyprus. But due to some reasons after the 50s, I started living in Magosa. I was married then, in 1953. I was a chauffeur in Magosa at that time. In 1955, when I was in Magosa, I was working as a taxi driver. And new lawyers came from London. Three people originally from Pladaisyon, its present name is Balalan. Osman the lawyer, Çifcioğlu and Orhan Zihni. They were looking for a new office. I had a telephone at home as a taxi driver; as I had a phone at home, I could be called. And I met with Osman, lawyer Osman. He said to me, "Why don't you bring that phone here so we can open an office? You would be my lawyer clerk." I didn't know anything about that. But I knew Turkish, English and Greek almost intermediate level. We agreed, he opened the office. I went to him; to become a lawyer's clerk you need to have a licence. The head judge of Gazi was then Vasililiou, from the Greeks. He used to do the interviews. He did mine in Greek. I passed, obtained the licence, started with Osman. Villagers started coming. Of course Turks started coming to the new lawyer; I did my best there.

They came [the three lawyers] as Barristers of Law. It was like that then, and the villagers would come there. I used to deal with deed issues, passport issues, sometimes other contracts and so on. But mostly it was passport issues. Then it was the English period. We used to obtain English passports easily. When someone would send us an invitation from England we used to give it and the passport, and we used to come easily. I sent them and we used issued passports but we needed a ticket as well. To get tickets, well. I was obliged to buy the tickets, but the Turks didn't have an agency. From the Greeks there was Amathsus, a big office. As I knew Greek I went, they accepted me, we agreed. With a small commission. Then tickets were 32 lira, I can remember still that today, 32 liras from Cyprus right up to Victoria Station.

2. JOURNEY - REASONS

IBRAHIM DERVIŞ: After the War there was a collapse in the job market, and unemployment – because the work for the army ended. The War finished, and Churchill had said, "Be very cautious with your money – that is to say you will suffer poverty, financial straits, and so on...." We used to hear Churchill's speeches on the radio. Those who came out of the army were unemployed – and over there they had priority. In the midst of this, we – my uncle and I – decided to migrate to England, because it was really tight living altogether in our house.

We made an agreement. My brother *rahmetlik* Ali Tahsin, said, "You stay near the family and I'll go and try, and see if I can be successful. If I am unsuccessful I will return," he said.

We used to get ideas about coming to England to work. As you know, we had to be come by invitation. Someone from here had to be your guarantor, and invite you over. They even had to write a few words about you and you had to speak a little English. I was interested in English. I used to read *Reader 1, Reader 2* and so on. I studied a little and this really was a benefit. There was the *Story of Titanya*. I memorised them.

NEVCIVAN JEVAN: *Vallahi*, at that time it was the fashion to come here. Everyone used to come to London to earn money. I last stayed in Larnaka. We had relatives here. Later on my uncle was about to come, I came with him and my brother. We stayed at their house. After that my uncle had a friend, he was here as well. Later on we met and got married. I came by boat. It was Italian. *Adriyatik*, something like that. It cost about 30 lira. Well. As a matter of fact it was around 1952 when we came. So I don't know how much it cost exactly because I forgot it. It is not today's story. My parents paid. I think, if I am not wrong, it took 13 days. I did vomit on the boat. I was sick. You know. I regretted after I came here, I kept crying for two years. I didn't like it here.

IBRAHIM AHMET: Before I came here I was living in Serdalı. Before I came here I had a job in Cyprus. I used to produce Turkish Delight. There is no capital. As I didn't have the capital to expand the job, I came to England to save money. We used to hear from this and that the money was a lot here. We tried this and we tried that to expand but it was no good. We were left with Turkish Delight, which was not enough. So we decided to come here. My brother came earlier than me. He was married here for 11 months. We sent him over and he came here. From there [Cyprus] you can't come here. My brother smuggled. When you arrived here they didn't ask you why you came whereas you couldn't leave Cyprus saying that you were coming to England. There was an agent called Behzat in Cyprus. They used to board you onto cargo ships. Both the captain and the agent would be bribed. After visiting the ports, within 15-20 days you would come to London. There is nothing secret about it. Once you came you use your British passport. It was just very difficult to leave Cyprus without an invitation. So you would leave as if you were going to go to the sea, but the goal was to come to England. Because you couldn't leave Cyprus to go to England directly. You would go round and round... from there we found a way and went. You had to have an invitation as if we were going to work for somebody in England. When I had my passport issued, I was allowed to go to England direct because I had a working visa.

My brother came in 1954 and I came 11 months later. He came in February in 1954. I came in January. He came here to work as well. All of us came here to work. Not for pleasure and not to travel. Most of us came like that. I came direct, that is why I paid £23. When we came a bachelor man would have £7 10 shillings. There were very cheap houses after the war. More or less you would buy a house for £1,000-1,500. You would pay £10-12 pounds per month. The people coming from Cyprus started using old carpets and bed and four or five people used sleep in one bedroom.

OSMAN TAHIR: [I was born on] 1915, 12 November. [I come] from Aytotoro in Cyprus. I got married and I had all of my kids there in Cyprus. I was 25 when I got married. I did everything, I did shepherding, also labour work, *neşberlik* as well. In the end, I had cattle, you know Greeks started EOKA, they used to slaughter the sheep outside. I thought and thought, the time I thought about it, I said, "I am going to sell them and leave." They butchered them all the time, villagers wouldn't do that. They knew us, they were good people but foreigners used to come and do that. Anyway, I sold them and left. Later on I brought all of my family over.

I sold the cattle and came in 1960. I sold the cattle, I took the money and came here. I left because of the problems with the cattle. My children were small, I had cattle, we used to live very well. When at the time they started EOKA, they started to kill a couple of them [sheep], slaughter them outside; I thought on my own that I am going to sell to leave. Of course I was scared.

When I came and found a place and bought a flat, I brought them. I found a flat in Elephant. Elephant and Castle. But all of them have been demolished. They built new.

DUDU HAKKI: I only came here for a holiday. I did have an interest in coming here because in those years dressmaking was made sense here. Dressmakers used to make lots of money when they came here. There was troubles in Cyprus.

REŞAT NIAZI: I was about 15 when I came [to England]. Bright music, rock music, bright lights I mean, made me want to come here. There was no television when I left Cyprus. I was very much a car man. I like cars, I still do. I have got more than 100 cars. Vintage cars. I was interested in cars – I used to go around Ledra Palace Hotel, and another hotel, I would look in their dustbins and find magazines. So I knew quite a bit about London. I thought myself English as well.

When I was about 14, in 1956, they put a bomb in RAF camp there. They sacked all the Greeks and took Turkish people in, in the RAF camp which has the airport around.

In Ledra Palace Hotel and in another hotel, and there was a officer club near the palace. English people used to go there, Cypriots didn't. But also I worked in the RAF camp, even though I was underage. Of course in those days anybody who worked for the British Government, anybody working in government, including the army and the police, this was a very well paid job. Better than a teacher, let's say.

Well, at first they came and told me to tell everybody to come to Nicosia and Kyrenia Gate. Something like recruitment. Then they took them all to the RAF camp. I worked in them in the tea office, and motor transport, as a messenger.

My intention in coming to London was to make a lot of money. That was in my mind.

I arrived in London in December 1958. I came by boat to Marseilles, from Larnaca. The name of the boat was *Theodor Herzl*. I think it was a Jewish ship. By the boat I think it took three or four days. Then train to Paris, then from Paris, a train to Victoria. It cost £25 or £27, something like that. My family had a bit of money. My mother had a pension. But we weren't badly off. So I got the money from my mother.

Always when you are too close to the sea, you want to go places. That is why the Greeks spread all over America long long ago, before Turks. Because they have all the islands. I was in a café, a couple of people were going. I said "I'll come." Other people were talking about going in the evening, and around lunch-time I said, "I am going as well."

My mother was crying. I have one brother younger than me. I left the family first.

On the boat we came, I suppose there must have been about as many as 10, 12 or a few more Turkish, plus some Greeks as well. It was a boat that carried passengers as well as immigrants. When we came, we used to go walk on [deck] and see behind the motor *roooor roooor*. Forty in a room, they give you a blanket and a pillow.

It didn't take me to get to realise that they had two compartments. One is a ordinary dining room for immigrants, let's call them immigrants. The other one was a luxury compartment, and we wasn't allowed really to go to the luxury one. But I did. I met a Turk who [lived] in London; he went to Cyprus and was coming back [to London].

The boat was occupied by mainly Jewish. I had a girlfriend on the boat. Really. A Jewish girl. Nothing happened, because she was Jewish. I loved sitting in her room. Luxury compartment. It was two girls in there.

I don't know if the other Turkish people were wondering where I was, I didn't mix very much with them, how can I say? There was a coloured man. I forget his name, from Nicosia; he was black. Not Arab Ali. He had been [to England] before. So he acted like a guide. Nice guy actually. Gambler. He was a gambler in

Cyprus, gambler here. Never worked. My conversation with them on the boat was, "I am coming to London to work."

You had two lots [of people on the boat]. You have first class, second class and no class. Now those who was in no class, these are immigrants – they have very little money.

EMINE AHMED: My brothers were here, my eldest brother and also the one younger than me. As they were here, my dad sent me here as well. My elder brother had been here for three years. He came three years before me, he had done his military service for two years. He left the army, when he left the army, my other younger brother came as well. He invited me, I also came. I had no intentions for coming here. Nothing, nothing, nothing, I didn't have any intention at all; as if I came to travel. Nothing, there is nothing.

My dad said, "You go there as well," he said, "you work as well," he said. "You would help them," he said. That is to say, how should I say to you, cook and so on. We came, all of us got married, stayed here. We first lived in Dalston.

I came by plane. As a matter of fact there was only one plane then. I think it was British Airways. Because at that time English planes used to land in Cyprus. English, Cypriot. There was one airport, it used to be used by everyone. I think I came by British Airways. From the old airport in Nicosia, yes. I don't remember how much it cost at all. That is to say, I don't remember how much I paid for it. My father got my ticket, he paid, that is how I came. Because I am telling you, we used do farming, that is to say we didn't use to do anything, that is to say we didn't earn money. We used help father, himself, he used to do his job, he used to hire labour then, that is to say we didn't use to see money.

CELAL HASSAN: I left Cyprus because they knew there was no future for me there. My job and then, there was poor people, you want to make some money you see. If you couldn't make money, you can't live. I wanted to go back after I came to stay in England.

I planned to live in England for a while and go back to Cyprus but unfortunately it didn't work that way. When you came to England, I intended to work, save money, help my mother, my father, my family there until they get better. It was 1955 when I left Cyprus to come to England. It was the end of the summer. I was planning to come here for a few years, five or six years, go back and then live over there.

HULUSI MAHMUD: At that time [1958] they was taking on military police, the British Army to help them along in troublesome Cyprus. And then my dad said to me, "No, don't go there, don't go to army." He sold the lambs, he gave the me the fare and said "Go to London to your brothers." And I accept that and I come over. My father suggested to me and I didn't refuse what he said. It was his idea for me to come over. My intention was to just carry on life, to lead a comfortable life, we don't fear, we are not gonna killed, whatever. Fear from get killed in Cyprus, you know the trouble they had, the Civil War so to call.

Not many foreign people were coming here. Only a few. My brothers didn't tell me nothing about London, they didn't tell nothing. "If you just wanna come, you come." That is it. I had a British passport, and fee to come. I was hoping to go to

Australia, but I didn't get the invitation I wanted, so I come here. I left from Larnaka. It took four days to come by boat. The name of the boat was *Messapia*. It cost £38. I came to Victoria station with £8 in my pocket.

HULUS IBRAHIM: I came here in 1958. The EOKA situation had started, the TMT had started, the situation in Cyprus was the Greeks wanted Cyprus, and the Turks were dividing Cyprus. How were the English going to deal with this? Of course they had closed down our *Emekci* newspaper before I came to England.

As members of the Union we didn't want the two communities to fight against each other, and our view was that the Cyprus situation should be resolved by roads of peace. But there were people who didn't want us to be friends, be it the English or be it the local militants and nationalistics – these had something to gain from the fighting. We used to obstruct this and because of this we were the biggest – in other words there was no other opposition at the time. It was essential for us to be removed from the middle. They started to shoot and kill. Because of this, we either had to get guns, which we preferred not to – or we could leave the region to them and abandon the country. And those that didn't abandon would be under their orders. They were going to get done what they wanted in Cyprus, and this is how it happened. Us forward-thinking Union members were forced to abandon Cyprus in this way in 1958.

The journey wasn't easy. There were no planes at that time. There were boats. 29 liras in that era. But 29 liras was big money. Of course I had an amount of money. I used to get a good wage. I used to get seven or eight liras.

I saved some money because I was going to go to Europe, to a Meeting for Youth. Seven people from the Union. had been selected. There was a group of seven. It was going to be in Warsaw, Poland. I saved to go there, Warsaw, Poland, it was going to be there and we friends met three or four times to talk about us going. We were going to explain the situation with Greeks and Turks in Cyprus. I was the only Turk that was going to go. That's why I saved the money. Pocket money in other words. For clothing and such.

I worked overtime for two weeks. I used to get 12 liras. Then I had some social security benefits. My boss at the time said [to the other workers], "Look, this friend of yours has worked amongst you all for all these years, he struggles, he fights, his life is in danger now. Help him," he said. "How much money do you need?" he asked me.

"*Vallahi*, money isn't the problem, as long as I get on the boat." I said. "Food," I said, "I can think about, I can find some from somewhere," I said to them. The workers gave me seven liras. The boss and the workers gave me 22 liras between them. Then my brother heard that I had to leave and gave me two liras, and my mother sold her gold and gave me five liras, to buy my ticket.

MERYEM SHEREFETTIN: Well, it's life. We think we were going to have a better life here in London, and we left Cyprus. Oh, the way we hear about London! We think it was a heaven! Plenty money! Freedom! That's why we decide to come to London, England.

GÜLSEN LARKINS: I was born in 1937 on the 19th of the ninth. I am from Akıncılar, Lourigina. I came to England in 1959. I was single in Cyprus. I did not work in Cyprus. My dad wouldn't allow it. You know the people used to work for the rich people. My dad wouldn't allow me or my mum. Oh yes, my dad worked. Dad, he was a good man. He was a labourer.

My dad came first. In 1954 my brothers came, five years after my dad came. My dad came in 1956, and in 1959 we came. Not only me. My mum, my little sister, my little brothers. The youngest one. We came by boat, my brother younger than me, he came before us. Three brothers were already here. We came three of us. Six altogether.

I was 22. We still got our house there. I packed my clothes, that is all. Nothing else. My dad paid for the journey. He paid for three of us. It was my first journey. I was all right, my mum wasn't well. She passed out on the boat.

She had the cancer in Cyprus and we didn't know. We had a private doctor. You know in Cyprus it was private, he used to come to village. The same day when we were leaving from Cyprus. We had to cancel the boat. My cousin cancelled it for four hours. We waited for the doctor coming over. She has seen the doctor, he gave the injection. There was doctor on the boat. Armenian woman, she said "I know doctor is here". People who used to work there said to me, "She should be all right." I said "No, No." Anyway. One used to be able to speak a little bit Greek and I said to him, "Listen. I can't leave here, she passed out." "All right," they said. Carried her around, take her upstairs, doctor will come. I can't forget, I can't get over it. I tell you, on the boat worry worry.

They left her on the top deck. It was summer before we come. It was nice. After then, doctor came. You don't have to pay, because we already paid. She come round. Three days she was round, three days after we had three days left for the journey.

I never get over it. After she was all right. When we got there she was ill. She wasn't that bad. Little bit better. She was better than she was. My brother took her to doctor.

We got to London. We come to Victoria by train. They come pick us up. My brother, he took us straight to hospital. Straight away. Anyway. Doctor told me, "I think your mum has cancer." In the [woman's private part] and she refused to take it out. I can't tell her.

No, I know from Cyprus. My uncle he brought the private doctor. Don't say to her. My uncle turned around and said "Doctor, don't say nothing in front of her. No." Nobody knows. It is only me and my uncle. What he done, he wrote a letter for my brother. My oldest brother. He read the letter. It is all right then. She is coming all right. My brother said, "What we do is bring her there by plane." It is very very expensive on that time. My dad said, "I can't afford it." Because he already paid the ticket you know. Already been paid the ticket. We couldn't bring her over there by plane. So we come by boat. Six days. Oh my God it was a hard journey. Telling me. Very hard.

My brother he was only 14. He was only a kid. I had to look after my mum and my brother because I was the oldest. I had to look after both.

My dad, my brothers. My two brothers, my oldest brother came to meet us at Victoria. He took her to hospital, it was near, St Thomas Hospital. Oh my God. I worry myself. My dad he was all right. He was saying don't worry. She'll be all right. He was crying himself. My two brothers were upset.

No one knew she was ill. There weren't any phone at that time. It was letters. I couldn't read letters to my brother. My brothers told my dad that she has got [cancer]. It is terrible, isn't it? Read the letters after was already on the boat. My uncle.

She was there in hospital about, keep her two weeks. It used to be two weeks.

When we first came we lived in Elephant and Castle, Pollock Road. I stayed with my brothers. First week I didn't go out and doing nothing. I didn't go out the door. I used to go visit my mum, that's all. My brothers took me to see mum.

I must be clever, sensible. Because my brothers said I am very sensible. "I'll be looking after her," I said to him. The first day, because I was upset. Don't worry, they'll look after her well. I couldn't stay. My brother stayed with her. Because he used to speak the language. Second oldest. It was a nice hospital. They looked after her. Ye. Everybody looked after her and she got better. We used to not bother her, it wasn't easy you know at the beginning.

SÜHA FAIZ: The reason why I go to England is because [my parents] have a baby of 18 months. I ended up coming here for something like three years, no, three years. In 1930, I'm born in 1926, I think 1930 – my father is now a barrister, he comes back to Cyprus, and then I go to school in Kyrenia School and I stay there until 1934, this is the first definite date I can vouch for. And my father decides, and I am sure the family as a whole, Münir Beys, Fuat Bey are all talking what are we gonna do, and don't forget it is now four years after the Treaty of Lausanne. The British were not legally in charge of Cyprus until Lausanne. They had been not [doing it] illegally: under the agreement of the Sultan, they were administering the island, they annexed the island in 1915, but in International Law you cannot annex a territory of a country at war. So from 1915 until Lausanne they were in a sense illegally ruling the country. But with Lausanne they effectively now are in charge of Cyprus.

We have become a colony under the orders of council in 19-whatever, 1925 it is, because I was born in 1926, so I was born British. My brother, who was born in 1924, is not. But to make the point about the surnames too. When therefore they decide we go to school in England, I am eight and my brother is nine-and-a-half. To a boarding school, that is a separate business we can go into if you like, but when we go of course, what's our surname? So our passports, My brother and I had a separate passports for the first time: I am Ahmet Süha Faiz and my brother is Mehmet Sedat Faiz, which is our father's name, not a surname. My father's brother, the judge Fuat Bey, Mustafa Fuat, so I have cousins, who are also at schools in English here. Our fathers are cousins but we have different surnames.

My father and mother brought us here in the autumn of 1934. I was eight years old, I didn't have any family here. Looking back on it I am surprised how very, how shall I put it, *phlegmatic* I was about it. Don't forget from the ages five to eight I was at boarding school, in Kyrenia. Nevertheless I am used to be taken to school and left there and then they come back. So I am not all that. And don't forget I had a brother with me.

I have no memory of the actual information that we are gonna take you, but obviously preparations were going on for a long time. And even to the extent that we get photographed in our new school uniform in Cyprus before we go. I have got the photographs by Mangoyan, the famous famous Armenian photographer.

EMINE AHMET: I am from Serdalı, its former name was Çatos. I was single. I came here and got married. I was not working there. Our father was a farmer, *neşber*. Nesberci Cemal.

I came here to get married. My husband is from my village as well. We got married here. We came here and got married here. They said go to London and get married. That is how it happened. You have never heard, nobody told you. My husband sent me the invitation. I came by plane. I came on 29 October in 1959 from Besmil International Airport. We came to Gatwick. We had someone from the village and we came together. We were three people. A woman came with as well. Mrs Senay lives in Hackney, Clapton, now. My *efendim* paid the ticket fee. He sent it to me and we came. It was £44 then.

We had Nehir Abla from our village. I stayed in her house until I got married. That was in Highbury Park. When I first came to London I felt like a stranger. I knew my husband and I knew Nehir *Aba* because she is from our village.

I wasn't excited on the aeroplane. No, no, no excitement. I was a bit shy.

HATICE FETTI: When my sister-in-law went to London, I wanted to go, I used to say to my husband, "Go. If it is nice, we can come as well."

He said, "OK." He prepared passports but an incident occurred. A man was killed in EOKA then. Someone who my husband worked with said, "I know them," which meant that my husband knew these people as well, who had done it as well. They took him and imprisoned him, my husband, for two weeks. As soon as he came out, his passport was ready as well, we sent him immediately here. This was in 1957.

He came to his sister's house. He stayed with his sister. After quite a long time, a letter, before there wasn't telephones or anything. He sent me a letter. My sister-in-law sent me an invitation. The invitation was a sheet of paper saying that they know you and that person is going to host you in their home. She was to host him [the husband] in her house, she sent an invitation to him and his passport was issued.

You needed to have an invitation to come over here, to show that there will be somebody that you can take shelter with. It was necessary by somebody. That is how he came. After that for a long time he stayed here. He wrote a letter, he is saying, "I am going to come back. Because nobody would rent a house with five kids."

"No," I said, "Stay, I will come, we come back together." I told my mum such-and-such, I said, "Mum, my husband Fetti wrote a letter, so he will return, but I also want to go." My mum said, "If you want you would go." Because we used to stay with my mum in the same place. My house was separate from my mum's, but we were within a yard. She said, "Go, you go, we will look after the kids." They were her first grandchildren, so she loved them.

FEZILE AHMET: I left Cyprus in 1962, on 29 June. We used to harvest over there, we used to pick melons, pick olives. We worked continuously. I decided to come here because my brother was here. I came to work here, I wanted to come, to see it here. I was married, but didn't live together with my husband. He came here before me. Actually, if you want the truth, a friend of mine tricked me into coming here. I want you to know that I was in Cyprus, and my husband was here. My husband's sister wrote me a letter saying, "Your husband's getting married, come." So then I came.

A friend said, "Let's go together, let's go and see, we can come back if we don't like it." I then prepared, I bought everything I needed, and then she changed her mind. I swear to god, at the last hour she changed her mind. At the very last hour. I mean the roads here were going to close. That day they were open, I remember it was a Saturday when I came. I came here on a Saturday. My sister pawned her sheets and coverings to get the money and gave it to me. I swear to God, I'll never forget. She took her sheets to the lady as collateral and got five liras and gave it to me.

"Spending money should be found in your hands," she said. That's how I came. I had one and a half lira left till I came and found my brother.

HATICE IBRAHIM: My mother in the village was old; I had a brother in Pergama who was a teacher on the farm. He used teach about agriculture. I couldn't stay in the village, my brother had three children, I couldn't burden him.

Remziye, Emine Hanım's sister [who was living in London], knew me from the time that I was staying with Doctor Adnan in Cyprus. She wanted me for her brother. She became the cause. Letter after letter after letter she would send from London. She came and got me and we came here.

At the time they asked me if I wanted to get married. I didn't want to. I didn't want marriage, I didn't want to come to London. But I said, "I was alone for a very very long time. Without a mother, a father, I was with others."

One day winter's day as I was walking in Pergama with my mother and my brother's wife, at the beginning of March, my brother's wife turned to my mother and said, "Take a look at your daughter, search her, maybe she is not right [i.e. a virgin] and that's why she doesn't want to get married."

When I heard this I thought, "I will get married, and I'll show them whether I'm a virgin or not." I don't know if you understand this question of virginity? I came from this point, and was burning. That was my reason for coming to London.

SÜHA FAIZ: When I was married and came back I was appointed and they had never had this before it came more or less the same time. They started to appoint an assistant to the district commissioners.

In Limassol there is a district commissioner English called John Reddaway – I was his assistant. In the Limassol Sovereign Base Area there was a political officer. British civilian administration advising the military and they had Cypriots there, in fact I was offered the post of Turkish one, I refused it for a reason because I decided I was gonna leave the island. But I was in Cyprus and I was the assistant district commissioner, Limassol district, from 1952 onwards. And it was while we were there that EOKA started, on 1 April, 1955.

When I left in 1960, you know the reason; we left as a family in 1960. I had no trust whatever in Makarios. Before the republic, but not very much, but because of the government, I didn't trust Makarios. I told the governor.

What happens is I have been in Cyprus with a slight gap. I was in Limassol, and then I went to the Secretariat again, but I was in the main government office, the Secretariat in Nicosia, but in the time when I went back in whenever it was, 1960 and 1952-53, after getting married. We were there, effectively I was in the district administration, my secretariat became later. It was while I was in the Secretariat that they had this great agreement, if you remember it, between Zorlu and Averof in 1959. In the sort of corridors of either the NATO meeting or something, and they decided this is gone too far and I was then the secretary. Averof was the Greek Foreign Minister and Fatin Rustu Zorlu is the Foreign Minister of Turkey. But very correctly recognising that Britain is the ruling power, they are not gonna do things, they are putting a marker down. It is not in the interest of Turkey or Greece that there should be a war, as a result of what is going on in Cyprus.

And I come into this, my personal story, I am then the secretary of the executive council, rather the clerk of Exco. The Exco is consistently a governor-appointed British Attorney General, appointed British financial secretary, they're the senior officials, half a dozen of them. I am the person who merely, I don't take part in discussions, I am a junior member of the senior administration. They have weekly meetings. I prepare the papers, for the department, they take the decision, I record them, send them back out. I am the clerk of Exco, quite a responsible job and I remember personally one meeting of Exco. The governor that comes in is Hugh Foot, by now the emergency is technically over, like the [recent] Irish ceasefire, sort of, and he tells us we have just heard from London about Zorlu and Averof come to this agreement, and the British government will agree whatever they agree with, you know. In other words, we have had enough, he didn't say it openly. Britain is going to agree to this – obviously we are going to have to meetings, and all sorts of discussions.

Basically the Greeks and the Turks have decided this is enough is enough. That is towards the end of 1959, as far as I remember. No, towards the beginning of 1959. Because almost for a year the government of the island is taking place in sort of two levels: the ordinary administration, such as it is, the governor, the Secretariat, obvious the individual departments, Forestry, Agricultural Ministry, but two bodies are now set up which consist of Greek Cypriots, Turkish Cypriots, not the British government, representatives of the Turkish government and the Greek government called the Transitional Committee – and they are now to work out the detailed arrangements of the constitution and what is to happen for the movement from Cyprus from being a British colony to whatever what it is going to be as a new state. And that Transitional Committee goes on and I am not part of this but I know people who were, Necati Münir for example, he was part of it. And of course Clerides was part of it. And the more important Greek and Turkish – including very very senior constitutional expert professor Nihat Erim, who subsequently becomes even the president of Turkey. These people are working on this and they produce what eventually becomes the great agreement in 1960, which is the Treaty of Guarantee, the Treaty of Establishment, the actual constitution itself – it is very carefully worked out, planned, which eventually is the basis on which the government is to coming into being. The new state. While all this is going on, and these committees are meeting, Governor Foot decides purely on an administrative basis to expand Exco, while bringing in as it were preliminary to their learning what government is all about to this committee, which you saw in the photograph, which used to meet every week.

I forget what it was actually called, maybe it was a transition committee of another sort. Hatice has seen it, there is the photograph which was taken very early on, a Government Information Officer came in, you didn't see me. I am sitting in the window. It had joint secretaries, me and a chap called Takis. I think. We had joint secretaries of this committee. I cannot see this without any light, oh boy, and on the very far left is your friend [Georgios] Papadopoulos.

So this committee is meeting every week, and every week I am there, and I am seeing these people, and I am looking at Makarios, listening to him, he says very little, very little indeed and I am of a firm conviction that this thing is not going to work. Because Makarios will see to it that it won't work. And I am married and I have two small children. Not a hope. I won't go into details, it is in my book*. Anyway, firm conclusion this will not work. I decide to resign and I told the governor, and I want not to be in the island when the republic comes into being. Now, it was due to come into being on 1 January 1960. So I know we left before then, very soon before then. In 1960 I am in England by January. And I leave, I mean there is no job, I resign without a job.

And [Turkey] jolly near came, in 1967! And I think about three times they nearly came in and the Americans held them off. And eventually we know in 1974, it finished. So I don't blame myself at all, nor has anybody ever told me in Cyprus or blamed me. The fact that I left in 1960 was correct, subjectively for myself and as a correct interpretation of what was likely to happen.

SEYIT MEHMET: I lived in Larnaka in Cyprus. I was born there. I was single when I came to London. I was in the army. I was in the army during World War Two. I was in the army and I demobbed from the army in 1947. I enlisted then. I finished, they call it 'demob' in the army. I enlisted in 1942 and I demob 1947. I was in Egypt, in Palestine, Italy.

I always wanted to travel abroad because Cyprus was too small for me. I was in Italy, you know, a big country. I want to come abroad… to see the world. I didn't know much really about England before I came. All I knew about London was Arsenal really. I remember when I was a little boy during the 30s, Arsenal was one of the best clubs in England. And the Queen, and the King. And they teach us when I go to school, primary school in Cyprus and the King George V he died, before he die in 1936, I used to go to school in 1935 and then they began to teach us the English anthem in Turkish and Greek anthem in Greek. The English [anthem] starts like this in Turkish: "Yasa, yasa hakanimiz cok cok yasa. Cahil mesut olsun, uzun omur olsun, hakanimiz mesut olsun cok cok yasa."

I wanted an adventure. Yes. Because my dad was a policeman, you see. They wanted me to join the police force. I didn't want to because I wore a uniform for

---

* Recollections and Reflections of an Unknown Cyprus Turk, Süha Faiz, Avon Books, 1998

five years in the army and I didn't want to wear uniform again. And just to please my mum I passed the examination – I couldn't go next day and put the uniform on, I changed my mind. And that's why I came to England.

HATICE FETTI: In Cyprus I lived in Tuzla. I was born in Iskele. At the age of eight, I came from Iskele to Tuzla. As soon as I finished school I went to the Master Craftsman and graduated as a seamstress within three years. In 1946, at the age 14-and-a-half my marriage [had been solemnized]. I got married at 16. I gave birth at 17. I wanted to, I wanted so much to come to London. When my sister-in-law went she stayed there. I used to say to my husband, "As your sister went, let's go as well. Why should we stay in this country?" Because my husband was a quilt-maker and his business wasn't going very well. I used to [say], "Let's go!" Because the people who went and came used to praise: "London is better." They work there. I used to say, "We should also go." I wanted to come. Well, my husband one day decided to go. I had dreams. I had many dreams, I used to say, "Let's go," to my mum.

I used to dream that I would I cross over the sea so I could do better at work. I liked it, I mean I would like to put smart clothes on, have nice car, a nice house. I used to want these, long for them. I used to say, "I am going to cross over the sea"; she would say, "*Git işine*", she would say, "Where are you gonna go with five kids?"

"I am going to go, wait, you will see, one day I will go."

ÇETIN KAYA MUSTAFA: When I was born in those days there was a sports club called Çetin Kaya sports club, football club. So my dad gave my name, Çetin Kaya. I was born 18 April, 1944.

I come from Limassol. In our time, when we were kids, we used to hear everyone was going to London, we were curious. We said, "One day, when it suits us, we will go as well." For example, we wanted to go, and we said that when we grow up a bit we should go to London. I was 17 years old. But before I started thinking about going I hurt my foot in Polemidhia, a village of Limassol. I jumped from a ladder.

Where I jumped there were stones, round like this – and they weren't steady. When I jumped, my foot dislocated. This leg infected in the plaster because of the heat. I stayed in Limassol for a long time like that. Later on my elder sister was gonna go to London. I said, "If it is possible I would come with you. I can have my foot examined in London, if I am gonna have operation it would be better there."

KEMAL AHMET DAVRANDI: I was 17 when this happened [the non-proposal of marriage]. The girl was the same age as me. My mum hadn't asked for her, actually my mum didn't approve.

Later they married the girl off to someone else. So I left there and went to Pile. I worked at the RAF camp. And from there I bought a ticket, got on the boat and eight days later came to London. October 1959, I don't know the exact date. I left because of the girl situation. I thought London would be like my own home when I came here. I mean, I thought it would be like when you leave one village and go to another village.

£7 10 shillings in my pocket*. I spent £5 on the boat, so £2 10 shillings was left. We got down off the boat at Dover, boarded a train and came to, what do they call it? Victoria. We came to Victoria and everyone was being searched. And we had a small suitcase. We took the suitcase and went to let them search it. The man said, "You walk. Go out," he said.

---

* For explanation of shillings, see text note about currency on page 79

3. JOURNEY - DEPARTURE

ALI HASSAN: When I left Cyprus I was 22 years old I think! If I'm not wrong. I left in 1957, so yeah, I was 22. I came with my child and wife in the same boat. All together in the same boat, they had passports as well. I can't tell you why I left from Cyprus.

I came to England with the intention to work and get by. While I was in Cyprus I used to hear about England. My brother-in-law was here. I used to hear that England was a good place. At that time someone needed to invite you before you could come here. But because I was a police I came without an invite. I didn't need an invite.

I found work really easily in tailoring. We came here in three days with a ship, we came to Geneva. It was a Jewish ship.

After sometime we was forced to take our child because we couldn't find a place to stay, because we had a child. It was £33 to come in three days. I earned my money to come here from tailoring and a bit of policing, you know. We had a few pounds saved up. Our first intention was to buy land. We was going to build a house there [in Cyprus]. At that time land was £60. With both of our money put together [him and his wife] we could have comfortably bought the land. And as a family we had a bit of money as well. And we said we should buy it and wait a bit to build. To sell it, and some of it you'd put in yourself, and make a house. And of course the bank would give a bit. That's what we were trying and while we were trying all this happened.

There was people on the ship that we knew, Memet the Quilter, our Şeref's uncle was there. We came together. We used to call him Mehmet Yorgancioğlu. He used to sell fabric. There was other people we knew, friends. In fact we even went to weddings with them.

On the journey we were scared, scared that we might get lost. We didn't want to get lost or anything, actually we kind of [stuck] with each other. We all slept altogether and did things together. The weather was hot, all of us used to sleep outside on the deck. We all slept close, close together, so no one would bother us and stuff. We all backed each other up. All of us. There were people who knew bits of English but very little. In those times in Cyprus nobody knew near enough any English at all anyway.

'Halladale' arrives at Dover c.1960. Image courtesy of Dover, Museum

IBRAHIM DERVIŞ: I came on the *Teti* up until Pile, and then from there the *Korinthiya* to Marseilles. After that a train to Victoria – no it wasn't Victoria, but near Liverpool Street. Or the station near Tower Bridge? I have forgotten its name. In any case it was a big station.

She [my mother] came here and received good treatment. But there was no community, no neighbours. That is to say she came here, but everyone had to leave the house to go to work, so she was very bored.

In 1949 I went [to the sister left in Cyprus] and said, "*Allaha ısmarladık*, I'm going, I too have prepared for travel." But in preparation I had also obtained a passport for her too, just in case. It cost around £5 then.

"Where are you going to leave me?" asks my big sister. So this time I go to her *Bey* and ask him what's happening?

He says "*Valla*, you're going, I don't have confidence in myself [Who's going to look after them?]"

"OK," I said, "We'll take her as well." That's how it happened. I brought my sister and her child with me, and her husband stayed there.

KEMAL AHMET DAVRANDI: I was fed up. They had married the girl off to someone else. My escape to London was because of the girl situation. That's why I left. Everyone was going on about LONDON, LONDON, LONDON. So I thought I may as well go to London. I got my passport from Iskele, got on the boat and came to London.

At that time it cost £25. I used to save some money. I used to save for eating and drinking. Marriage didn't used to enter my mind at all. The money I saved I spent on myself!

There were four more Turks from Nicosia on the boat. We got on the rowing boat and as we were going towards the ship they were crying. I mean I could hear their families crying on the shore. But I had nobody. I didn't tell my mum or dad that I was leaving that night. Nobody. I said, "Hey why are you crying? Look, I don't even have anyone crying for me. You can go and come back." This is what I said to the friends. I felt faint when I got on the boat. Faint i.e. [saddened].

Vallahi, Believe it or not, I left thinking Cyprus would never come into my thoughts again. That much hatred had come to me.

DUDU HAKKI: Lefkara was our village. Lefkara. I was single. I was a dressmaker-seamstress and I used to sew my mother's dresses, my nephew's trouser and embroidery, *Lefkara işi.* I came here [to London, in 1960] for a holiday with Nahide *Aba* and Mehmet Emin *Abi.* My aunt's son was here, and his wife came over to Cyprus with their children. She wanted to take me back to London but my nan wouldn't allow it. My nan took hold of my passport and tried to throw it in the well. The neighbours ran and took it off her. That was my Nanny Ayse; she wanted to throw my passport in the well so I couldn't come here.

I bought my ticket, but then I changed my mind and didn't go. My Nahide *Aba* left Lefkara with the children. Two boats collided the day they left to go to London, and three people died. Their boat was then cancelled, and they came back to the village. When my Nahide *Aba* came back to the village, she told my dad, "It's her destiny to go. You see, you won't let Dudu come to London, but we went to go there and the boats collided, people have died, and we are back. This is why it's her destiny, her destiny is to go to that place." And that is how he allowed me to come. I came intending stay for one or two months and then go back.

GÖKMEN MEHMET: In Cyprus I was a dressmaker and hairdresser. In any case my family were hairdressers. I came in 1954; I used to live in Nicosia. I came here because my sister lost her daughter in London, and I come to make her company. I also had a brother here. My family paid for me to come here. My dad paid for me.

I used to get letters from my sister here, so I heard a bit about London. I came by boat. My husband came with the *Mesapya.* Mine was a different boat, an Italian boat. It was the first time I was leaving Cyprus and I was happy. I liked to see London. I travelled on my own. I was laughing, I was only 17 when I came. I made plenty of friends on the boat, and everyone was excited. If I told you what I was like on the boat you would think I was a snob! I was wearing a different dress every day, and some couple from Köfünye, they were Turkish used to be in the ship as well, I was very close with them. Other people didn't do that on the boat [change their outfits everyday]. I like being smart. Many people were English tourists on the boat.

CELAL HASSAN: I travelled by a ship called *Mesapya.* It was an Italian ship. I went to Limassol to get the boat. Ye, my cousin Remzi was there [at the port]. He came here for holiday. He brought me there. I was crying when I left there. Because I never knew something better. I was born in a village, till I was 16, 17. I was 19 actually when I left.

The ship stayed in, half a mile say, and we used to go with a small boat there. So we went there. [Only a] few people that you know. No, we never knew anyone on the boat, but I knew few Cypriot people, you know. It was more Turks than Greeks. But I didn't know them, you see, in those days. It was different village, different towns. There was no one from my village. The journey took five days. It went to Greece, from Greece to Italy somewhere. And then we went to Genoa, we came to the train, and then we came to Victoria station.

When we stopped in those places they didn't take on more people. Not really, mainly it was from Cyprus that they used to take but not many. It cost you £25. My wages in those days in this country was £4 10 shilling. My brother got the ticket for me, and gave me £5 in my pocket, pocket money to come here. So when I came and I worked I paid my brother slowly slowly.

MUSTAFA HÜSEYIN: I lived in Kalebrunu. I was single before I came. My job was farming over there. I was 18 when I came, in May 1953. In those days, in the 50s, everyone was coming.

They came to work and to find a better life. We were four siblings; two boys, two girls.

I came by ship. It was an Italian ship. It took ten days. It was a cargo ship. It was also bringing passengers. It wasn't that classic. I probably paid 18 lira for the ticket. Either 18 or 20 something. My dad gave it to me. When we came there were Turkish people on the boat. We were four Turkish people. Probably there were three, four Greeks as well. We didn't arrange to come together. We met on the ship.

We were leaving Cyprus for the first time we left – of course it felt abnormal for us. How can I say to you, we felt relieved, because we left Cyprus, leaving the depression to find a better life. Of course there were things I heard about London. I had my relatives here. They came here in 1932. Mustafa Misiri. He is deceased now. He came after the war. He came back to Cyprus in 1945 on a passenger boat to see the relatives. He was my aunt's son. He told me nothing about London to put it in my mind when he came. He just came. It wasn't even in my mind. I was still going to school. I didn't know anything.

EMINE MEHMET: I came here in 1952. I actually come from Anafodiya, though I was bought up in Nicosia. I was five when I went to Nicosia, and I went back to the village when I was 15. And at 18 I got married, my dear. I was not working in Cyprus. I left Cyprus because my husband had got skin trouble, and we wanted to come and see a doctor. He came and stayed here, and after he sent me an invitation. I came six or seven months after him. I came by boat. It was called *Abbazia*, an Italian boat. They stopped using that boat, and started using another called *Messapya*. It would take and bring people. I can still remember the boats' names, after 52 years. *Abbazia* was an old boat so they stopped using it. It was a passenger boat.

We came here in eight days, and I travelled with my husband's brother and an eight-month-old baby. My baby. I had given birth and brought him with me when he was eight months old. I had been out of the hospital for eight days when my husband left, and I came here with an eight-month-old baby in my arms, together with my brother in law.

I was very happy on the journey, as I had never gone abroad, you know. I was very happy, happy because I wanted to see my husband. That's how I came. Anyway we were newly-wed, we were married for one year when he left. I was this young girl with a new baby, and they put me on the bottom bunk. There was a Greek girl on top. She used to go down to all the parties all night long. I was lying down with my baby in my arms. I was afraid to walk in case I dropped my baby from my arms. One day this baby of mine did not want to eat a thing. I used to breastfeed but I had very little milk.

There were other Turks on the boat. They were all on another floor. They all stayed in the same place. The room I was in was a bit more expensive. My husband, now deceased, sent me the money. So I stayed in a special room.

I stayed in a room for four but there was only two of us in there. The *Cıracik* on top and me and my baby on the bottom. At dinner time we would leave the cabin. There was a sort of veranda and we would go and sit there, but the *Abbazia* boat would shake us. It felt like my intestines were about to come out. We were young, the *cıra* became very ill. They took her to hospital in Italy. She was old at that time. We [made a successful journey] because we were young.

We first docked at Venice. You know there's those black-nosed things, they put us in those and took us across [i.e. Gondolas]. We got to the other side in one of those. That was the first time I left Cyprus. When we left Cyprus we first passed by those mountains of Greece.

With the baby in my arms I was unable to pluck up the courage, and I saw from the opposite side that they were buying gift dolls. I was holding my baby and was scared. As if I was going to drop my baby somewhere. I did not budge anywhere.

Later we boarded the boat; at last we were going to come [to Britain] and they said something about the baby in my arms. And I looked very childlike. I was 23 but looked childlike. The French ladies would look at me and look at my baby and say something. Who knows what they where thinking at that period of time. Then they stamped the passport and we got back on the boat.

We then got a train to Victoria. My husband, God rest his soul, was waiting for us there. When he saw his child – the last time he had seen his child was in the hospital – he tried to hold him but the baby went towards my brother-in-law. The baby had never seen and did not know this stranger – he was a stranger to him anyway.

HULUS IBRAHIM: I made the journey together with a friend called Ferit. I came together with him. But what was strange was that on the boat there was a German. And when we got off the boat in Athens, we bought a magazine and in that era on the cover of that magazine was a photograph of Kurt Sef [possibly Khrushchev]. And when we was on the boat, this man would always sit opposite us and watch us. Ferit said to me, "Look here, talk to him. You know a little English."

I said, 'What am I going to talk to him for, I don't recognise or know him?"

"Ask him where he is going, ask him where he is coming from and so and so."

"Oh, leave him alone," I said. "Maybe he doesn't want to talk to us," I said.

Anyway he spoke to us before we spoke to him: "Hey youngsters, where are you going?"

This German was a member of NATO in Cyprus. He was a policeman. That German, come what may, wanted to take me to Germany. "I'm going to England," I said.

"I'll pay your fare as well," he said.

"I have no business in Germany," I said. We last spoke in Marseilles, and he offered to take me again. "Where has this man come from, and where is he going to take me?" I said to myself. "What am I going to do in Germany?" I had an English passport and an invitation.

MEHMET ALI BEKIR: My name is Mehmet Ali Bekir. I was born on 25 March, in 1940, in Larnaka, though I lived in a village, Pirga Larnaka.

I've been here [in Britain] 45 years, I came in 1960, before the Republic was set up. I was 20. I was a second-class mechanic in the military zone in Icelya. My passport was an English passport then. While I was were wandering around, with friends, young of course, one of my friends said, "Come, let's go to England!" I said "Come on! Let's go!" Not for holiday. In those days, an invitation was necessary to be able to come. My mum had a niece/nephew [not clear in the transcript] here. He/she used to stay in Shoreditch, and he/she sent me an invitation. And I was holding the invitation in my hand, and my passport was in my hand, as well. English passport. And when we were wondering with friends, one of my friends said, "Come, let's go to England!" That's how that idea came. He told me on Saturday, we set out on our journey on Wednesday.

MEHMET ŞEREF ALI: I had an elder sister in Cyprus at that time widowed, she used to say, "I am going to England." Such and such. The rest of their business was there [in London]. I said, "I would come as well, let's go together." We used to sign a contract for six months. After the end of first six months, in the middle of the second six months, I came to Cyprus thinking that we were gonna go to Cyprus. This time, my elder sister gave up.

I went to Behzat, he used to issue passports and so on. I went and said to him, "I would like go to Australia, England." 90 lira. It was 90 lira to go there, passport and so on – and 65 lira to come here, to England. He used to send people. I wanted to go to Australia. I didn't have any relatives in Australia. In fact, there weren't any here either. In fact, in reality there was a nephew here, maybe that's why I changed my mind so that I came here. I wanted to go to Australia to Well, that is to say, to work.

My elder sister used to talk about England. I said, "Wait for me to come, I would come with you too." I came, she would say that she had given up [the idea of] coming to England. About a month passed. I had some money since I stayed, worked for nine months. I said I would go to Australia. Because I used to hear, I said that I would go to Australia as well. Behzat, that poof pimp [*puş pezevengi*], excuse my language, Behzat said to me, "What are you gonna do in Australia, the other side of the world? In England there are girls in the parks, and so on." So I thought, "I know English and as English is spoken there, well!" A couple of friends that I had made in the camp in Egypt at that time [were there]. That's what happened. And also I had a cousin. We received the passport and came to Victoria Station.

We came on a ship called *Avenia*. The Italian ship was *Buenotrias*. Not Italian, this was a Greek ship. Was is it *Ionia* or *Avenia*, something like that? We got on from Limassol. Of course it went to Italy, then Marseilles. To Genoa by train. From Marseilles by train. I travelled through four, five ways. There weren't any Turks on the ship. I knew some English.

MELEK KAZIM: She [my mother] came in 1952, we came in 1955. My sister came later. There is 14 years between us. She was born here [in England].

We came altogether on a boat in eight days. It was a Jewish boat. I have forgotten the name now. We caught the boat from Iskele. I remember because all my uncles, aunties came to see us off. From the past, it was our first excitement. But we started to walk, go up the boat. I didn't want to go because all my aunts were there [in Cyprus] and they were crying. I didn't want to go, but I was going to see my mother. We felt forced to go. At that time my mother was on my mind, and my auntie use to say to my sister, "How are you going to speak to the English?"

It was the first time I was boarding the boat. Oh, there was lots of [Turks], neighbours, and people from other places and villages on the boat. The journey went very well. I didn't feel seasick. The olders were often feeling ill, we [children] would often play up on top board. We came as far as Southampton on the boat, because some people were going to Italy, France, Marseilles. We saw other countries too in eight days.

I remember we stopped in Italy because there was a well there. I remember we stopped there, and we went to Napoli. We stopped there and I remember we got off the boat and we visited the shops around there a little. My father held our hand. I held my sister in my arms as she was small. We only stopped there in Italy. In Southampton, my mother came to pick us up. She picked us up probably in a bus, there were trains then. With a train because I remember my mother came to pick us up alone. Well in three years she had got to know the streets. My mother was very streetwise. She stayed with my aunt [dad's sister], with my father's family. In Stoke Newington. Because I remember when we came. We stayed in Stoke Newington for three months, until my father bought a house in Tottenham.

We bought our house. £600 up front. In those days houses were very cheap. After my father sold up in Cyprus, we got the money and brought it here. Anyway my father had money. His status was good. Anyway, we came, Mum oh what a beautiful thing! We saw my mum. We cried. Anyway, we used to always cry. Everybody used to cry whenever you saw someone or whenever you saw someone off. Previously tears from happiness, however, now from hardness. We came from there to Victoria by train. In those days people were more loving. We would show each other love and respect. Even if it was a stranger, there would be love and respect shown. In other words if that feeling of love and respect was never ever found you in some years, there would be no feeling, no longing. None. We hugged everyone and caught the train to Victoria from there. From Victoria we caught a thingy, a taxi. We carried baskets. I had within my basket a doll. Until this day, within my heart is a doll that my mother sent me from here to Cyprus. I never had a doll. It was a really beautiful doll. It was big and in a box. It had blue eyes and blonde hair. I have had blonde hair since I was young. I forgot the doll in the excitement. I forgot it there, and until now it is within me. I didn't manage to love my doll.

The basket contained our bread, olives, onions, Turkish cheese, tomatoes. Whatever there was, we put in the basket because they told us there was no food available en route. Therefore you bring your own food. Some people would starve as the train journey was for three days. Well, a packed lunch, a basket full of things. We covered this with a towel. There was everything, including figs, we brought everything. We came in March. There were oranges, apples, tangerines at that time. We brought them all. They gave us food on the boat, but not on the train. Previously this was a steam train. Coal, they would pour coal.

Other than food and the doll that I forgot, we bought over only our clothes. My mother had brought over most of the photos. We then brought over what was left. At that time, there was nothing like this [friends giving presents because you were moving to another place]. There was not much of this and that.

4. JOURNEY - ARRIVAL

MELEK KAZIM: We came here from Victoria by taxi with our baskets. We had old-time suitcases. Those which clicked when opened. I had one of those. It's beautiful. You should see inside this, it's beautiful, it has pockets and everything.

GÖKMEN MEHMET: The journey was nine days. Long. My sister came to Victoria. To me it doesn't look different. Only the houses looked small. When I went to my sister's place in Bermondsey, it was very small. Because I used to got a very big house, my dad's. Bermondsey had small houses and small gardens. In Cyprus I got no Turkish neighbours – I was living in a Greek part. In London all my neighbours were Turkish. It was all Turkish, everywhere. I was surprised. They were Turkish Cypriots.

REŞAT NIAZI: I arrived in Victoria. I have a cousin here. I forgot his address. I lost his address. I couldn't find his address. Then somebody I met in the boat, who I knew, he had a brother. I knew his brother. But he didn't want to go to his brother because his brother didn't like him. He was a bit on the naughty side like me. We both didn't want to go to his brother, but we did.

We got a bus to Hammersmith, no, sorry, to Streatham. It was night time as well. Early evening. It was freezing cold December. No overcoat, no nothing. There was this much ice. Dry snow, and he wasn't at home. He always liked drinking. So we knew he was drinking somewhere. We waited until the pubs closed about 10. Then he came.

He said "What the hell are you doing? You have got no money, you have got nothing, that is why you came to me." Then he said, "Come in for a few minutes. That doesn't mean you're gonna stay." He put a little gas fire on and he said "You stay here. Tonight. Tomorrow I will take you somewhere else." That somewhere else was Ramadan Güney, who I also knew from Cyprus.

He lived in Vauxhall. He didn't charge us. Next morning I bought on the way an army coat. There were shops all around London.

After a few nights in Vauxhall, I went to my cousin. Because my father died in the British army, they have legion office there, so I went there. They put me to school to learn English and find me a job in Lyon's Corner House. 99% of the Cypriots pass from there.

A big Trocadero. A very big building. There used to be several in London and outside London. They had about 10 restaurants in there [Lyon's Corner House], Wimpys, restaurants, self service, music and dancing. That was in Piccadilly, Coventry Street. It's called Trocadero. It's the whole block.

I went to a Language school in Tottenham Court Road, somewhere. I stayed with my cousin about a month, now I am going to school and working. £3 10 shillings a week because I was not old enough. Four people in the room and when I saw Piccadilly I was shocked, because it wasn't what I expect. London was dirty, filthy, cold. I wanted to go back. I was going to save ticket and a few pounds and go back and I am still here.

ALI HASSAN: Of course there was fear [when they arrived in London], we didn't know the roads or anything. Were they going to look for us, how were we going to go, how were we going to find it, we was wondering, of course. But when we came, for example, we came with a ferryboat. We got a train again and came to Victoria Station. My brother-in-law was there together, with my sister-in-law. They got us and we went to there home that night with the train. When we first got to England we came out at Victoria Station, when you come with the boat to Victoria Station. My brother-in-law Hasan Pasakoylu met us there. There was no one from my family here. Nobody, just my one brother-in-law. We came to his house. We stayed there for a while.

MEHMET ŞEREF ALI: We came to Victoria Station at night time in the dark. Possibly it was nine. I had my nephew, he died here. I had a nephew. I had his address with me, we came to Victoria Station. I looked everywhere, I couldn't find his address. I said "*Eyvah*, it is all up with me! I am done for!" I couldn't find the address in the dark. In those days all of the English people, both men and women, used to wear hats. Were they called Edwardian, those old ones? I keep looking like this. As if I went into a coalmine – there was so much fog, mist at that time; the weather was awful. I looked, what are you gonna do then?

I put my hand into my pocket, I looked, I had £40, I remember it like now. I saw a taxi which had empty seats, in Victoria. I said, "Hotel, I wanna hotel," I said.

He kept looking at me, the suitcases are in my hand of course. He asked me, "Do you have money?", I said, "I have." There is also another taxi on this side, opposite. Black cab. He said to me "Turkish?" "Yes," I said. "How did you know that I was Turkish?" I said. "Come in," he said. I went in. It went from Victoria, we passed through West End, we came to Denmark Street. [At that time], there was Cyprus Turkish Association – he took me there.

It was a cul de sac. Probably they moved to D'Arblay Street afterwards. I saw a sign with a star and crescent on it , and writing, 'Cyprus Turk' – I said that this was a Turkish place. I went upstairs, and found a friend. The man opened my palms and took – I don't know how much he took. It was around seven shillings and sixpence*, that is to say, that is my guess. Anyway, there was a friend there from Aytotoro, who I met in Suez. It was a coincidence that I was in the club. "Welcome!" I said: " This is my situation." [i.e. referring to the death of his brother in Egypt].

"God rest his soul!" he said. "May he rest in peace!" he said. He understood of course. In those days Turks were very few, they knew each other.

---

* That is 37.5p in 'new' English money. See text note about currency on page 79

Locomotive spotters at Victoria Station, London, 1950. Image courtesy Museum of London

HULUS IBRAHIM: We came to Victoria Station. We were going to be met by a friend from Larnaka, and I had a friend called Derviş from here. He was going to meet me at Victoria Station and show me around. He wasn't going to leave me alone. We were going to arrive at Victoria Station at seven in the morning. We came to Victoria Station at 12, 12 midnight. The people who were going to meet me had left. When we reached there, everyone's close family and acquaintances came, met them and took them away. I was the last one left, with two suitcase, a quilt, sheets and so on. There was a English ladyfriend, 25 – 30 years old: "Do you want help?" she said. Now I don't know London, my first step in London, and she thought I was rich, I thought she was now going to take me to mug me. We used to watch some films!

I said, "No thank you." But there was no one left around. There was only one Greek who I recognised, and I had met him on the boat. "Hey you Turk," he said. As there was the Turk-Greek fighting then, Greeks would stay away from Turks and Turks stayed away from Greeks. But as a Union member, Greek, Turk, Armenia, I would talk to whoever. My intention was to meet them. I had spoken to him on the boat, young he was, my age as well. I saw him and called him. He had been to London before and stayed here for three years. "He knows London," I said to myself.

My friend Ferit had met a French girl on the boat and stayed in France. He was a tailor, and wanted to learn design. He was going to come to England but changed his mind on the boat. At Marseilles their train for Paris started to leave before us. I suddenly remembered, and as the train was moving I ran and gave him my address in England, and said, "Come and find me in London if it doesn't work out in Paris for you," and so Ferit parted from me and I was left alone.

There were men at the station and the Greek told me to hire lockers for my luggage. They gave me two lockers, and I put my luggage in them, and begun to follow him. We went to a Cypriot café, a Greek café, and there were some people that I knew there. He was staying there. So we went there but I was starving, my stomach was rumbling from hunger.

In the morning I said, "Take me to a Turkish café if you know of any." In Angel, there was a Turkish café opposite the park. He took me there, we caught a taxi and went there. He paid the 10 shilling fare as well. I thanked him and he left me there. I take a look around, a load of gamblers, and I was not a person who went to cafés in Cyprus. I was always involved with the Union. But I sat and drank a coffee.

MEHMET ALI BEKIR: My new friends were Tezel, his brother Ahmet, his brother Halil, mechanic Mehmet, Hüseyin Boyaci. There was deceased Basbartu; his name was Vedat Basbartu. Mustafa is another friend. I met them after staying in Angel for a while I moved to Newington Green . Because the place where I worked was in Newington Green, a garage, called Jet garage. I moved to Newington Green. Tezel, Mustafa and I were staying in the same room in Tezel's elder sister's house. On rent. Since it was three of us, we used to pay less.

EMINE AHMED: We came to Heathrow. Nobody came to meet me there. We came to inner part of London with a coach, I don't remember that place, we came to inner part of London and Sultan Abla picked me up. My nephew's wife came picked me up. We came to Dalston by bus. She came and picked me up from there. English buses took us; it was a special coach. It takes and brings all of them there [the airport], from there everyone picks up their families, they don't go to the airport. Sultan Abla brought me to her house.

There was of course, there were of course Turks and there were English people, there were Cypriots. All of us were mixed on the aeroplane. Then, in '61 we were all mixed. Separation started in '74. I wasn't scared on the plane. I was pleased, I came as if I was coming for a holiday. Nothing came to my mind, nothing at all.

ÇETIN KAYA MUSTAFA: I had my brother-in-law and brother in London. Before we came here, they had come. They came in 1959, and we were coming here because they were here. My brother-in-law and my brother were here. My sister, her little son and I. Three of us came here.

We came by ship. Ship *Moledet*. It was a Jewish ship. As a matter of fact, Jewish ships used to always come in those days, and the price wasn't that expensive. 32 and a half lira. 32.5 and a half lira Cyprus money. That was towards the end of 1961, it was winter then.

It took us five, five-and-half or six days, something like that. First I think we went to Italy. After Italy, I think, to France we took a train. We came to Marseilles. From there we went to Paris. We went on the train for a while, for two hours, something like that.

On the ship, there was Hüseyin Yapici from Anoyra. There was also another one, Ali, the one who plays *zurna* [a reed instrument] in weddings. It was Ali Yapici, he was Yapci as well. Yapici – his hair looked like it had been dyed with henna, something like that. He looks like English. There were a few people. My sister was there and her son called Cemal, they call him Cemal Dunny now. Anyway, after that when we boarded on the ship we liked it, but it was very cool as it was winter. It was rough, wavey. Every two minutes up in the air, and down, and up in the air down. All of the people were having diarrhoea. They would give a special tablet for us, so we wouldn't have diarrhoea.

All the passengers were Cypriots from Limassol in Cyprus. From different places in Cyprus. There were Greeks as well, they were going as well I think. Greek, Turkish all were mixed. The passengers were Greek and Turks; we didn't see any other foreign passenger. But foreign passengers would come from, for example, Italy. Other passengers joined us in Italy. You go to sleep at night, wake up in the morning it is sea again. For four days sea all you see is sea, four days. Every day sea, every day sea. It was nice, we liked it. Food was very nice for example, they would change the bed sheets every single day.

The food was a bit different for us, but we were eating whatever we found; for example you like or don't like, you would eat not to starve. Sometimes you would ask to get something else if they give you something you don't like. Sometimes, if we didn't feel full, there was egg or cheese sandwich or rolls, on the ship, we used to buy sandwich, or rolls with our own money. It was nice. For example the ship had a hall, they used to play music. Hüseyin Yapici had his *saz* [stringed instrument]. For example he played his *saz* with his friends. He was playing *döblek* [a type of drum] with his friend they were doing something. We used to play that song called 'Ya Mustafa Ya Mustafa', it was famous in those days. We used to sing that song. Then Hüseyin sang other things on his own. That is to say it was nice.

After Dover, after Dover we took a train, came to Victoria Station. My brother came to meet us. Mehmet Mustafa. My brother and my brother-in-law also came and from there we picked up our suitcases.

SEYIT MEHMET: I came here by boat in 1949. It was passenger boat. It was Italian passenger boat. I think it – what was it called? They used to call it something. We come to Venice; from Venice we took the train, we travelled to Paris, only way from Venice. From Paris we come to Dover in England.

It was an Italian boat. There is one *Mesapya*, one *Catanya*, one *Athropy,* something like that. Maybe *Mesapya*. I am not quite sure about that. The journey was five days. We come to Venice. We come to Venice, we stay one night. Next day we took the train. Five days. It cost £18. I saved the money. I was saving money. I travelled with friends.

I came with friends. We meet everybody in the boat because they travelled from Larnaca, you see. The boat was coming from Larnaca. There was only one person from Larnaca, he was from Larnaca. He was Greek Cypriot, and his name was Jumbo. Greek Cypriot. And it was only him and me who could speak Italian. So when we come to Venice they wanted us stay one night. So it was about 40 of us, something like that. Nobody could speak Italian. So we went and made arrangements in a hotel. We stayed there during the night and next day we come out you know.

We arrived in London, Victoria Station. It was, it was foggy, it was dark because it was winter, it was three months before Christmas. It was something like that. It was misty everything like that. I didn't like it at all.

I had a sister who came six months before me, and some other friends. They came to meet me at Victoria Station. An invitation was sent me by Mr Ali's wife. Mr Ali, he is from Anglosisdes. Anglosides is near Aytotoro a couple of miles apart.

His sister and my brother were married. So we were *dünür*. In them days you needed an invitation to come. When I first came I stayed in Edgware Road, they used to call it Roundel Avenue in Edgware Road, before you go to Cricklewood. They had a flat up there so I stayed there. I had just my sister here, no other family. Mr Ali's sister was my brother's wife. We call it dünür [in-law]. I stayed there about six months I think.

EMINE MEHMET: My dear, it was I think a month before August when I came. We left towards July. I came in July. My *effendi* [her husband] did not have a place, of course. He rented a room in an English house. It was two and a half lira a week in that period of time. In Kennington, I still remember it. I can even remember where the house was. It was English lady, she put us up in the house. And in that period of time you were afraid to buy a single thing. I was scared. It was as if there was no money around. That's what it was like. I mean I saw a different kind of life here.

KEMAL AHMET DAVRANDI: When we arrived at Victoria, believe it or not I had no thoughts. There was a friend from Baf who on the boat asked me, "Where are you going to go?"

"I've got an aunt, I've got a [milk brother]*. I don't have his address but I have Topcu's address," I said. I showed it.

Apparently he lived in Manchester, over that way. Well, how was I to know? I paid the train fare, which was £1. I had £1 10 shillings left. The brother from Baf also lived in Manchester.

We got on the train. *Tak, tak, tak, tak*, it goes. Then stopped in a place. "Come on, we've arrived," he said. Well, how was I to know where we were, or what had happened?

"Come on, Kemal *Dayı*, get down!" he says.

I got down off the train. I said, "It is all pebbles and stones around here." We got the suitcase down off the train too. They too were trying to get off the train.

"Oh my God! Oh my God! Get on! Get on! It's not a station!" he said. I was going to die on the first night! *Ya vallahi*, the train would have gone, another train would have come and hit and killed me. But the train had stopped, but it wasn't a station. I got off and onto the stones. Luckily there was no electricity. I quickly threw the suitcase back and got on the train again. The train moved on again. We went until the early hours. What time was it? It was 1am by the time we got there. *Tak tak* I knock on the door. No one's opening.

Tak tak, I knock on the door, nobody's opening the door.

---

* A boy who has been breastfed by a woman other than his mother becomes the 'milk brother' of the children of the woman who has breastfed him. A girl in a similar situation becomes the 'milk sister'.

"Kemal *abi*," the [lad] says to me, "It's now one o'clock, you can stay at ours if you can't find your cousin. I will find him tomorrow for you," he said. "Don't worry at all," he said.

"OK," I said, but as we were talking, I looked and saw a black lady come out.

"Does Ibrahim live here?" the boy asked.

"Yes", she said.

"Please can you call him, his cousin has arrived?"

"OK," she said. The black lady went upstairs and called him.

Down came my milk brother. "Welcome cousin!" We hugged and kissed each other. He lived in a small room. Half the size of this. "To be honest, cousin, the bed is small, but we will see it through to the morning," he said. We both got into the one bed.

MUSTAFA HÜSEYIN: We came to Victoria. We took the train from Calais. I first stayed in Aldgate, we used to stay in Brick Lane. We came with my sister together. I think she came before me; she came one week before me. Her husband was here. God rest his soul and I stayed in their house for a long time. From 1953 till 1956.

FEZILE AHMET: We sent a letter to my brother telling him that I was coming to London. The letter arrived three days after I arrived. The letter didn't arrive in time and my brother didn't come to meet me at the airport. Nobody came to meet me at the airport. Nobody, have you understood? Nobody.

Listen, listen. I came out of the airport, where should I go? I got out I went and looked at my suitcase circulating, only my suitcase was left, I have one and a half liras in my pocket, where should I go? I went downstairs – as I was going down, you know the escalators, I went to step on them and fell. I wasn't used to them. I'm telling you because you'll laugh. I fell over. The Englishman said, "Sorry, sorry mum." But who knows what 'mum' means? Who knows what 'sorry' means? You don't understand, you don't see.

A man lifted me up. Another man started shouting "London, London! London!" And I started to cry. Aren't we in London I thought? Where are we I wonder? I had a letter from my brother I showed the man his address.

The man said, "Yes, London." He took my suitcase and threw it in the back and then put us inside. It was a coach. It took us to the West End. We got out at the West End, there was this little place where the buses would terminate and where you could get a taxi and go. Probably Victoria, I don't know. I look around. Everyone's gone and my suitcase is still there. I was waiting for the man to give me my suitcase. You'll never believe it, I was looking at my suitcase and was crying. What was I going to do? What should I do?

An English child, may God bless him wherever he is, was *vir vir vir vir* saying some things I don't understand. He was saying, "Don't cry," and indicating something with his hands to me. He was a young boy. I took out the address and showed it to him. He took my suitcase and put it at the edge of the road. He stood beside me, a child, a young boy. What could I say? A black taxi came and stopped and I showed the address to the driver. The taxi took me to my brother's house. He was staying in Hackney at the time.

The driver knew that I didn't understand English. He signalled to me to wait. Then I look and see that the driver went and knocked on the door. God helped me and who do I see but a woman, that woman was Nadire Aba, now deceased. She was coming with her daughter Sidika. "Walk, further" she was saying. I was hearing Turkish. "Walk, further" she was saying.

"Ah this girl has come from Cyprus?" she was saying. I swear to god, you won't believe it but she came and it was as if she had known me for 40 years. "Welcome my daughter," she said.

Thank you. "*Hoşbulduk*", I said.

"What are you doing?" she said.

"What should I do? What are you doing?" I replied. [How are you?]

"Who are you looking for?" she said. I was still waiting in the taxi. And she was walking past on the street and came over to me. They were talking to me in the taxi.

"I'm looking for the butcher's son Kemal. I am looking for his address," I said. I told them that I gave the address to the driver who said he would go and talk to the house owner.

"Don't worry," she said: "We will get his address off the taxi driver. You can come to us if you don't find your brother and then we will take you to him. I will have your brother found tomorrow," she said. The taxi driver came back and said to them that my brother had left the house. In other words he was a lodger at the woman's house, but had left there and gone somewhere else.

"I don't know where he has gone but my husband does," the woman said.

"Don't worry at all, let's go to my place," said Sidika. "I will find him for you," she said. She went and asked the landlady where my brother was living now.

She said, "I don't know but he lives in Ahmet the barber's house."

Sidika said, "Don't you worry at all, I know where he is. Come, I'll take you there."

I swear to God it was like I say. We went, but what should I do with my suitcase? Sidika said, "Leave it here, and your brother can come and get it." So we left the suitcase right there in the landlady's house.

We knocked on the door of Ahmet the barber's house. The man, the barber was there. We could see him there shaving someone. He came to the door and asked, "Who do you want?"

"We are looking for the butcher's son, Kemal," said Sidika.

"Yes, he has just gone upstairs," he said.

"His sister has arrived,"

"OK," said the barber, and opened the door for us. We went up the stairs. But I was dying, I was worrying, "Where am I? What's going to happen to me?" I was hungry and thirsty. They gave us pork on the aeroplane. I didn't eat it. It was an English plane. Well anyway we went up the stairs and my brother's door was slightly ajar. I went to barge in.

"No! No! Knock on the door!" Sidika said. We don't have knocking on doors before entering in Cyprus. I knocked and my brother said from inside the room, "Come in." I went in when he said come in.

"Where have you come from? Where have you come from?"

"Look," I said, "Don't ask me anything, go get my suitcase, and come and show me somewhere to sleep." I didn't sleep all night. I slept, woke, slept, woke and spoke to my brother all night. That's what we did with my brother.

I found my husband later. He came over, he heard that I had arrived. Two weeks later. He came two weeks later. "What have you come for?" he said to me.

"What do you mean, why have I come?" I said. "I have come. Like you, I have come to the foreign land".

My brother then said to him, "Take your wife and go if you want to, but I don't want you staying here with me, going to and fro as you please."

That was that, he never came again.

HÜSEYIN HASSAN MEMOUR: I lived in Lurigina, now called Akıncılar. It used to be Lurigina when I was there as a young boy. The first time when I left [Cyprus] was in 1952. I went to France for three years, did specialist studies to become a priest – but not Orthodox, but Protestant. I was away from 1952 – 55. I completed my studies in three years and then I went back. I am a priest. Not Greek Orthodox, not Catholic, but Protestant. I used to come here [to London] every summer when I was doing my studies in France. No Common Market in those days. So I had to come here and work, and I used to spend my summer with my sister. In England. North London, a place called Southgate.

SÜHA FAIZ: The boarding school – I don't know how on earth they selected it – it was in South Devon and it was called Ashburton Grammar School. Now my cousins who came here, they went to different schools. They must have had their own information or advice. I have a kind of guess, which I think is probably right. While my father was in England becoming a barrister – and don't forget he had his elder brother some years before him – and this probably means my father went back to become a barrister in 1927, because I was born in 1926, 28 December. His brother must have been there, Fuat Bey must gone, not in the late 1890s, Münir Bey maybe, but sort of five or six year before that – so there was a kind of, by now a kind of tradition. So I am sure that when my father was being a barrister he met a bloke, who must have probably known Fuat Bey and he was a refined. His father was a Lord Merrivale, lord because he was a senior judge, the head of the probate division in High Court. And you become a lord in those days. And a proper lord, hereditary. And this chap was his son – my father and his son were friends. The peerage that this Lord Merrivale took his title from was a Devon place, it is a village in Devon. They must have been people from Devon. And probably through him, father gets us into this grammar school in South Devon. The interesting thing is within less than a year the headmaster of that grammar school, Jack Evans Prosser, becomes the headmaster of a public school in Shropshire called Ellesmere, and we go with him.

So we go to Ellesmere, really my education starts in an English school at Ellesmere in Shropshire in 1935. Just the two of us. Because obviously the arrangement has been made between my father and him. And the reason I mentioned that is also if you go to a boarding school and you have got no family, where do you go for holidays? Well it so happened that Evans Prosser must have arranged – with or without my father's knowledge, but I am sure with knowledge and approval – that we stayed at a rectory which was only about, less than 20 miles from Ashburton. In South Devon, at a little village called East Allington – an English vicar, rector actually and wife, and in those days English clergy were not exactly rich! They had three children of their own, and they were trying educate them in private schools and the British Empire is in being, lots of British people serving in India, in Burma, Africa, who send their children home. So there is quite a flourishing tradition of families who are not well off taking children of overseas parents as their foster parents. So my brother and I spend five years from 1934 until the war – with one gap which I'll explain – in school in Shropshire, holidays in South Devon. And very nice too, I enjoyed myself!

Süha Faiz at Ellesmere College, Shropshire, 1937

Sedat Faiz, Adam Rassim and Süha Faiz, East Allington, Devon, 1937

We communicated with Cyprus by letter. But two things happened. One is my brother got – in fact we all got, one did in those days – measles, chickenpox, mumps, all the rest of it. And from measles I think it was he developed pneumonia, this is at 1936 and he got very ill, he nearly died in fact at school. He was very ill and when he got better, father came and took him back, because the doctor advised he can't spend another winter here after what he had, and he spent, I should think six or seven months, anyway two school terms in Cyprus. I stayed on by myself. And then when he came back, until 1939, I never went to Cyprus at all from the time I came here in 1934 till 1939, five years which is a long time, from the ages of, what? Eight till 13, something like that. We went out for the first time for a holiday on a P&O ship from London to Port Said. That is it, we get a little ship from there to Cyprus on the *Fouahdieh* and then the *Khedieval* lines – and this is ship was absolutely full, I think it must have been chartered by parents, because it was full of schoolboys all going to their parents god knows where – Gibraltar, Egypt – and it went on to India, all these places. All these children were being dropped off. It is my memory of it. But it was a regular P&O liner. Now they are all cruise liners. But this is a proper passenger ship. I remember the name of it too: *Ranchi*.

Anyway, my brother and I come out for this holiday – this would be in June, July of 1939 – and my father has now finished the superintendent policing in Larnaka, covering Famagusta as well. And of course what happens in September 1939 is war: World War Two.

Now, curiously – this is a side issue – my other cousins, Münir Bey's sons, this is Necati, Cahit *sizlere ömür*, there is five of those families, two of us in Cyprus. They came out as well, Necati and Cahit, on the same ship as us, and they stayed. But my father, God knows how he managed it – after all just think about it you already invested God-knows-what – he sent these pupils to school. I don't know on what basis this happened, because there were two other people on that ship, who were English boys, one of them I know pretty well. I think they must have been the sort of a symposium of parents, English and us Turkish. Münir Bey, for all I know he didn't send his children back. Anyway, we went back on a ship. It was an Egyptian ship. We went from Cyprus not to Port Said but to Port Alexandria in this little boat, it was a sort of postal boat. And from there we had an Egyptian boat called Muhammed Ali el-Kebir.

Now, we are going from Cyprus. It is now wartime. This is January, late January 1940. We are in Cyprus on holiday. Supposedly for about three or four weeks we get stuck. So from July 1939 to February whatever 1940, we are in Cyprus and this thing is organised and we come back. We arrive back in England, having crossed France by train. Think of our parents! My father and mother are over there, they now hear – we are back at school, let's say in the Easter Term in 1940 – and in April you get the [Easter break] and then you come in. So that is how I come, and by then of course, we stay in England, my brother and me. He, I have to cut it short, he joins the navy, anyway when he leaves school, he goes to Oxford for one year and in 1943, he joins the navy.

My brother is called Sedat. I stay on at school, I then go to Oxford, this is wartime. It is 1943-46 I went to Oxford, of course war ended in 1945. I then get my degree, war is over, long story and then I come back to Cyprus.

OSMAN TAHIR: I stayed here for a week, within a week I found a job in the bakery in Waterloo. We used to earn good money but it didn't take long, they moved from there. It went somewhere far away. We stayed, you know, then we still didn't get used to the streets, roads.

I learned language, slowly, slowly, some of the words that we used for work we learned and got used to but there are some [words] that have never passed through our mouths that we don't know. Here you don't learn without going to school. Like that, while we speak, we stole [words] from here and there.

What do I know? How can I know the price of the journey? We came here by train, passed Dover. We came to Victoria Station. We got off there, my brother-in-law was there, he picked us up. They brought me home and my son as well. Victoria Station was enormous. We didn't know then, we came as a stranger. What did we know? They used to come from outside, get off in that, in Victoria Station.

HATICE FETTI: I came seven months after. I came by ship. It was 30 lira then. Of course my husband paid for it. Of course, he sent it to me. It took nine days by boat.

For example, when we came to Greece, before I left there was a neighbour. Her son was married to a Greek. He loved a Greek girl, a *ciracik* and he married to her. When this conflict occurred he was afraid and he went to Greece because the girl, the girl was Greek. The neighbour used to go and come to London so she knew the journey. She said to me, when I was going, "It is going to stop over in Greece. There are cafés. It is easy, you can ask someone," because I knew the language well. Well, I got off, asked, if there is such a person and that I know him. They said, "OK." They called him. He came like this, indicating not to talk in Turkish, as he didn't say he is Turkish. The Greek people knew me as a Greek Cypriot. My Greek was excellent. With me, there was my sister-in-law as well. Well, I was talking. He came, they asked us what we would like to drink. I said,

"Please, give us something cold." I mean, they were hospitable. I said, "I have a letter, I am going to post". He said, "No, I can post." But as I didn't want them find out that I am a Turkish, because the name was written on top of the letter, I said, "No, no, it'd be better if I post it. Then I would know that I have posted the letter." They said, "OK." Afterwards the boy came. They asked something to the girl [the sister-in-law] next to him. I said, "She doesn't understand, she can't speak. She became ill suddenly; we are going for a treatment." They said, "Oh, it is such a shame. How beautiful she is." I said, "She can't speak yet. We are going for a treatment." I mean, if my sister-in-law understood, she would have laughed a lot. The boy came. We talk in Greek. From there we went to the ship for an hour.

We didn't reveal at all. He took us for a walk. There is a place in every town in Greece, he showed us around but we didn't speak in Turkish because in a foreign country you speak Turkish. When we went to the ship I started speaking Turkish. Well, he asked how his parents are, if everything is OK. I explained to him that they don't have any problem. That is it, because the ship was going to leave, we were going to go inside. He went back.

There were other Turkish people on the boat with me. One of them has died now. The other one is too far away, I don't see her at all now. The journey was nice. Our journey was very nice. It was a passenger boat but it was also taking cargo. It was an Italian ship called *Mesapya*. I don't remember what countries we passed anymore. We went to Paris. We got off, we walked about somewhere. It was my first time leaving Cyprus. Second time I left Cyprus with my children, we stopped over in Italy. We walked around in Italy. We weren't scared when we left because we used to walk with a crowd. We weren't afraid of anything.

I came to Victoria Station. I saw my husband; they picked me up. But before I came here, that is to say when I immediately got on the ship, on top of my sister-in-law's, her sister-in-law used to stay and she had a daughter who was ill. The flat was very high. There were 72 steps for her to climb the stairs from downstairs to upstairs. It was very difficult because the child had a heart problem. And there they had applied to be given a better flat. When I was getting on the boat, a piece of paper was posted to them. A letter. It was necessary for them to leave. They gave them a flat by River Thames. One storey. When it happened like that, my husband offered them to sell it [the flat] for £50. Then they sold that flat to him for £50. We stayed there, two rooms were [inside each other]. Our gas cooker, everything was in there. I was going to wash the kids on Saturday, there was a bathtub made of iron. There was a passage outside, there were taps. We used to heat up the water in the buckets on top of the gas cooker and we used to wash the kids inside, we used to have wash as well. One day, a friend of mine said to me, "I thought about coming to you." It was Saturday. I said, "No, I don't accept guests on Saturdays." She asked me, "Why it is like that?" I said, "Because one of them is going to have a wash in the bath, I can't host you inside." I said. We stayed for a fair amount of time, upstairs. Afterwards council gave us one more flat downstairs.

The flat was in Farringdon Road, Clerkenwell.

HATICE IBRAHIM: The journey was 12 days. I came with my father-in-law. He came to ask for me in Cyprus and then we travelled to London together.

Vallahi, unknowingly. I swear I was completely unaware on the journey. It was as if smoke had lifted me and was carrying me. In that manner. It was as if deep down I knew this was not going to be a good thing.

On the contrary there was this young man who was pursuing me. He would always come and stand near me [on the boat]. "Why are you going to your fiancé?" he would ask. "Have you lived together?" He would ask.

"Yes, we stayed together for five to six months," I said. Lie. I hadn't even seen him. I wanted him to distance himself from me.

He then said that he was a plainclothes policeman, that I should give up my intended and have him. He was Turkish. I was not bought up like that. I did not grew up canny. To see and grab someone else. I very tragic thing!

So we came to Victoria. I had an unmarried brother here called Ibrahim. When we arrived this plainclothes policeman said, "When we get to London and I see your fiancé, I'm going to tell him that you're not a nice girl so he won't have you." This was the situation. We got off the train and were waiting to see who was going to come and collect me. My fiancé's father, who was on the boat with us, said, "Go girl, go embrace your fiancé." My fiancé then came over and half-heartedly embraced me. The plainclothes policeman saw this and walked away. I looked down the train tacks and thought, "I have fallen into a hole. I am finished."

I did not fancy my husband at all, but I didn't know the plainclothes policeman very well. I didn't talk much with him. I just told him that I had seen my fiancé. A lie.

At that time my brother was unmarried and had a rented room. We went there with a black taxi. My other sister-in-law Remziye, my brother, my fiancé and me were in the taxi. He bangs on the window and tells the driver, "200 Farmers Road," but my brother says Kennington. Driver gets annoyed and stops the taxi and says, "Tell me where you want to go. Which address?"

I was tired and said to my brother, "Leave it *abi*, as they paid for my ticket, I'll go with them. Let's see what's going to happen and then we can make an agreement." He let me go with them. My first sister-in-law was a lodger upstairs.

HÜSEYIN HASSAN MEMOUR: I came here because it was my home and I had the British passport. It was my home and all that. No, not as an extension of Cyprus. England is a unique country. England has a very very unique history. The number one Protestant country in the world, [though] not now.

ŞABAN LEFKARIDI: We came all together. My intention was to come here for one, two, three years and go back again. To work of course. I left my house to my brother to look after. We had an olive grove, a farm, there were more than 200 olive trees in one of our fields, beautiful trees. That is to say first class, we had a very nice property in the village. We still have property on the Greek side, in Larnaca. It is still ours.

I paid for the ticket myself. We came here by a ship. It was 90 lira I think. Altogether. I think, my child was one-and-a-half, or two years old, something like that.

We left Cyprus from Larnaca. The name of the ship was *Mesapya*. I think it was Italian, or Jewish, I don't know. There were both Turkish and Greek passengers. We were all mixed anyway. We went to Italy, the ship went to Bari. Afterwards from Italy we took a train and came. I think we came to Victoria. I can't remember how long the journey was.

Well it was the first time we were going a journey, the sea was rough and wavey as well. Everyone was going from one side, another side. We had those kind of days, that is to say. It was my first departure from Cyprus. I didn't think of going back on the ship. That kind of thing didn't come to our mind, that is to say. We had to continue, we were obliged.

When [we] came to Victoria, my sister's daughters Emine and Remziye were here to meet us, they were here. My brother's son Halil was here as well, he is deceased. I can't remember which one of them came to pick us up, but one of them came. I used to stay at Halil's house first on Farness Road by Kennington Park. It was his house. My brother's son used to hold the lease. He gave us a room as well, we used to stay there. Afterwards I bought a flat in Elephant and Castle. I came in 1955, four or five months, something like that. Later I bought an apartment in Elephant and Castle, I myself moved there. It was a flat, flats were very cheap in those days. We used to stay in one room. We thought we would be more comfortable if I bought a flat with two or three rooms, at that time, it was very cheap. Everyone used to give commission for people to rent their flats because all of them were empty.

We bought it by rent. Rent was £25 per week. They used to let flats easily because there weren't people to rent. Where we used to stay in our flat, all of them were empty. All of the apartments were empty. There was a Turk, Fuat from Aytotoro. His English was good. He had graduated from an American Academy, and the agent used to give him commission for him to find a customer to rent. Because they were empty.

We found our flat like that. Our neighbours, they were Turkish as well, same as us. All of us were tenants. All of us were Turkish in those flats. We went to Elephant and Castle in 1955. Five, six months I stayed there. I think it was Timgiri street – now all of those places have been demolished and new buildings have been built.

There were lots of Turks from different villages, all different, Turkish and Greek from Cyprus. We all ended up there because those places were empty. Mr Fuat would receive some commission, because he would find customers for the agent. Anyone who heard about that went, anyone who heard about that went. Turks and Greeks from Cyprus used to stay altogether there. There were cafés there, a lot of cafés. Turks, Greeks, all of us always used to go the same cafés around there. The women were at home. They used to go to their neighbours, to each other, because all of them were Turkish around there.

HULUSI MAHMUD GÜRÇAYOĞLU: It was my first time here. When you see everything, they are strange places to you. You just have to get used to it. My brother came to meet me. We went through Greece. We stopped at Greece. We come to Italy. We got to the train to come near to Calais. It was all right seeing other countries until I come to London. Because in London, in those days the weather was very bad. Foggy, and so on. Burning coal, you know. Some days you can't see where you are going. Buses used to stop, they had tram buses, which is run by electric. I wanted to go back and started crying. He said, "No, no don't be silly, you are not going back." My brother told me. I started crying as soon as I got to England. I wanted to go back straight away. Yes it was very foggy, it was some days. I didn't like it but gradually got used to it.

We were only a day in Italy. We come off the boat and get the train and come to Calais. And from Calais we got the boat again, across the sea, the channel, two hours from Dover by train to Victoria. There other passengers on the boat, some going to New Zealand in Australia. But London, I don't know. No one came to London with me.

I wasn't scared on the boat, but I was ill at first when aboard the boat. After that I was on deck, just observing the sea and so on. That was so nice.

When I came, I went to live with my brother in Highbury. My brother died now, he passed away. My oldest brother. His wife was living there at that time, the boy their child. After that I went to another brother. They were living not far from there. Islington. I lived with them about four years, two years. Then I got married after that.

IBRAHIM DERVIŞ: We came to Liverpool Street. We came to our home. My sister's husband had some government bonds with the Turkish Bank. By luck there was a prize of 400 Cyprus liras, and just before I came he won. I immediately informed him by telegraph and they bought a house with the money.

We were all together at one time. We were in a little bit of a tight situation. We tried to organise ourselves and so on in our house. The house was on Charlton Street, off Malden Road, in Camden Town. There was Queen's Crescent, In any case, the house cost something like £400 – we paid for it with the money that we had won. The price was cheap then because there were lodgers in it.

I missed my friends. I missed my motherland. There was nice weather, but the yearning for the motherland, far from friends – because in Cyprus, there had been a good community in Fikret Baba's scout group. I left all that and came.

By now of course, my responsibilities towards by family had all finished. I thought I could now return. I missed Cyprus. But I couldn't entertain that thought because the house need repairs and so on.

DUDU HAKKI: We came by boat in eight days. I think the boat was called *Mesapya*. It went from Cyprus to Greece. We stopped in Greece, two hours in Rome, then Belgium and then England. I made the journey with Nahide *Aba* and there were her sons Memduh and Ismail. Nahide *Aba's* husband had left Cyprus a long time ago. He came here to work; there was more work for men here. In 1960 they had already been here for 13 years. 13 years after they left Cyprus they went back to visit.

The boat came from France to Dover. From Dover we came to Victoria Station by train. We took a black taxi with Nahide *Aba* and went [to her] home. Her husband Mehmet Emin *Abi* was waiting for us.

When I got to Victoria, I thought it was very bad. Mist, fog, dark and raining. You couldn't see your nails from the fog. In any case, we got out of Victoria Station to get a taxi, but even as we got off the train I said to Nahide *Aba*, "What is this place that we have come to? I'm going to go back. I'm not going to be able to stay here at all."

"Your *Abi* used to say that, but let's see what's going to happen," she said.

That day when we came, 11 people came from Cyprus, from Lefkara. They all dispersed to their families. I went with my Nahide *Aba*. I stayed with her. I came here for a holiday, but I didn't go out sight-seeing anywhere. Even when I went to the market with Nahide *Aba*, Mehmet Emin *Abi* would immediately shout "Come back quickly now!" So where could we go out?

ALI GASBAR: It was a three-day boat journey, a Jewish boat called *Zibra*. A one-day train journey but I don't remember the name. It departed from Limassol by boat, Greece, Italy, Trieste port. From Italy we would board a train. We would get down at France, Calais and by ferryboat come to Dover. From Dover to Victoria by train.

Firstly we arrived at Victoria. Munur Asim, my uncle's brother, met us. Three friends and myself, our two other friends, had decided to stay in Germany. We stayed at our friend's Munur's house in Newington Green. We came to a place that at first darkness, weather not resembling Cyprus's weather, rainy, snowy, cold. I was saddened because I left behind my family, my loved ones, and my relatives to come to this foreign city, it upset and scared me. I did not leave the house for three days. Neither did I acknowledge that it had been day or night. Tiredness and reasons for sadness meant I had been unable to pull myself together.

CELAL HASSAN: Ye, there were some other people from my village in Victoria. They came and picked me up and they bring me home. In this country I had my brother, I had my cousin but he was on holiday that time you know. But we knew some people in this country like Madriko, three or four people. Not many Turkish people here, no. Turkish people was after that.

When I arrived in Victoria in London. They took me straight home. It was in near Goodge Street, a place called Goswell Place. Used to belong to one of the village. It was all men in those days. He was here before during the War, you know.

We called him Tahtacı. Nickname. He was from Gorovya. I stayed in one of his rooms. I stayed about two years. Well, I don't remember where I went after that, but I went to another place. You went to live with my brother you see.

MEHMET MUSTAFA: I came here in 1960. I just finished high school then. It was during EOKA time, the time when EOKA was a hot subject. I came after Cyprus Turkish Republic was established.

16 August 1960. It just happened, I went to Doctor Küçük's, we were invited as students, at school. I have photos of them.

Of course there was discrimination, when I came here, I used to tell the Greeks. 70% of my customers are Greeks. I said there isn't prosperity here for us. Everyone used to go. Young people as well.

There wasn't many, there were just a few. There was Ibrahim Mapushanecilerin here. Their family came to pick me up from the train station. That is to say, there were a few people here. They used to know the arrival time of the ship, train; specifically they used to go to Victoria Station and wait to see a familiar face, a Muslim face, a Turkish, a Cypriot face. They would enjoy it.

The name of the ship was *Theodor Herzl*, it was a Jewish ship from Israel. The ship would come from Israel to Limassol, from Limassol to Naples, from Naples to Marseilles, from Marseilles to Paris, from Paris to London. We took the train from Paris. There were even 21 Greeks. Their tickets were in my hand as well, because I was the only who could speak English. That Cypriot told me not to disappear because our life is in your hands. There was a Greek, he used to take you specifically from place to place. "But I came to Marseilles. I am gonna go back." he said. "You take it from here," he said, as I can speak Greek, I can get on with the Greeks and I can speak English. He said to me, "Take these, when they come to Paris, they are going to ask you, you are going to give these tickets, after that you'll get to Calais, from Calais to Dover". We boarded in Dover.

They take you from Dover to London automatically. That was included in the ticket. £32 10 shillings sterling. All the way. By train. You used to go to Victoria for £32 10 shillings sterling. Now this is very dramatic. I came to station, everyone is around. I was sitting down, I said, "Why should I get up? I have got nobody to come get me, there's nobody." I look up and iron poles, these bolt-upright things. There nothing like these things in Limassol.

Oooh, those big big irons [railings]. Allah, Allah where did I do wrong? I came here, where am I gonna go now? Everyone is in rush, to come out of the train and go.

No, no one knew that I was coming. My brother-in-law here three days before he went to Turkey. Supposedly he is gonna come here from Turkey and we are gonna meet. As something like that can happen. Neither did I take any address, nor nothing. We are going to meet. He doesn't know the streets. I would sit like this, I wouldn't look. I wouldn't look, I wouldn't get off either. Where am I going to get off, where am I gonna go to? Because it is not easy to get off the train in an enormous country.

It is not fear. "What are we gonna do?" we said. "OK, you came up to here. On the basis of what did you come here?" I say to myself.

I had £27 in my pocket. I got it from this Çetin Kaya. He had a book [savings book]. I look, like this, suddenly; now look at the greatness of Allah, I saw someone through the window, there was deceased Ibrahim's brother. He had an accident here. "My Mehmet, it is you!" I thought, "Allah spoke to me!" I look. Where is he, who is he? Elmas is his sister, she is here, 75, 76 years old and ill now. Ibrahim as well, three of them, we were neighbours, next door neighbours.

Their window was opposite us: "My Mehmet!" Their happiness was more than mine. Because they saw a Turk. They picked me up, he says, "Let's go." We left, went, he took me into a bus to Tulse Hill. They used to stay there. Their house is antique. It wasn't their own house. What do they call it, squatting? They squatted; it was an open area in the middle of something. Train goes through there. When the train passed by we used to hold the table as it was shaking like this. I stayed there for a while. We play cards, hold the table not to lose any money.

But there were 20 rooms in the squatted house. All of us loved it, we could accommodate 100 people. That is to say 100 people are welcome, like that. The people who come and go can stay. They were also a big family, they were five, six people. They picked me up, took me. Their mum, Meryem *Aba*: "Welcome my Memed!" Their mum was in this squatted house as well. I guess squatting wasn't heard of. It was an empty house, they moved in. They used to stay, neither rent money nor nothing. It used to shake when a train passed. Who would live in that? You had to hold the table; otherwise money would drop off.

I didn't stay that long, because I will tell you later. "Now, who was going to come and pick you up?" he said.

NIAZI OSMAN: We used get on the boats from Limassol or Larnaca ports, there were Jewish ships called *Zim*. Italian ship called *Capidoccio*. But the ships are very nice. Their service was five star, Their service was like hotels. We used to go in, send our passenger with 32 lira, but they used to ask for a courier as well. They didn't know, five, ten people as a group we used find a courier and send them. I mean to take those people. Helping them. We used to get on from Limassol, after a nice life, a first class service, arrive in Italian and French ports. Either to Marseilles or Venice. After we got off, we used to get on trains with lot of trickery.

We would carry our own luggage ourselves. We used to go into trains from Venice or Marseilles. After spending one night on the train, we would come to Paris, from Paris again to another train. We would come to Calais to the West ports, from Calais again by boat to Dover. In Dover of course, you don't know what to do in somewhere you visit for the first time, but the courier would help us. We would come from Dover to Victoria. We used to meet our relatives the ones who sent us invitations. We used to meet our relatives in Victoria and go to their home. When I came in 1958 the old apartments in Elephant and Castle were really very awful at that time. There was only one toilet for the whole apartment, they didn't have a washing machine. All of them used to gather in corridors, they used to wash their clothes. It was very difficult, very difficult. They didn't have bathrooms.

I was not a courier. I used to come from time to time. I didn't come every time they say. We used to find another courier and bring the passengers. We used to mix our passengers with Greeks. I came, as a passenger, and I helped my customers a little bit.

It would take six days, four days on a ship, and the other one is six days. We used to for example, then I saw there wasn't a Turkish agency here. I made my mind up to open an office here. I came in 1962, I found my relatives here. My siblings' children were here. I found deceased Fuat, Hüseyin Onbası, there were our other villagers. In the end, with their help we searched from this and that, we found that place on Old Kent Road. I settled down there. I came with my family, together. I didn't have kids. I had money. I used to earn then. Deceased Sermet, my first cousin, met me at Victoria. My uncle's son Sermet, he is dead now. He met me, after that we went to his house, I, the kids were there. It was in Haringey. When I first came I stayed in Haringey. After that we had kids, thanks to our Fuat, we settled there. He had a place in Elephant and Castle. I didn't stay long in Haringey because I went as a guest. Fuat, my sibling's son said, "Come and stay with me until you find a place, settle down." That is how it happened.

HÜSEYIN YUSUF: I am married to my second wife. My first wife was English, when I got married here. I was single when I came here. I was only 18 when I came here. I came here in 1949. I was working, in a small, like a station, I don't know it in English. There was a stopping place for petrol, something to eat, coffees, things like that you know. I was working there. I did catering, serving, selling petrol in gallons.

I was a young, ambitious person. Like everybody else when they are young they wanna see the world, excitement, things like that. My intentions were, I come from a big family, brothers and sisters. My father was not a well-off person. Well I came to improve my life, my living. And also help my family here. Ye. I was one of the first one in my family to come over.

I travelled here by boat from Larnaka. My first impression of Victoria Station was a very bad first impression because it was a foggy night, hardly you can see anything. My uncle, my cousin, were supposed to come and meet me. He didn't come. He didn't because he forgot about me. He didn't remember because his wife was having a baby. Very same day he had a daughter. He had a baby and he would have possibly forgotten.

I must have arrived eight, between eight and nine. In the evening. Nobody came to pick me up, so I took a taxi. People were coming and going. I was really bit disturbed. Because no one came to pick me up, and I began to think about things like environment, atmosphere if you can call it. It wasn't anything that I was used to. I was a bit upset. I took a taxi and I had his address. So taxi took me to his house. I didn't have no money to pay taxi – I rang the bell, after while he came down. He said he was annoyed because he just went to bed actually. He didn't recognise me at night.

"What the hell do you want, who are you?"

I said to him, "Don't you know me, recognise me?"

He said, "No, should I?"

I said, "Yes, I am your uncle's son."

"Oh," he said. "Sorry," he said: "I forgot all about you". He didn't see me for over a year because he didn't come to Cyprus.

I am his uncle's son, his uncle's son. First cousin. It was something, believe me.

He lived in 49 Upper Street. I still remember. I went from Victoria to Upper Street, Islington. It was a café, and a couple of storeys above we used to live up there. I stayed there for say about six months. I remember when I woke up I was straight down to start work, washing plates in the café. And it was a very busy café. We start in the morning, seven o'clock in the morning and we didn't finish until about two, three, four o'clock in the afternoon.

Well, I didn't actually know I was going to be working in the café.

The feeling goes through your whole system. I get goose pimples, do you know what I mean? I don't find it hard to talk about it, actually it is just a reminder of your past. It shouldn't be hard, it shouldn't be a problem. Some of the things, you kind of forget you know. I didn't know I was going to be working in this café. Coming to a blind spot, as you say. I knew he had something to do with catering but I didn't know where he was, what he was doing? Where it was situated? I didn't know anything!

I didn't get to see the customers, I didn't talk to the customers. No, I couldn't speak English anyway.

5. WORK

The British currency changed in 1971. In the old money, 12 pence was a shilling, and 20 shillings was a pound. In the new money, 100 (new) pence is a pound. Old pence were written 'd'; new pence are written 'p'. Hence seven shillings and sixpence (7s 6d) became 37.5p. Interviewees use lira and pounds interchangeably in conversation, so it won't always be clear which is meant.

OSMAN TAHIR: There isn't any job left that I didn't do. In the end, I worked in baked beans for four years. Heinz, I worked there; later on they moved as well. They moved outside. I went to Lambeth Hospital. Later on I went outside London. A place where they used to make augers and gimlets. We used to carry iron. That was our job. I worked there for a year. I left and came here, to London. We used to grind peppers in London. We used to grind everything. We worked there, but tears used to run out of our eyes. Tears used to run. Fire. From there I went to the beans.

In 60s, my wife used to do dressmaking. She was a finisher. She used to work during the day. She used to come home at night with a bundle, she used to work at night to make some money.

KEMAL AHMET DAVRANDI: "Hey Salih *Dayı*, find me a job!" I said. "I can't be unemployed," I said.

"I doesn't matter, my son, I'll find you a job," he said. There was a Necmi that he knew, Salih *Dayı* found him and asked him about work. "I'll ask about," Necmi said. "There's a cake factory in Kentish Town that my friends work in. I'll go and ask the boss there. Maybe he'll take him on," he said to Salih *Dayı*.

"Alright, take him and go," Salih *Dayı* said to Necmi. He took me and went, Necmi I mean. A person never forgets a person who does good. He put me in the car and took me away. He went and spoke to the boss. I don't know what was said but he gave me work. £3 a week. I started by cleaning in there. They used to make cakes in there. We used to scrape the sinks, carry the cakes to the sink. The sinks would be sticky, sticky! We used to scrape that, wiping, sweeping. I used to help at the ovens as well.

It took six weeks to two months to find this job. It was all Turks in there. There was a man called Kemal, God rest his soul if he has died. His wife was called Naciye. He was a baker, the head baker in there – and then we had a foreman called Ted. I didn't know any English but they made me a porter. Whenever he wanted something I was to go and get it. He told me.

But what do I know? In short he would say *redjump*, I would go unlock the room and look for *redjump*. *Redjump*, what do I know? I come and go in the room. I lock it, take him something. The pimp screamed at me and gave me a punch. "I'll shit in your mouth," I said in Turkish. "You are going to learn English!" he would say to me. This pimp's gonna kill me, I thought. "This is red jam," he said, and showed me red jam. For God's sake, I swear and I'm telling you the truth. And little by little I learned what he was asking for. After that they put me to help with the cakes.

The factory was called John Daley. I'll never forget.

DUDU HAKKI: After I came, my Nahide *Aba* started work. "I'll immediately take you to work," she said to me. She took me to work, to dressmaking. It was right at Christmas time. I worked for two weeks, four days a week, and then they made me redundant. I worked for a Jewish man over in the Bethnal Green area.

Nahide *Aba* had a lodger who worked at a cobbler. "I'll take you to my work," she said: "I'll ask the foreman if he needs any workers." She took me to the cobbler. They made really nice slippers for Marks and Spencer's. I used to dip the brush into the chemical and then use it to remove the excess glue from the edge of the slippers. I really enjoyed that job. It was really nice. I used to work on Saturdays, as overtime. I used to get £7. The Turkish lodger took me to that job. There was us two, and one other Turkish person working there. The rest were all English, both men and women, all mixed. There were more Turks in the first factory that I worked in. We used to sew really nice dresses for new expensive shops. When I got engaged in those days, I paid £7 for my dress, that was very expensive, and then my ring was £7 too. In 1960 that was very expensive, because there wasn't much money around. When I told people that I bought a ring for £7, everyone would say, "Oh my God, oh my God, that's very expensive!"

GÜLSEN LARKINS: I got a job. I wasn't allowed to go out. Same in Cyprus, isn't it? When I started working. I started working year after. No, I wasn't 22, I was 21, I told you. I got married 23.

I worked in Bermondsey. First I went to learning dressmaking. After my cousin took me to making jam. Not making, first packing. My first cousin, she used to work there.

EMINE AHMED: My dad gave me either five or 15 lira then. "Take it," he said. "When you go, send it back to me, because I borrowed this," he said. When I came, I sent that money back. I used to work for four-and-a-half lira, later on the foreman raised my wages to five lira. My first job was in Dalston. Dressmaking. I used to do dressmaking in a Jewish factory. Sultan Abla found me the job. She also used to work for the same foreman. She was working as a finisher for the same foreman, I also went there. I started working as a finisher. I started to work a couple of weeks after I came here.

CELAL HASSAN: I worked in Charing Cross, it used to be a coffee house there, belonging to Tahtacı, and I worked about six months, and then some other friends, they told me to take me to Trocadero. They used to call it Trocadero, but they changed it now, I don't know what they call it now. It was a company. Lyon's company. A restaurant, a kitchen upstairs.

They served mainly to rich people, poor people couldn't go there in those days.

Ye, I was living with him [Tahtaci] and give me some money as well but when I went there I got £1 more in the job. So that is why I changed the thing.

I didn't find it difficult working in an English restaurant, No, because there used to be a few Turkish people there you see. And then suddenly I got a letter from the English government. They say to me I have to do National Service. Once you are in this country – so I took my record there, we talked to them to the office. They said you have to do it, we give him six months. He has to leave the country or he has to do the National Service.

I'm not sure what year was this… I think, I am not sure, I used to work in Trocadero. I remember it must have been 1958, 59 something like that. And then in that six months time suddenly I had a letter, they abolished the National Service, no National Service, you can stay free in this country they said.

SÜHA FAIZ: I am a Turkish Cypriot, I am back in Cyprus. I'd like to work here, I have got a jolly good degree, I was as good as the English people who were doing whatever it is. But Münir said no, basically no. Because you would then be regarded as local appointee. You shouldn't be a local appointee, what you must do is join the Unified Colonial Administrative Service, which means an appointment in England by the Secretariat State.

Not in Whitehall, by Whitehall, I mean the Secretariat State for Colonies. That state is still a colonial empire. Kenya, Uganda, Gold Coast, Nigeria. And for many people this is their career. So Münir said, "Go back, get your appointment from there and they will appoint you somewhere and then after a sometime you can ask for a transfer to Cyprus, and then you are in Cyprus as a proper colonial British whatever." It was wise advice, which I took. So then I go back to England with my mother, because she hadn't seen England, she wanted to see England, so we went back together on a ship.

I am now back in England in again – it was January 1947 with my mother, and we are living in a little hotel, in those days you can live in a hotel in London near Notting Hill, Bayswater, from where I made my application and I am appointed. As a cadet officer, appointed to the Gold Coast. Well, therefore, my mother has seen England, her son is now safe, her elder son is back from the war, he goes back to Oxford, everything is OK. She goes back home. And now my mother is back in Cyprus, my brother is at Oxford after a while he served in the navy and I am now about to go to the Gold Coast 1947.

And at this stage I could speak Turkish, but I won't pretend that my English [isn't] infinitely better.

HATICE FETTI: Work, as soon as I came, I came on Thursday, I had a cousin in Elephant and Castle, on Sunday we went to them. She said to me, "Do you know, there is a factory here, I will go there for and if they need workers, you can go." It was a sewing factory. I said, "OK." She went and looked. On Monday night we stayed there. They had space. It was only their kids. My cousin, my uncle's daughter went and looked on Monday. She came and said, "I found a job for you." £1 a day. I said "Oh, how nice, £1 per day!" I used to get £5 a week. I used to go but it was easy. I used to take bus number 62 from here, it was Elephant and Castle, I used to come by one bus, straight away. There were other Turkish people there as well, and of course English people. There was, but first when we came to this country, in factories there were mostly Cypriots. That is to say, we didn't have any difficulty because we didn't know English, when we wanted ask something to the bosses, people who knew English used to help. Our boss was Jewish. We used to sew men's clothes, and they would put the men's clothes inside bags. I used to sew them on the machine. I worked there for seven months. I prepared, I bought clothes for my children. Before there was such a thing: if you saw something you wanted to buy, you would put it on hold, you would go and choose, put a deposit and then we used to go there every week to pay it all off. When we went there and I bought for all of my children.

In one shop I found, it was all children clothes. I bought clothes for all of them, I put a deposit on them first. Then I used to give £1, £2 each week because I used to get paid £5.

EMINE AHMET: I started work in January, March, one year after I came here, my husband didn't allow me to work anymore. Before I started working in Highbury there were some other people who Ibrahim my husband knew. I used to go to her to learn how to use a machine, she used to work at home. I came out of an institute* in Cyprus and came here. There weren't electric machines, there were manual ones in Cyprus. We used to embroider on the machine. I did those. Three months before I got my diploma, I left the institute and came here.

When I came here I didn't find it too strange. Because I used to go to an English class in Cyprus. I could understand the things said. I didn't have too much difficulty. A couple of months later I went to that friend of mine, we used to sew. After I helped for a week or so, she called me and wanted to pay some money. Because she says, "You are not a learner, you know the job." I didn't take it. There was a friend who came here the same year I came. She said, "Let's go to work, let's go to work." A week later she took me and we went, we looked for a job in a couple of places. They employed her, they didn't employ me. My husband was working in a restaurant and he was sleeping during day. I went in the morning. She found a job in a Greek factory, of course I took a bus and came back home. My friend's sister-in-law Mrs Hava said, "I am going to take you to work." There used to be a flour factory called Harilla. They didn't give me the job. When she saw me the woman didn't employ me. As I had newly arrived, she was concerned a lot. She says, "You came here recently, how are you going to find your way, how are you gonna come to work?" I took a bus and came home, my husband was still sleeping. I wouldn't get lost, because I know the language. I have got the courage. I came home, a couple of months passed. I said, "I would like to work." He sleeps during the day, works at nights. I was alone at home;

---

* Vocational and training colleges in Cyprus were called institutes.

Nehir *Aba* was working at home. I said "I am going to work." Because my father was a *neşber*, we are not used not working. We are village people. We used to do a lot of work in the village, we used to embroider on the machine. Anyway, I looked for a job. I found this job myself. I worked for a week.

It was making dresses. My first job was that. Gross money was £6, he gave £4 per week, net. Fifteen days later that was closed down as well. I left that job, I stayed at home to find another job. When the factory was closed down, they sent us to a factory called Green Foot which was on top of Midland Bank on the opposite side of the road. They used to sew jackets and coats, I was deployed to sew lining [for the coats and jackets]. When I was sewing the linings he said to me, "You know the job, I am going to deploy you to sew the arm of the jackets." He put me in that department, until I became pregnant. I was six months pregnant, by coincidence it was Easter. He told me that the factory is going to close down, it is not worth it for a month. Because my pregnancy was difficult. I stopped working. After that I didn't work outside. I gave birth. My first child was born in June 1962.

ALI GASBAR: For the first four months I was a tailor and pattern cutter. I used to earn £2 and 10 shillings a week. In 1957 like many of the first Turks who came here, I worked in Park Lane Hotel as a washer. Midnight Saturday night, in January 1957, after being involved in an event in a park, I immediately returned to Cyprus. After staying in Cyprus for two months, I bought my ticket for 27 Cyprus liras, with the 30 Cyprus liras that my dad had given me. The boat that I came with this time was called *Gabidaklo*. Two weeks later I worked in a butchers in Leyton for six months. In 1958 I started to work as a painter in a factory managed by Şükrü Ahmed. In 1960 I got engaged and within six months I married. 1963, I worked for a year as a *makascı* in Hüseyin Lido's factory.

In 1964 I set up my own factory in Kingsland Road. And when my friend Mustafa Avcı, who I love a lot, returned from fighting for the cause of the Cyprus campaign, I set up a partnership with him.

MELEK KAZIM: Parkhurst school was the last school I attended. After Parkhurst, I became a hairdresser. I would train on Fridays. On Saturdays we had a Polish lady with us. She took me near her [to work]. I use to go and help. After I finished school, I worked with her. Every day. Although my hands struggled with the chemicals. They were strong chemicals at that time. The doctor asked me to leave this job.

My hands would be covered with dermatitis. My hands would be covered in a red rash, and then my skin would disintegrate. The gaps would peel due to the chemicals and therefore I was forced to leave.

Then my mother suggested that a new, small Tesco had opened in Tottenham. There they taught me to be a cashier. The manager liked me so much that, she said, "We should train you to make you a manager." I was 17 years old at the time. I was married by 18 years old. I did not want to be a manager. I changed the job to work with Jews. It was a similar job, but smaller. I stayed there for one year until I got married.

NIAZI OSMAN: I found a place on Old Kent Road. And through Uncle Enver Emin, he is a very good foster brother, as a nice person he helped me. He made me take loan, then I bought that place for £7,000. The house, office altogether was freehold. Altogether it was for £7,000. We gave £3,000, I took £4,000 loan from the bank for five years. I used to pay £70 per month for the loan. After I lowered my loan, within a couple of years it decreased to £50. I found it difficult, because when you first come there isn't a job. I employed an assistant as well. English, part-time. My deceased wife and I employed a good assistant as a part-time secretary. Because I used to give the correspondence to the secretary, she used to correct it and send it. In short like this. I came in 1962 and the same year, I opened it in 1962.

As a matter of fact the customers who I brought here knew me. They were the ones that I sent from Cyprus to here. I made an advert; immediately they found me. But there weren't enough [customers] at that time in London. Of course the expenditure was then as much as today, but it was accordingly expensive. That is what happened. After that towards 1969, Turkish Airlines came. They set up in Hanover Square the office that they still have to this date. They opened an up-to-date, very nice contemporary office. Immediately their manager Mahmut Bey, may he live long, came and found me.

"We are glad that we found you, we are going to help you, we are going to make this place head office but without money, for the appearance." But he helped me a lot with tickets. They used to give me tickets for wherever I want, for a fair amount of time 30%, 40% commission, they helped me a lot when they first came. Two, three years had been like that with Turkish Airlines.

From 1962 to 1974 I was the only one. I was the only one. It was all me. I used to issue passports, deal with Home Office issues. Until now, I worked very honest with passport office, Home Office. They used send me forms by post as much as I wanted.

The name of the business was Zodiac Travel Service. Until now, it is still there. The same office. Zodiac Travel Service. I gave that name, yes, in 1962, I bought the name in 1963.

Because when I opened I registered that Zodiac Travel Service. And in order to buy this I was thinking what to do. I used to ask friends. There was Sergeant Yakup from Iskele, my foster brother. He said, "Give it the name Zodiac" I said, "Zodiac?" and then I thought about the stars, I said "OK," I accepted. It stayed, on top of the stars.

We didn't have any English customers because we needed ABTA (Association of British Travel Agents) membership then. We weren't ABTA then. English people, didn't come near us. Later on, what did I do to attract English people, I used to sell coach and train tickets. They used to give me their national travel tickets and I used to sell them. They used to come. I used to make some packet tours to Spain, and Turkey. We started those as well, after that I found it appropriate to obtain ABTA. I undertook and bought membership. This was probably in 1976, 1977, I bought ABTA membership and after that of course more business came. We continued.

The Turks used to come as a customer. In 1963, 1964, when the problems occurred in Cyprus, correspondence and telephones were cut off from us. Red Cross took the work. I heard that Red Cross helps, and I went to Red Cross. I approached, they recognised me and said, "OK Mr Osman, whenever you need help, we will help you." I brought many families for free at that time. From there to here. I go to Red Cross, I used explain it to them, Red Cross here would agree with the Red Cross over there, they used to find the families and bring them here. When the families got to England the families used to shelter in their own families. Everyone had a family here. They used to shelter with them. Something like that happened. In 1963, 1964, we had a big stroke here. That is to say, Cyprus correspondence was cut off. Neither telephone, nor letter. We heard about what was happening from radios, television. We used to watch what was happening, on television. We used to always see and through the Red Cross. I felt terrible because our relatives were there.

My villagers used to come every day from Cyprus. I always had customers. I did an agreement with Estate Agent called Cooper, and I used to find cheap houses for them.

I used to find house for most of them. I used to get mortgages for most of them, help them. Sometimes our old mothers used to come, I used to open bank accounts for them. They used to trust me a lot.

As a matter of fact, I didn't have much time to go to café but business required of course, for business we used to meet with an appointment. Some of them couldn't make it to my office, for business, I had a car, I used to go, find them, agree for their work, I mean either they would want ticket, or passport, or Home Office issues. I dealt with many Home Office issues. In 1960, England gave a due date of two years for Cypriots who want to become English. There are Turks, Cypriots as well, the people who want to become English, the people whoever wanted could remain Cypriot, not all of them knew this.

This was in 1960. There is this agreement on 15 August 1960, this agreement happened during Makarios period, and Cypriot Republic was established. Cypriot Republic was established then and until then it was English passports. When I came, I had English passport as well. I didn't change it at all. It was necessary, Anyway I was in Cyprus, in 1960, most of them used to come and that's when I started working with Home Office issues, from then. When I came here after 1962, that period, the people who had been staying here for more than five years used to obtain English passport through the Home Office. People who were married for three years used to obtain. I helped a lot.

Always I did the forms for them. The Home Office used to send me the forms, passports, I mean it was nice thing. But I didn't put adverts often. I used to only publish a booklet myself, a diary, and I would put the address on it and other things. Somebody else used to publish it and I used to put something in it as well. I used to deliver it to my customers as a present. We used to put small circles for adverts and for other things. I used to find the heading of my own advertisement and write other things. I used to do that, and deliver it to my customers as a present. I had a stencil and I used to do adverts with that too. I used to write and draw them myself and I would distribute them myself.

No, there wasn't anyone else bringing Turks over. Later on they came and opened agents. I continued. I wanted to help my people. I helped people from Turkey quite a lot, as well because they used to come as workers. They used to obtain labour permits and I used to help them a lot. They used to come from Aksaray, Ankara, from I don't know where. They used to come a lot and buy tickets, I used to sell them workers tickets.

Until 1988 I stayed in London, I didn't go at all. By God, it didn't take that long for me to feel like this country was my country, because I was attached to my job. As a matter of fact, I started this job there. I found my permanent customers here. I had relatives here, I didn't have difficulty to accept this country. I used to mix with my relatives every week. Every week I used to have a car, used to find them, or they used to come to me. I used to mix. We used to go to each other's house. Then all of us didn't own a house. Some of them were tenant, some were on council flats. And the Jewish agency used to obtain houses and give them to people with money. He used to get them for free and then you would give £50, £100, and then he used to give the flat to you.

When I came, I did try to work here but I didn't like it. I tried to be a mechanic because I know about mechanics. In those days, in Cyprus, a professional licence was necessary so that you know about automobiles, machines, and when I went to get my licence in Lefkosa, they gave me a certificate in Greek. And after that I learnt mechanics, how a machine was, and I used to repair my car a bit in Cyprus. When I came here I looked for a job as a mechanic first.

I wanted some money to start that travel agency. I used to want to earn a little a bit more money. I looked for a job to work, but then said to myself, "No, I came here for this aim, I am gonna do that." I searched from left to right, I found the Old Kent Road. But before this I did look for a while to work for someone in a garage. I didn't find one.

It's not just because I couldn't find that I did the Travel Agency because I did want to be a travel agent. And of course for how long are you gonna spend from your pocket? Until I found this job, I both looked at this and that. Later on when I couldn't do that one [car mechanic], I concentrated this one more.

I didn't go the job centre because there was, there was an acquaintance. There was a job centre. I didn't go and register because I was thinking of opening the office, and I was looking for a place. A couple of places. I looked in North London, in Newington Green, on Essex Road. I gave deposit as well and I lost it because I wasn't experienced then. I gave deposit, but to the owner of that place who was leaving and I didn't get the place. I didn't give the deposit to the solicitor. I went and [made an agreement with] the owner of a bicycle shop. He said, "I will transfer you to somewhere else, give me £20," and I lost that £20. I lost that deposit but it had been a big lesson for me.

The Travel Agent was an electric shop first, someone called Mr Taylor, he used to sell radio, television. As a matter of fact, he wanted to sell the freehold and I bought the freehold. Through this Enver, Enver Emin used to do these jobs. I bought it through him. I settled down there, but I don't know, you might want to know in 1964 we had Turkish Cypriot Association. It is in West End, in D'Arblay Street. I was registered there. I wanted to agree with a Greek friend, because as a matter of fact we used to deal with Greeks in the past, ships, planes, Olympic Airways etc. Turkish Airlines didn't used to go to Cyprus. Later on it happened. We wanted to do charter from time to time, through our club. And with that Greek guy, we agreed that we obtain the licence from the Association and we can go to Cyprus, Lefkosa. It was Lefkosa Airport then. Nicosia airport. We found our passengers, we found the plane from Caledonian Airline. We found the plane, made it full. The Cypriot Government didn't give us landing permit as we were all mixed. "No," they said, "They can't mix with the Turkish Cypriots, what will the Greeks do in that group?" and his passengers didn't go and they made him go bankrupt. My passengers went, but I didn't have any profit because he gave the money back to his passengers. The plane went, with only Turkish people. It didn't take Greeks, because they didn't accept that Greeks should go. He put down most of the money and he lost a lot.

They gave us landing permit after the Greeks were not involved.

This happened in 1964, June or July. We got the plane from Caledonian Airline. It doesn't exist now. We did charter from Caledonian Airline, from Gatwick to Nicosia Airport. The airport is still there but not in use because it is in the middle. They didn't give permit for that.

IBRAHIM MUSTAFA: We used to pay £3 a week. My wages were £9 a week. We used to get good money, but then people complained, I know some people, I won't mention their name, they complained that I was younger, but I am earning more than them. So they cut my money to £6 – is it £3 a week or £6 a week? I was in piece-work plus bonus those days. And they complained, and they cut my money because my age was under 21. But when I reached 21, I got the full money then. I got different money – that is, piece work, then I used to earn bonus. Even in wintertime they used to let us go home early because of the fogs, snow and everything. When I was in Stoke Newington I used to walk [to work]. But from Caledonia Road I went by train. Railway, from Caledonia Road to Dalston. Ye, I remember them, the trams, I used to travel on them. It was the 641, now the 141, it changed. From Green Lanes, Newington Green, further down. For over a year I was walking to work. From my sister's house to work, it was only five minutes walk. I used to walk. We used to get on buses, we used to pay, it used to be 1d in those days. 3d, we used to pay 3d for a fare, we used to pay and go. It used to be 12 pence a shilling*. I never used to go to the underground a lot, because there is no underground station in Stoke Newington. Only when I used to go the West End we used to go from Caledonia Road, get on the underground and go. It was fun. We used to enjoy it.

REŞAT NIAZI: After I was working at Lyon's, they had a catering school. All over the world the Lyon's company made tea, coffee, bread, I don't know, desserts, ice cream, they made everything. It was a big company. It went bankrupt in the 70s. They were called J. Lyon's. They went bankrupt. They sent me to their own catering school, as well as Westminster College. I became a Catering Manager through them. At still only 21 years of age I became a Hotel Manager at Strand Palace, at Cumberland. At the end I made a no-star rated hotel into a five-star

---

* See text note about currency on page 79

hotel for a Turk. It was called Biggley Manor, and it is still there. I know the children very well. In those days you had RAC and AA. It became a five-star hotel from both. At that time I sold my own E-type Jaguar to buy a rug for the hotel.

I left from Lyon's, I saw the Jaguar and said I'm going to buy this car. I left my job, I had a diploma and I had been a Hotel Manager. They used to open restaurants, London Steak House I think, and I went to them as Manager. I gave up Lyon's and worked in three jobs: one in the city during the day, one in the evening in Leicester Square and at weekends I worked in the Casino. I made an arrangement, the city one was closed at weekends anyway. And I arranged not to work weekends so that I could work at the Casino.

I used to serve drinks. At that time drinks in the casino had just started. In those days there were lots of casinos. There used to be a small room and I used to buy the drinks and the customers of the casino would give tips. I also had a girl working for me. I used to make very good money. In one year I bought the car and it was second hand.

I left Lyon's Corner House about 1963, something like that. The time that I came the Turks were in Angel. There was a bar or club, it was a coffee shop, a gambling den – I never used to mix with them. I was always with the English to learn this job. I still have not met a Turk or Greek that knows as much as me about this job. Whiskies, France's wines, cocktails, the world's catering, I have cooked very good, very very good meals.

After I left Lyon's, I departed from the casino, I said I have my car so I left. This French lady said to me, "You work a lot," she used to shout at everyone, everyone was scared of her and she would throw customers out. She never said a word to me. "I want to make you rich," she said to me. "But I know you and that you borrow money to these gamblers. So if you don't give up on these gamblers you will never have money."

"Stay" she said "and if you change I will take you out from here and you will make much more money than you do here." She was the owner of the casino. It was Jewish there. French Jewish.

Most of my life I have been self-employed.

I lived in Dolphine Square and there was someone called Tarbaz who had a restaurant in D'Arblay Street that belonged to the club. A shop and a basement. He opened a restaurant that he couldn't run because he had other restaurants as well and he wanted me to go and work for him. I would not work in places like that. I worked in the best places. I didn't get the best pay because the best places like the Savoy and things like don't pay well. These places still pay low. They pay low because people from all over the world go to work in those places for two months, three months, five months to learn and for a reference. I still have connections there. I have always made a lot of money. Ask any of the oldies; when I [first got] a car there were only four or five Turks who had cars.

When I went to Turkey by car in the early 60s, I used to get £25 or £30, it was good money. The waiters used to get £5.

ÇETIN KAYA MUSTAFA: We came to Stoke Newington, Neville Road. There is a church on the left hand side of the Aziziye Mosque at the end of the street.

The coal, yes, yes. Automobiles [i.e. lorries] used to come, there were holes like this in front of the houses. They used to open that and empty the coals into the basement. Anyway, my brother used to work there. I used to go out to nearby Aziziye Mosque not to get fed up. I didn't know English either. I would go out from near the Aziziye Mosque but at that time the Aziziye Mosque was a cinema then. I went there quite a lot. We used to go to the cinema quite a lot. I forgot, what was the name of the cinema? Was it Essaldo? Something like that. Well, it was a cinema. And I used to go from there – from the right-hand side of the pavement until Shoreditch so not to get lost. I used then to cross over, to the other side, and I used to come back home. What can I do not to get fed up at home?

We didn't have a job either. I told my brother, "Look, take us to work as well." but I think before that I saw Hüseyin Yapıcı. There is Wimpy in Dalston, now it is like a gambling place. Right opposite the Dalston market. Next to the bus stop there was Wimpy then, Hüseyin used to work there. He used to take me as well. I used to wash plates there. They took me as a kitchen porter. We worked there for a long time, for a while, but afterwards we left there, where did we go? I stopped after that, and my brother said that he would take me to spectacle factory in Angel so I can work there. We went, when the man saw me. When we went there, the guy asks, "Who is the person is looking for a job?" He shows me, the man doesn't want me, he wants Mehmet, my brother. We said, "Why?" Well, he saw that neither can I talk, nor something. I used to look like a silly fool person. Because when you don't know English, it was difficult. My brother was full of life. My brother said to him that I have come to get job. He asked if he [my brother] works. My brother said, "Yes".

"If you want I can employ you." And he didn't take us and after that, he employed my brother, but he didn't like the job. Afterwards he left there. And then my brother went to work in hotels. Knightsbridge Carlton Tower is just before you get to Harrods, it is just in Knightsbridge, and my brother worked there for a while, he took me there as well. I also worked there in plate machine [dishwasher]. In those days it was like that, when you don't know English. We stayed there for a considerably long time as well.

I think that was in 1963. We came to London at the end of 1961. I worked there, I worked in Wimpy, after that I went into a hotel. What year was that? I was still a child in those days. I wasn't very old, I was single in 1962. One year passed. Afterwards I left the hotel, I think I left the hotel, I can't remember it clearly. All of the other workers were foreigners. I had no friends. No, I could talk very little [English] anyway. From Cyprus I knew hello, mello, a few words like this.

HATICE ISMAIL: Have you seen my diploma? The one I obtained in Cyprus for dressmaking. In 1955.

I keep it as a memory. As you know, you go and learn here. In our Cyprus tailoring and dressmaking is different. You cut, sew, button up, you do fittings. Here, they straight away cut it, and put onto a machine. Sewing was different. But again you still receive some help because you know, its right and left sides, front and back side. When you become a tailor, you discover the shapes, patterns.

Later on I used to make samples, she/he said to me "You," she/he said to me, "You went to a college, went to a tailor so you learnt." She/he says to me, "You can work in West End well," she/he used to say. "You should stay." One of them wanted me to go to West End, she/he had a showroom but my husband didn't let me go, he was a little jealous.

I didn't show my diploma to get jobs. They didn't know, didn't understand it at all. They don't want to know. I told you even here when I first stepped on the machine, the machine was like *virrrrrrr*, how many needles were going in and coming out from here [shows her fingernail]. Because the machines in Cyprus are different. There we were used to sew with foot. Here it is different, but I received some help and learnt. I was curious. Whenever I went to the factory, when everyone was sitting down to have their lunch, I used to go from one machine to another machine and I learned with my own effort. I learnt overlocking and to use the felling-machine, I learnt button hole, button, I had become specialist. Afterwards, I started going as a specialist machinist. I both cut, make a sample, sample machinist, designer. It wasn't necessary to sit down and work as piecework. I used to make only just sample, and also alteration. The new workers used to do it improperly, I used to tear and repair them.

Hatice Ismail's dressmaking diploma awarded in Cyprus, 1954

MEHMET MUSTAFA: There were rooms, as many as you want. We went, after three days, my brother-in-law said to me, "Let's go to Stoke Newington." We went there, stayed there for three days, a couple of weeks. Afterwards we were looking for a flat, because Çetin Kaya started writing letters to ask, "Send me that money." Only three days had passed and he was asking for his money back! I wrote a letter back, I said, "Hey" I said to him, "You have heard that London's streets are full of gold, full of money, but I haven't made any money yet, I haven't found it yet. I will start a job, make money so that I can send your money," isn't that right? Before three days passed letters started to come. Anyway, I came here in the tenth month and in the twelfth month, or January, I sent him his money. As a warehouse man I used to get paid £7 per week. They were Jewish.

It used to stock goods for shops like Sainsbury. From there they would load, take them to shops, deliver. In the house I used to stay in, the man said, The boy should take you, they are looking for workers there. Back then they used to look for workers, it wasn't like today. When you took somebody, they used to give a couple of pennies to you for finding them a worker. It was like that until 1972.

Afterwards I worked there for a while. Yet of course, if I were to analyse, I used to walk from Stoke Newington to that place and I would get there one hour early. I used to get paid four shillings per hour. Four shillings is now 20p. One hour. I used to get up early in the morning. I used to get up an extra hour early so that I can walk there. I used to take a bus, there used to be fog during wintertime and I used to pass the place that I wanted. I wasn't even aware of it, I would go pass it. This time I walk back, I pay the money, I walk back. I said, "No, it is not right; I am going to walk so I can see in front of me". There was fog as well at that time. Fog, there was fog. There isn't now. Coal was burned. Anyway, I used to go like that, I used to earn £7 per week. An extra hour was paid, another 20p. £5, £20. And then, there is Chef Kemal from Limassol. He let us know that there was a job in Carlton Tower in West End in Knightsbridge. We said, "OK, let's go and work." We went there as a kitchen porter. I started working in the hotel Carlton Tower as a kitchen porter. It is a big hotel. Makarios stayed in there as well. There was Topcu, Şakir Topcu the eldest. Well, he was in there too. Later on we brought Çetin Kaya there too, he was working together as well. The responsibility for the coffees was theirs. Now I am a chap who graduated from high school. I wash the plates, I can't stand it. I continuously wipe the floors with a mop. I used to work, I mean, I used to work very hard. At last he made me angry, I was almost beating him [the boss]. I said, "I am leaving." I left. It didn't last long. I worked for about a month there, on this side. Three, four months, in 1961.

On one hand I finish in the café at one o'clock on Saturday. We used to work five-and-a-half days. In the afternoon I started work. Same hour I got the train I went there, I started working there again. After that I left. But I became unemployed, I left there, a [bit of] news came to me, a telephone call if I wanna be a waiter in the same place? But a comi waiter. Chef Kemal phoned me. He was also staying in the neighbourhood. We said, "OK." We went there as comi waiter. I dressed. All those ice creams was under my control now. I am a waiter, above him. There were Arabs in there as workers. I said, "Ice cream for everyone. Whatever you want. Because I have got the authority now. Lots of ice cream to all of you." He couldn't touch me at all. Because he knows that I am above him now, you see. I take my revenge. Anybody wants, I give it to them. Anything you want. "Are you sure?" he said. I have no work problem. I give it to them. I stayed there for a little while. For a while. But we used to work from morning till evening. Between one and four no work, we go to Hyde Park, lie down, I take some from handkerchief serviettes, but expensive one like this. I lie them down, I lie down until four o'clock, and I come back and I work hard.

And then there was Adil, they are from Aynikola. They are three, five brothers. Adil, Yusuf. Adil is same as me. Yusuf is same age as Çetin. They used to have a car next to my father's shop, they used to cook shish kebab. We met there in Limassol. When we came here we were very good friends. We used to go to English girls' houses in Limassol and so on. They used to stay above the bypass. He said, "Come." He says to me. he said, "There is a job in Lyon's Corner House for you. The tips are a lot."

He took us to Lyon's Corner House, we started working there. I worked there for a fair amount of time. It was wartime, there was war in 1964, I left the job, went to Cyprus to do army service in Limassol. But you couldn't go to Limassol directly. It was the very time of the war. There had been war for three days in Limassol. Do you remember, in February. I set off on 10 February. We were 21 people. We also took one person from Turkey. The Cyprus Consul's son was in Turkey, anyway we took his son from there. We came to fight, we are soldiers there. We even used to pay for the ones who couldn't pay the journey fee. That is to say, it was like that. The journey fee is £30. The people who went from Turkey went to Erenkoy. We came from here.

IBRAHIM AHMET: In our time you couldn't come to England without an invitation card. The people who came here in those days didn't know the language, no place, they used to stay in the streets.

ŞABAN LEFKARIDI: My first job was in a hotel. There was a hotel named D. E. Evans. I worked there for four weeks. A friend of mine found that job for me. A Turkish Cypriot used to work there, he took me there as well. We used to wipe spoons for eight hours. I stayed there for four weeks. Afterwards, there was this paint factory; they used to paint motorcar pieces. I stayed there for two weeks because it was a very dirty job. I used to change clothes twice a day. Later on I went to Unigate. I worked in their factory in Vauxhall.

When I first went there, I worked there with quite difficulty for the first one or two years. I was about to leave, but later on they brought new automatic machines. There was a Scottish man working there, an officer. He used to be a major in the army before. We became mates because he used to like entertainment and I used to take him to Cypriot places. And while they were setting up the machines, he put me there to follow the job. And after that, when the all machines were set up, I knew as much as a mechanic would know, even more. I learned, that is why it was a very comfortable, clean job. The money was good as well. I worked there for thirty three and a half years.

I retired from there and they even gave me this watch that you can see. There was a few that stayed as long as me, but a few because they used to be take a payment and leave. We didn't leave.

I started in Unigate in 1955. There were other Turkish people there, before I started there were three people, there were people who came after me as well. But only I stayed there, the rest of them left. Unigate had a General Union Committee. Within that there was Transport General Union. I was in that committee. This was afterwards. We used to go the meetings about managers, labours. We used to talk there.

MEHMET ALI BEKIR: My dad wasn't working when he came. I found a job for him. For a while in Upminster as a mechanic – after that I found another job. We used to make the back of the trucks and I took my father there to work. Of course as he was old, he couldn't work. I was 20, 21, he was 50 years old. In the end he bought a house and he had a café, he used to stay there. He opened a café himself.

I went somewhere near Euston Station after working in Upminster. There was a painter called Hüseyin. He took me to his own work place alongside the English. I started working there. I began to learn painting. Not house decoration, automobile painting (dyeing/colouring). When the English left the job after a month. I worked there two, three years.

HATICE IBRAHIM: My brother took me to work in a television factory in Oval, Kennington. I used to stick thingies into the televisions. I liked the job but I became allergic to the smell when I became pregnant. I worked there for about a year, and then went back after I gave birth. I gave my child to a childminder. Then I was pregnant with my next child. I stopped work, gave birth and went back again. And then when I was six months pregnant with my third child I fell and fainted. I was unable to go back after that. I was there for some time.

Out of the English, the manager was really nice to me. The English women were really nice to me as well. There was even a record that I really loved. 'Volare' in Italian, and also 'Guantanamara'. I really loved these two. They realised this and gave me them as presents.

One of the managers that I told you about said, "Go to English school, I want to be able to talk to you." Well, I was pregnant, about to give birth, married, how could I?

SEYIT MEHMET: I got a job in a restaurant in Wardour Street. Piccadilly Circus, there was a restaurant there, I was working in there making coffee and tea. I didn't like it at all, that is why I left, after a couple of months I left and I went and found my own job. Well, relations found the first job for me. Mr Ali was actually the owner. His wife who sent me the invitation gave me the job in their restaurant. She was Italian. They died now, both of them.

It was in a place called Number 2 Park Street. It was a hotel, and it used to belong to the government. That time it was the Labour government. I worked up there in Steer room. The Steer Room is where you make tea and coffee only, only beverages. They call it Steer room, you see. It was a hotel, they used to come for government. It was a hospitality to all the dominion what they called in them days. Countries like in Africa, including South Africa, was British dominion. Colonial and they used to be, people were there representing their colony, they used to come there as a hospitality. I mean the government used to cover all their expenses.

Number 2 Park Street was in Park Lane. I was there about six months and there was no future left there. So I left, and I got a job in Club Man 2 in Bruce Street. Piccadilly. I was a comi waiter there. I started as a comi waiter. It was a five-star.

So all the menu was in French. Nothing in English. So I found it very difficult until I learnt it all. What I used to do… I had a big menu with 30 different kinds of soup, 30 different kinds of main course. Everything in French. And when I started, I didn't know what I was doing. I couldn't speak French, you see, and I used to take the menu home and every night I learned something. In six months I learnt the menu writing down and speaking. I was there for nearly a year. From there I went to Mayfair Hotel.

I was a waiter in the Mayfair Hotel. And then from there I left it there, I went to get a better position and I went outside London, I went to Maidenhead. There was a hotel there called Skinbill Hotel. Because it was so good there, after nine months I become a head waiter. I have always been in catering.

ÇETIN KAYA MUSTAFA: After the hotel I think I went to Morning Lane. They used to make furniture, for example their skeletons. I was helping as a porter there as well. For example either carry a piece of wood or I don't know what, and the craftsmen in there used to do the rough work. They called it piece work. The more they do, sofas and chairs – quick quick – the more they used to earn. No, no, there wasn't any discrimination there, there wasn't such a thing. As long as you did your job properly, nobody would say anything to you.

MUSTAFA HÜSEYIN: There was an acquaintance. He took us to Lyon's Company. There was Lyon's company. He took me there to wash the dishes. In Piccadilly. It was Trocadero before, now it is still Trocadero. Its name has never changed. They had a big restaurant. There was Lyon's Corner House, and nearby that there was Tottenham Court Road. It is everywhere. There was one in Camberwell, one in Marble Arch. They were a huge company. They had teashop, you used to go and drink tea. Regent Palace was theirs as well. There was Strand Palace.

Many Turks worked there in our time, when we came; Cypriots used to work there and the blacks. The blacks were very rare and they used work in the kitchen. Under the ground there was a kitchen, they used to work in there. The acquaintance that bought me there, he passed away, he was from our village as well. He took us to office, he talked to the man, staff manager. He took us for the job. Then I stayed until 1956.

Afterwards I left and went to the army. A soldier in the British Army for two years. From 1956 till 1958. The army was a good thing. Discipline, everything. I came here with a British passport. Then Cyprus was under British rule.

Of course we didn't go abroad, yet we went almost everywhere all over England. When I went, I was the only Turk. I went somewhere else; there were other Turks in other groups as well. There were also three, four Greeks, Turks as well. Mixed.

The English treated us very well. We were always close to each other in the army. There was sympathy to each other. I left the army because it finished. It was compulsory for two years. National Service. It was compulsory. Whether you want or not, you had to go. If you don't go, you have to go back to your country. I was a private. In camp I was, how should I tell you? I was a commander's caretaker. I used to clean his shoes, iron his clothes. Like a Commander's assistant.

I left in 1958 and went again to Trocadero. I left [the army] in October, I worked there until New Year's Day, I left there and went to nightclubs. I worked in the nightclubs. I left there. I found a job as a chef in a electrical company. I worked there for 27 years. After that, I retired.

GÖKMEN MEHMET: My first job was terrible. It was a jam factory. Only two, three weeks I worked there. Because I wasn't used to it. I can't remember what I was doing in there. It was 51 years ago. My husband's sister found me that job.

I was working in a shirt factory in Aldgate, on the machine. That was nice. My last job was in Tower Hill making trousers. It was Jewish called Adastra, in 1957. My last job before I got married. It was all Turkish girls that worked there. I enjoyed it. I was doing piece work. I used to like it because it was better than the jam factory, clean and nice. I used to get the number one bus from Bermondsey, it would go straight there.

FEZILE AHMET: I stayed one week with my brother Kemal. Believe me, I used to stare out of the window at home. The outside. Crying, crying – my eyes were going to pop out. Exactly one week after, there was a woman called Pembe *Hanım* downstairs. She had two children. One evening she sent her young boy upstairs to me: "Auntie?"

"What is it, my son?" I said.

"My mother wants to see you," he said.

"OK," I said to the young boy. "I should go," I said to my brother.

"Well, go," he said to me. "It's not as if you're going outside and will get lost. I won't be worried." We went.

"Welcome," she said to me.

"Thank you, *Hoş bulduk*" I said.

"What are you up to?" she said.

"What should I do"? I said. "What are you up to?" I said. We spoke. She asked me if I wanted work.

"Yes I do," I said. Look, I sit around all day. What can I do? I am forced to ask for work.

"OK," she said, "What work do you do?"

"Pardon me, but I'm not yet capable of any work."

"Can you cut cotton?"

"If they show me how to." I didn't know what to say.

"Well, then be prepared for Monday morning and we will go to work together." She used to work for the Jewish boss and we lived on Caledonian Road.

"Look Kemal, I'm going to work on Monday," I said.

"What, what work?" he said.

"I'm going to go to work as well, what else can I do? I'm sitting at home and I'm going to go mad if I sit in here day and night." I didn't even last one week at home. Believe it or not, but from morning to night I used to sit alone in a small room, with only one bed because you couldn't fit two in it. So this is how I started to work.

The Jewish boss gave us £4 wages in the first week. I used to get three-and-a-half in Cyprus. I came here and they gave us £4 in the first week. The following week the Jewish man saw that I was quick and gave me £5. A lady there told me that I could take work home and get paid one penny per piece. We used to cut the cotton off bras. So I used to take bundles of work home and sit at night cutting the cotton off. Do you understand, what things we faced? What things! There were other Turks working there too. There was a Sema. She was born here and had beautiful English. She used to do translating for us. It was 1962 – she had been born here. She suffered a lot. A lot.

If the truth be told, I have never wanted to study. I can speak a little English, I mean I can communicate, I have no fears there. And that's thank God to that Irish lady. There was an Irish lady called Helen at work and she helped me a lot.

I wanted to learn English because they couldn't understand me at work. I had just started work recently and my liver was frying. I ask "Where's the water?" Nobody understands me.

"What are you talking about?" says Helen. I was dying of thirst and they couldn't even understand me when I was asking for water.

The afternoon came, there was no water on our side of the factory. It was on the other side. There were two parts to the factory. One side they would drink and on the other side they would sew. At lunchtime I went and saw where the tap was and drank water. Until lunch my liver burned without water until the afternoon.

I didn't know what water was, I didn't know how to say water.

There were very few Turks at work. I worked for the Jewish man for 12 years. From the time I came I stayed in the same place for 12 years. After 12 years he wasn't paying me much. I don't want to lie, I think £35. I can't remember. It was low pay. I didn't say anything, I went and found another job. I wish I didn't go to work for the Turks. Did they pay more? They gave me £40. I left my first job for £5. I had worked there for 12 years, for 12 years I worked for that first boss. We used to make bras. At first I used to be a cotton cleaner, but I could see *car car car* [Turkish sound of the sewing machine] them sewing. I wanted to sew as well but I was scared too.

One day, in half English and half Turkish, I told a lady there that I wanted to sit and learn the machine.

"Did you use it before?"

I said, "No." Anyway one day someone didn't turn up for work and she called me. She cut a small piece of material and drew on it with a pencil. She told me where to sit.

"You have to do it beautifully. Do it slow, very slow. I am not coming to watch you," she said. "I'll come and see you after lunch." So anyway, I sit at the machine. *Tik tik*, step by step by step I began to sew. She came back after lunch.

"How are you going, Fezile?" she asked me. She had a look at what I had done and said, "Very good, you sit on the machine," she said. So I used to sew on the little bows on the bras. I always worked with bras. At first I used to put the bows on the bras, then I used the Zig Zag machine, They didn't think I would be able to use the Zig Zag machine, they said it was very hard work. I said that I could and that I would. I tried and succeeded.

God's honest truth, the Jewish man would walk past, pat me on the back saying, "Good, good."

HÜSEYIN HASSAN MEMOUR: When I first came here I worked in the restaurants, and this and other things. First I got job as a porter in the kitchen. I had my jacket on over my lovely suit my dad gave me, and I was hanging them up in the cloak room. I was in the basement and the Irish man came and saw me downstairs and said "He got my job," and he went upstairs.

On that day, you know, like the other day, it was pouring rain, I went upstairs, "Where is my jacket?" He [the Irishman] took my lovely jacket. Spoiling my suit. And my overcoat, I couldn't walk out. He took my jacket because I had his job. I went upstairs, I told the manager.

"I think I know what happened." he says. "Anyhow, come up to my room, to my office." So I went to his office, and I found half a dozen overcoats left over. I tried different ones…

There were four lovely girls. Waitresses. "What is your name?" [they asked].

I said, "Memour."

"We call you little Moses," because I was singing all the time, like Moses. "We call you little Moses," she said. So that day I lost my thing [jacket]. I went back there Friday and I started whistling again. Sally came along, she was a temporary waitress: "Oh, little Moses, you must have found your jacket," she says.

I said, "No, but," I said, "fortunately my joy was not in the pockets!"

She says, "What?"

I said, "My joy does not depend on my overcoat and all that."

She was so impressed, she went around and she collected £5 and gave it to me.

I am still preaching, for nearly 25 years in the streets, and playing my mouth organ. I first started preaching in Hyde Park. I think the first time I did it was when I was coming here for summer between 1952 and 1955, when I was doing my studies. I would come with a cousin with the same name, and his mother breastfed me as well, because he is nine months older than me. So you would go down to Hyde Park, and I would put this case down there, my cousin would stay there in distance, and I would start preaching and then he will come nearer and nearer, pretend he was a stranger, but he wasn't a stranger. And you collect about 100 people, easy easy. It would be a short ceremony, ten minutes, 15 minutes.

I then went to work at the Performing Right Society. Somewhere near Goodge Street. I was also having open air meetings during the lunch hour [in Hyde Park]. Keeping records on cards and all that. Because if it was played yesterday, they have to pay some money. Your record was played, your cassette was played, they will send you a reward for allowing them to use the voiceover on the radio, on the television. After three months I was doing the same job like a big man. Very clever. So I asked for a rise.

MUSTAFA HÜSEYIN: The truth is when I first came, I wasn't glad that much. Because when I was there, I was working for the English Army. When I was there I used earn seven-and-a-half to eight lira. I used to earn that per week then. It was good money then. When we worked over time sometimes we used to get paid 10, 11 even 15 lira per week. When I came here, for example, we used to wash dishes we used to get three shilling, nine pence then. Either you are gonna pay for rent, or for room, or you would give laundry costs or you would go and have entertainment with your friends. It is a bit difficult. After the 70s I started to see the benefits of being here. Because the company I used to work for then used to pay very good money; in those days I used to get £15, £20. It was a lot of money then. It started then. It became kind of easy.

MEHMET ŞEREF ALI: I am happy here. I came thinking about work. I left army in 1959. I worked in a Wimpy Bar in our street, for about eight to ten months. Later on, I joined National Railway in Isos. I got married in 1963, in 1966 I went onto Mount Pleasant Post Office. I worked on the Post Office underground and railway. Tourists and big people used to come from Japan and places to see the Underground. It used to go to Paddington, Baker Street, Liverpool St, Mount Pleasant and Rathbone I think and maybe Holborn. It was five or six stations. There were wagons and we used to sort the packets.

EMINE MEHMET: My husband worked in a milk factory. There used to be a milk factory. He worked there for seven years. I went to work too. A year or two later my mother came here too. I left my child with my mother, and went to work. I used to get three-and-a-half lira a week. I used to sew on the sewing machine. This was in 1953, when I got work in the factory in Lewisham. I used to really like work. I used to sit at the machine happily, happily and work. They used to give us half an hour for lunch. I used to walk home, as it was close, to go home to see my child. I came and went from home so I could see my child. And then there was this heat, like the heat now. I used to faint in the streets from this heat. I worked there for some time. I had no money to buy my child clothes. I wanted a little coat, you would want to dress you child well, so I worked and got three-and-a-half liras a week. I saved £5 and bought a little suit and dressed him – his photo in that outfit still exists. I bought it with my own money and dressed my child in it. Because the man [my husband] worked in Vauxhall, in a milk factory and they used to give him £5.10 shillings.

He was either going to spend it on rent, or on this or that. It was not enough so I worked as well. I dressed that child.

For 15 years I worked sewing in Dalston. I came and went from Camberwell on the 171. I would get the bus at Camberwell Green. I worked for the Jewish there.

My mother looked after my children for a while. For a period before my husband worked in the milk factory and worked in the mornings, he would look after the children in the afternoon. So I mean we didn't have to leave our children in any strange places in this way.

HULUSI MAHMUD: When I came to Highbury I thought it was so quiet, not many foreign people in London anywhere, [not] in the area you know. I started working in the soft drink factory for a while, then I went to a restaurant.

I got a job more or less straight away. After a week or two in a soft drink factory. My brother found the job for me. Then I used to live with them there. Then we went to an interview, they said, that is, "OK, you can start." From thereafter, the money wasn't very good, they encouraged me go into restaurant work in the kitchen. Holborn. High Holborn.

I was in the soft drink factory for about three months, something like that. There was only one other Turkish person in there. I don't know what country he was from.

I started learning the language when I started working in the fish and chip shop. In the Italian restaurant, I started learning the Italian language. It was so good you know.

I started learning Italian before English, because nobody can speak English or Turkish, so I learn to speak Italian. It was so easy to learn Italian. I forgot it now. I was in the Italian restaurant in 1959, end of 1959, 1960. It was in High Holborn, a big restaurant, Carlos restaurant.

I left the Carlos and I went to Mayfair. I worked there for a while. From there I went to a fish and chip shop, there was more money in there. So I went to the fish and chip shop in the Archway. From Archway, I got married. And then I opened a butcher shop after the fish and chip shop.

I didn't go out much. I was still feeling strange in the area, you know. So when you work in night, finish about one o'clock in the morning, then you go home. We used to go cinema sometimes. I have never mixed with the bad companies.

I used to meet with Turkish people here, of course I used to meet. Most of the time I worked with the foreign people. I never worked with Turkish people. They are envious of each other, jealous of each other. Say for instance we work in the same place and the manager likes you better, when he give the overtime job to earn a bit more money, you get jealous of me like, "Why you do that overtime?"

IBRAHIM DERVIŞ: My sister's husband was a chef. He goes out to work, comes back at night and so on and so on. My sisters and mother stay at home. I left home alone and went to Warren Street. The number 24 bus went there. There were a lot of Lefkaralis there – Osman, our barber Aziz, who came before the war. And by coincidence, while wandering around, I found Musti the barber and the rest, in Goodge Street.

I told them that my profession was shoes, and so on. Ah, they said, "Yusuf – that is, Joseph – from Anglisia is here. He has a real need for someone like you." They took the telephone in their hands and called him. "Put him in a taxi and send him to me," Yusuf said. That's how it happened.

I started to work there. He said, "How much wages do you want? How many shoes can you make?" It was made-to-measure shoes and custom materials there. His wife Miryo was Jewish. In 1950 Yusuf Bey made shoes for £20 a pair, and wages at that time were £4 or £5 a week.

I said, "I can make 40 pairs and so on." I was good at my profession and really I could do 40 pairs, but we were going to work on models.

He said, "There are three people here, you cannot do this job."

"I have faith in myself," I said. "OK," I said, "let's try it out," I said. But at first I said, 'I'll work for one week, then we can see if we can agree."

The end of the week arrives and this Nicolas Makaridis has been watching my work. I really was good at it. Because I used to work on women's shoes in Cyprus, I really didn't find it difficult. Now this friend – who was a leftist and a joker – says to me in Greek, "I have seen your work, the work you do, the boss is in real need of an artist. Ask for whatever you want, without hesitating."

In any case the boss says to me, "I'll give not £12 but £14 a week if you make me 40 pairs a week." The others working there with me were getting £4 or £5 a week. He was going to give me £14 a week. Well in any case he liked me, of course, and the customers were pleased. He took me to lunch at the Atlantis Restaurant because he didn't want to let me go. So I started helping out at home.

MERYEM SHEREFETTIN: I got my first job in 1956, January 15. Yeah, I remember. All that I remember. Well, I been to West End because I had another job. In the beginning I have a job for one week, again in the West End. I work there one week at that place, it was Christmas and it was shut down. And on 15 January, I been to see the place, if it's was open, because in those days we didn't have any telephones to ring you know. And the place was shut and I was walking with my little girl in the West End you know, in Oxford Street. and somebody call me "Sister-in-law! Sister-in-law!" and I see one friend of my husband, and he says to me, "What are you doing here?" and I say, "So-and-so." He says to me, "Come on, I take you to one place and you going to be very pleased, and you're gonna work with these people and you're going to be very happy," and he take me to one Jew factory. A Jewish factory. And the next day, I start work, you know, and I work seven-and-a-half years for those people. I can't remember the name of the factory. We made dressing gowns. I was on the sewing machine, and I couldn't speak a word of English. It was terrible, they give me the bundle to start work, and I want to have a sample to see the style, you know. And I was trying to ask them, you know, explain to them that I need something to see and I couldn't say. In the end I say this [points at the clothing she is wearing], you know, and they understand, and they give me a sample and I start work. And those people, they was very nice to me. All ladies, they were working over there and they helped me lots. Most of it was English – the workers. The boss was Jewish, but the workers, it was, most of it was English. And they was very good to me, you know.

I worked seven-and-a-half years for them, and later they decide to shut the factory, because the father-in-law [of the boss] was rich anyway. And they recommend me, top of the factory was another factory that was making evening dresses. I start work over there, but I wasn't happy, me and another two girls. We left and we been somewhere else, you know. One factory after another factory, you know, we have very difficult times in those days, you know.

I start with £6 a week and after that £9 a week and after that they put us on the… what do you call it? I forget. It wasn't piece work but it was, if you make more, you was getting more money. A bonus! they put us on the bonus. £9 wages and if you made more than so many so many dress you know, you can have a bonus and I was earning about £12 with bonus.

I used to go by bus. By bus. My husband – he take me a couple of times by bus, and after that I been myself. Because I was taking the 14 bus from Caledonian Road, get out at Dominion Theatre and I was walking about a couple of bus stops to the factory. The 73 bus was going there, but I must get off one bus and catch another bus, and I would have to pay extra fare. I couldn't do that. So I would have to walk in the morning, walk in the evening again and get one bus only.

At lunchtime I carried with me sometimes sandwich, and sometimes the girls were going to a café to get something, and I was giving them money and they was bringing it to me. They [girls at factory] helped me lots. They teach me everything, or even when I have to buy clothes they was coming with me. They were choosing the clothes for me, which colour is suitable for me, which style is suit for me, and they were saying, "This one," and I was paying the money and I was getting the clothes. They were so good. So good. We would go shopping at lunchtime, quickly have the lunch and go shopping. I was saying, "Clothes, I want clothes," you know, to two English ladies. The one, she was about 59, she wasn't young and she was coming with me to Marks and Spencers. It was near to the factory, and they were choosing what is suitable for me, and they were saying this and that, and I was paying the money. They helped me lots. They was very good. I mean she's not living now, I'm sure she's dead because she was an old lady then, now I'm getting old.

In the beginning we kept in touch, yes. In the beginning, but after so many years you know, you forget. In the beginning we miss each other, and we was getting in touch with each other. And there was one Turkish lady. When I worked over there a couple of years after that, one Turkish Lady from Magosa, she started working with us, and we coming very close friends and we was together. We was going out lunchtime you know, and even with her I can't get in touch. She lost her husband from cancer. She has two children, one girl and one boy, even I don't know where she lives. We lost each other. Her name was Neriman.

Meryem Sherefettin at work at factory in Oxford Street, London, 1960

EMINE AHMED: This was in 1963, the year I gave birth to ŞENSAL. When you come from Angel, somewhere around Newington Green roundabout there was a three-storey factory. I used to work there. There was a room on the first floor and on the second floor was the sewing room. The third floor used to belong to pattern cutters. A couple of *Ciras* on the second floor used to chatter while we were living the building. The boss sent them upstairs next to the pattern cutters. They didn't want us. They used to bring up the troubles in Cyprus. The time I came first, when I was working with Greeks I got used to Greek language and I learned Greek. When I left the Jewish work, I started working with Greek people. I learnt Greek here. I didn't know Greek at all, because there wasn't any Greeks in our village. That is to say I can now understand 90% of what Greeks say. I can answer as well. But I can't answer as much as I can understand what they say. We suffered from it as well. Do you know what we used to sew there? Tents. We used to sew tarpaulin, the one you cover over a long vehicles. It had holes on the sides so you can tie it with ropes to the lorry. Oh, you keep sewing and sewing, turning and turning it round on the machine. Keep stitching together the pieces of clothes together, it doesn't finish. I think that is why I have become disabled. We used to sew piece by piece. They used to open holes, put rope and tie it to the lorry. We used to sew three-bedroom tents. Our boss was Lukaidis. How many years I worked there. He was Greek Cypriot from Limassol.

Our boss, we said to him we are leaving because we can't cope. We are not guilty. The boss said, "Leave it to me." He transferred two *Ciras* to pattern cutters room. We were two people as a matter of fact. We were three Turkish people, but they used to verbally abuse two of us. The foreman said, "You stay in your place." He left us. My boss was good. I was happy with my boss, if he is dead, God's blessing on him. We used to work per piece. You would get paid according to how much work you had completed. I used to get 10,11 lira per week when I worked per piece. I think we used to work from 8 till 5:30 pm. I used to go sometimes at 9am. I would take the kid to the child-minder, from there I would come to work. You would prepare the kid's backpack, you would prepare your own bag as well. You would put her in the pushchair, leave her to the child-minder, come back again, take a bus and pick up your child, go home, wash clothes, cook food, sleep. If you don't have a child-minder it is difficult. If you don't have someone to help you it is more difficult and if you don't have a car it is extremely difficult.

NEVCIVAN JEVAN: I came here from Cyprus in 1952. I got married in 1953, I gave birth to my daughter in '54. I gave birth to my son in '61. When I came of course I used to work. I used to get paid three-and-a-half lira per week. I used to work in a dress-making factory. I was a dressmaker in Dalston. There used to be a dress-making factory in Dalston. I don't remember how I found the job. I don't remember. But until my son turned two or three, I didn't work. Afterwards, we set up a factory and worked there, probably in 1964. I did work a little bit first, after that when I had the kids I didn't work. I got married here. My boss was Jewish. There wasn't English then, always Jewish then. I was machinist. I stayed in this place for one year, one-and-a-half years, something like that. My wages was either £7 or £9.

Nevcivan Jevan at the Hibbi Spots Factory, London, 1953

SÜHA FAIZ: The Governor actually tried to dissuade me, clearly from his point of view. I am not a senior chap, I am rare enough, well-educated Turk to stand visibly, but they made no difficulty. But on the contrary when I came to England without work within a month I had a letter from the Commonwealth Relations office. This is all in my book*. Saying, we had a letter, we call you for an interview.

I hadn't got a new job. What I have been interviewed for was a temporary appointment in the then Commonwealth Relations office, which still existed separate from the Foreign Office, and if I am successful, I would get appointed on a temporary basis, unestablished with a view to my then – if I want to – sitting the competitive, full exam for the civil service with a very difficult exam. And I am overage anyway, 30, what am I, 1960, 34 I think. Yes, 33 – 34. So anyway, I get the interview. While I was in Cyprus, there was another, these young people who played Assistant District Commissioner, they called Achillis Papadopoulos, who was married to a Scotch girl actually. He is a nice chap. EOKA were gunning for him. Because they are also going for people of their own side more, who they thought will not, you know –

So he resigned what I have, I am not involved, but I know he then had a job in the CRO (Commonwealth Relation Office) in the information department side, not administration. So I am aware of this. So when I get this interview, I am interviewed pretty rigorously at three levels. Desk Officer first, Head of Department another, and then the Head of Establishment at secretary level. Somewhere along that line, I can't remember it now, where it literally came up, one of them said to me: "You know Mr Faiz, your name would be a problem for us." At least the guy was decent and speaks openly. Now he is not making a threat, he is saying, in fact he couldn't really say, maybe silly to say we can't have you for that reason, they could just not appoint me and say, "Well he wasn't up to

---

* See footnote on page 43

scratch or whatever." But anyway, I have been thinking about this before for other reasons. Here am I, if you want to call it passing for an Englishman, I am an Englishman, as far as that goes. I am not English, for many reasons I would object to be an English, but other things apart. I have been thinking about this and I decided I would change my name officially by Deed Poll. You know you had to change your name. So I changed it but the simplest possible way, changing the "z" in my name to an "r", and indeed my signature when I do it, it is indistinguishable, I had the great advantage that I didn't have to sort of send banks, security, change signature, my name change but the signature was the same. So I have my passport, and I changed my Ahmet with Alan, because actually when I was at Oxford, my tutor used to say to me, "Ahmet, Ahmet, I can't call you Ahmet," and his name was Alan Brown, so as a joke he used to call me Alan. I wasn't known as Alan at Oxford, I was Süha, but I was Alan Faiz to him.

So anyway I changed my name. And it is so happened, they didn't know I changed my name. I changed my name, anyway I got the result, I am successful. So I joined the Commonwealth Relations Office as a temporary assistant principal, which is about as lowest as you can get above the clerical. It's the university entrance level at senior civil service. Very much over-aged, I am 34, normally you get it after 25, 26.

This is 1960. This is about February, maybe I am 35 now, if it is 1961, '60. At the time we lived in Kensington, because Lalage's sisters together had bought a house in Addison Road in Kensington West 14, we have seen them on leave. And I said to them, because I had some money, my Fuat Bey had sold, he was the *kabile reisi* then, Hürmüz Hanım died and all her children, the oldest one was Fuat. So anyway, he has sold, we had a field, which is Niapolis in Nicosia. That is now Niapolis. I can't remember how many *dönüm** it was but it went in those days for £66,000, a colossal sum of money, which my brother and I had a sixth share in. We only had shares in fields, you didn't get shares, because my father died before his mother, who had offices, houses, shops. I took, had no share. So this is really all I got from there, apart from a little field, in Zeytinlik, which is where I built the house. And my brother and I shared a sixth, which is £11,000 – I had £5,500, which in those days was a bloody lot of money. £5,500, which I deposited. We said if a house comes up round here we like it, who knows what the future is gonna be, buy it. So they telephoned, telegraphed us actually while we are still dickering. I can't quite remember when, the dates slightly vary on this. But we had a house which was let in those days. So we resigned, I come back to England. This is the time when we were living with a family member. So we went to live in this house as tenants. We there, when we got the good news I got the job. And I stayed there and I am the member of CRO. I had the children with us in this flat. Oh, yes, yes. It was pretty cramped.

I had a job. The point is I got to pass this civil service exam. I took it twice. First time I won't take you through it, but it is in the book. It is an interesting little story. I failed the first time, on the final hurdle, not on written or interview. And

---

* A land measure of 1,000 square meters (about a quarter of an acre)

the second time I took it, I got through. I'm now an established member of the Commonwealth Relations office. At a time when the Diplomatic Service of Britain, foreign countries had embassies, you would go there from the foreign office to be a member of Paris embassy or whatever; Commonwealth Countries like Australia, New Zealand, in those days South Africa, India, Pakistan and Canada had High Commissions, not Ambassadors.

They still have, which is ridiculous, because of the Queen. So anyway, while I am in the Commonwealth Relations Office, I am now permanently established, we get first posting abroad, because they always post it sooner, or later and we get posted to Canada. That is in the book, we don't need to go into that. But I am a regular member of the Commonwealth Relations Office and I have an overseas post in Canada as First Secretary High Commissioner in Ottawa. So I am really as [senior?] as you can get.

This would have been in 1965. We left Canada after doing just over half a full tour, which would have been about three or four years. In 1965, I am in England, thinking at long last, *Allaha çok şükür*, in our house now in Kensington, but of course it had a tenant, we had to, anyway, eventually we got in. We are back in certainly by 1966, '65 or '66.

I remain in this job. I am in all sort of stuff, I'm in the ministry, including a spell I had, as the Civil Service Commissioners which are the people who interview and select for the Civil Service. That is an interesting little story too.

EMINE AHMET: One day I said, "Let's buy a house, my feet ached and my back was aching. I can't carry things up and down anymore." I used to climb 20 steps to pour the dirty water and bring down 20 steps down. Before we bought our house, I asked the owner of the house we used to stay, "I would like to buy a sewing machine." His reply was, "I can't allow you to sew." He was from our village. I said that I wouldn't sew for other people, I would sew for myself as I was a tailor. He didn't allow me to sew. We said, "OK." When we had a child and she turned five/six months old we started thinking of buying a house. My feet started aching because of carrying things up and down. The cooker only fits one pan on it. Even that doesn't fit. It was a small cooker. When an Arab cooks, you can't cook. You would eat downstairs in your room. That is how I suffered. As we were tenants we didn't complain.

NEVCIVAN JEVAN: I didn't like my job. I didn't know the language, what was I going do? Sit down. You couldn't sit down, it was necessary to work. I used to go to work on foot. I am telling you, we used to stay at my sister-in-law Sultan's house in Dalston. I used to just cross the road and go to work. It wasn't far away. She took me a couple of times, that's how I learnt my way. It wasn't far away. I used to come home for lunch at lunch time. I used to cook meals as much as the time allowed me to. I also used to do cleaning because I used to stay in the guest room there during the time before I got married in 1961.

SEYIT MEHMET: The wages wasn't too bad because my wages were £6 a week. But I used to get tips on top of my wages. Then when I was living in Tollington Park my wages were £7 10 shillings.

MEHMET ŞEREF ALI: On your own suddenly. I would say it was both good and bad; the money had been running out. But my nephew said to me: "By all means! If you need anything and so on, call me on Wednesday, because on Thursday their wages would be paid. Money and so on, I would put the money in post, if you want." I said "OK!" I called him on Tuesday: "Nephew, such and such, we have run out of money, I couldn't find a job, either." He said "OK, come tomorrow and take it." Like this, on Wednesday I went towards the evening. He used to stay around Caledonia Road, something like that, I used stay in Archway. I know the way from Archway to West End. In those days, I only knew those places. I went to West End, from there I came back halfway through, in my pocket there was only one shilling left, as far as I remember. I went inside, I didn't talk. I went into the house, I looked, he used to stay with an Irish person in the house as he was single. I was so hungry, it was raining, cold, like this, I didn't have many clothes either, I speak the truth.

We sat down, talked about the weather, they set the table, I am looking forward to it. Either I had one mouthful or two mouthfuls, and he started saying I got paid today and I have paid this much for that and that much this and so on, as a matter of fact the money he used to get from there was £7 10 shillings per week, or was it £5 10 shillings? So no money left. So no money left to give to me. I am not a child, at the age of 26-27 – I was 25 years old when I came here. I said, "Aaah, I remembered something." I left the house, I didn't eat either. No, I don't cry but that is to say it annoys me. I took to the road. To the West End on foot. No money was left for busfare either, that I go to West End and come back to Archway. Thanks to God, I asked someone, the rain was starting. I said, "I am going to Archway, how?" He said to me, "Turn left, next right." Anyway I walked all the way and went upstairs, I didn't come downstairs for two days.

Anyway I don't know if the woman's still alive, but there was this woman, was she Naziret? Well, I can't remember. I remember her husband. She came upstairs, she knocks on the door. I was writing a letter so that they would send me money, so I can leave. I couldn't find a job. I couldn't find a job, I had run out of money, too. There wasn't any money left to pay the last week's rent. I think it was 15 shilling per week, possibly. It was a lot of money at that time. It was nearly £1. In short, she came, I think it her name was Nazir *aba*, she knocked on the door. "What happened, Mehmet Ali, are you ill?"

I said, "No!"

"So why haven't we seen you for two days?"

"Aahh, I will leave. There is no job, money has run out as well. Why should I tell you a lie, finished, I need to leave this week." They took me downstairs, into warm room.

"You are gonna eat, drink, sleep here until you find a job. Not going to think about money and so on." He took £5, gave it to me. He wouldn't be considered as a stranger. He is from my brother-in-law's village. It didn't take long. A week later, there was a friend, his name was Yasar. I said "Hey," of course I was looking for carpentry work. But he was a kitchen porter. I said, "Whatever you want, be it so; if only a job. Let it be a job."

It was in Lyon's Corner House, in West End, in Piccadilly, £4 10 shillings a week, including eating and drinking, too. It was good money. We used to wash these big pans in the basement. I think I worked in that job for six, seven months. I got used to it, I even managed to save some money. Also, tell the truth, I had great interest in buying a motor here. I said, "I should go from England by a motor." My dad was an addict for motors. So, was going to buy the motor and go back [to Cyprus].

"Where do you work?" [my friend Mustafa] asked [one day].

"In Lyon's Corner House, well, in that place, as a kitchen porter. As a matter of fact I understand carpentry." I didn't want to work nights any more. So he told me about a carpentry job and I went and worked there as a day job.

ALI HASSAN: My first job, my brother-in-law was already working in a trimming factory anyway, he visited all the factories mentioning me, saying I have a brother-in-law who's a tailor and so and so. We went, one to two weeks we worked there. This was in Aldgate. The factory was in Aldgate. It was a Jewish factory. In those days there were no Turkish factories. We used to sew and make trousers there, and work as a machinist. There were no other foreigners. It was just me there, the only one Turk.

There were Pakistanis, you'd find some. I wasn't working by myself all day. You'd say hello to the people working next to you. We'd speak half and half, we began to get used to speaking English. Like this and that. In the beginning it was difficult. Getting up every morning to go to work was something that had to be done. You had to go. Whether you knew the language or not you had to go. We had to go to work in order to save ourselves. To build our future. Because you could learn the English language, like today you'd learn one word, tomorrow you'd learn another one or two words. Slowly, slowly we progressed a bit.

At that time, in the beginning, my wife went to a tailor factory to work as well. With my sister-in-law. My sister-in-law was a machinist and so was my wife. She'd show her and slowly slowly she'd learn. Because there was a Turk next to her, with her speaking half-and-half she developed her English.

I used to go from Plaistow to Aldgate with a bus. We used to get up early in the morning so that if you got the bus before 7:30, the bus fare was 5d in those days. Actually 7d, but if we got up before 7:30 we'd pay 5d. At that time a shilling was 12d. We used to wake up earlier to go, so we could save that 2d.

6. FAMILY

ALI HASSAN: We couldn't find a place to live because we had a child. You'd find a place, and the person renting wouldn't want children there. This time we was forced to send our child back to Cyprus to my mother-in-law. Of course the Turks wouldn't accept us with children either. They didn't want you if you had children. I don't really know why, because they make racket, I don't know what they make? People never used to agree. After a couple of people said this to us, urgently I said I'd pay the money to send our child to Cyprus to my mother-in-law, for her to look after. And this would become her living, with that money. We sent her our child.

Our child stayed in Cyprus till 1966, until the age of 10. After that I bought a house. One year later I bought a house. I stayed for one year. One year later I got a house, but I was still staying in Plaistow. We didn't have any more children, because we still had to pay off our house and stuff. When we paid off our house, we sold it. We bought a better house.

In those days the houses cost £950. A three-bedroomed house was £950. £250 from us, like I said £50 from one friend and £50 from another. A solicitor sorted out the mortgage for us. An English solicitor sorted it out for us. We had translations. As a translator we took my brother-in-law, he used to study here and take English lessons, he knew some English so we took him. His English wasn't fantastic but it was understandable. That day we took him with us, we got the house, we was going to pay it off in seven years, we paid it off in two to three years. We sold it. We bought it for £950 and sold it for £1,100, we thought we made a big profit. But it was £10 weekly, and my wife used to get £5. So we was receiving £15 a week. In the end we sold it, and bought a better house. £70 worth better.

FEZILE AHMET: My brother got married after he came here. We had an aunt here called Mueccel, who had come to London before us. Her husband Ozkan was my brother's wife's first cousin. One day my brother said, "Shall I take you to go and visit Mueccel and Özkan?"

I said, "I'll go if you take me."

So we went to Mueccel and Özkan's home. Özkan's first cousin Emine was there too. Anyway, Emine and my brother Kemal chatted here and there, and then agreed that they liked each other. After that it was fate, they got married. They got engaged first and then married. We all lived in Haringey after they got married. One-and-a-half months after I came he got married, one-and-a-half months after that they had a wedding.

MEHMET ŞEREF ALI: My nephew had been here for one or two years by then. He said, "Come" – probably it was Saturday, if I am not wrong. That night. He took me to Tottenham Court Road, there was a Swiss Restaurant on Tottenham Court Road, he used to live above of that. He took me that evening. Anyway, we stayed there at night, you will laugh in a while, in the morning we went downstairs. That was my first day in London. I would look, a bus passes by, with 'Brook Bond Tea' written on it. My friend said, "Shall we go by bus, or we can get on an underground?" Of course how would I know the underground! I said, "Let's go by bus so that we can have tea as well!"

"Come and let's go by train," he said.

Oh God, I looked, feet are coming out from the ground. We went down to Mornington Crescent. We came out and found my nephew, deceased of course now. I stayed there for two nights, I think. Afterwards, there were people from Aytotoro in Archway.

My nephew, his name was Osman. Well, we talked, he said that Uncle Reşit had a house. Uncle Resit's house was on Road in Archway, I will never forget. Well, we went, thanks to them, all of them took me inside, but snow, cold, our snot used to get frozen!

I came here in February. I left Cyprus on the 7th. I came on the 18th, possibly about 11 days. Anyway, I stayed there for a couple of days. There is this much snow on the ground. Of course about 10 days passed. When I couldn't find a job. My deceased mum used to say, "My son, there isn't sun in England." Indeed, it has been a month since I came; neither there is sunshine, nor anything.

GÜLSEN LARKINS: I was allowed to go to work here, but I wasn't on my own. You must be joking. I was with my cousin who was here. Our bodyguard. Every time I used to have my bodyguard. She was married, she had kids. My first cousin, my mum's niece. Her mother, my mum's sister.

I had to give my money to my dad for rent. I don't keep any money. My mum used to save my money a bit and my brother used to come here. After I left [got married], my dad used to take every penny off me. My dad. He used to take every penny, because I was the only one who got paid full wages. I used to get a lot of money those days. Unbelievable. I used to work from Monday to Saturday.

The first things I bought was clothes, shoes. My mum used to, no, my brother actually said, "Don't give every penny, just give him £10." £10 is a lot of money them days, isn't it?

SEYIT MEHMET: When I moved from Edgware Road, I went to Holloway Road. They used to call it Tollington Park, they call it. My sister had a room. We shared a room. I used to pay £2 a week rent.

IBRAHIM MUSTAFA: When I went to see family I always went with my wife. We used to go, when the kids were young we used to go a lot for picnics. We used to go all over the seasides. We used to have barbecues. It was all the friends with their kids, and other kids. We used to play football and everything.

HULUSI MAHMUD GÜRÇAYOĞLU: I was a comfortable a bit later. When I was living with my brother, I felt a bit comfortable. Second one. It was in Islington, it is just opposite the Town Hall. The house is still there. The house is rented out. He owns it.

He [my brother] must have come in 1949, 1950-something. I know my oldest brother come in 1949, 1948. One of the first ones here.

Since we bought the home in Turnpike Lane, everything went into pieces. We move down now. My daughter got married and within six weeks they are apart, and after they got married my wife she wanted to divorce. I said, "Why are you gonna divorce now, we are gonna enjoy our lives together. No, I can do better without you". It is all right, if that is the case, I went and she stayed. She got the house, and I took my car and I come out. In 1990.

EMINE AHMED: When I first came here I didn't like it all. I came in the winter, fog, cold. I was going to the factory on foot as well, it wasn't far away. We suffered a lot. Three siblings used to stay in one place. After that we found a house in Finsbury Park, went there. We felt relieved. For each of us we found a room on the same floor, we stayed there. After that we went to somewhere else. We went from one house to another one until we bought a house.

Look, in the house which Sultan stayed, my brother and I used to stay in the guest room, my eldest brother used to stay on the upper floor. They used to stay on the top floor. It was both a living room, kitchen, and also a dining room. That is to say, they used to open a portable sofa and sleep there. They used to let all of the rooms. That is to say, us three siblings used to stay, and also a man with five kids used stay on top floor. His wife died while she was giving birth to her last child. The child who was born last was adopted by them, then the man used to stay there as well. That is to say, in a three-bedroom house a man with five kids, three of us and two of them. From there we went to Finsbury Park, in Finsbury Park we used to stay in a three-bedroom floor. My brother in one bedroom, the other one in the one bedroom, I was in one bedroom. In that one we were a bit more comfortable. After that we went to Haringey. I suffered a lot in Haringey. I got married, I didn't have a kitchen. We used to stay in one bedroom.

I stayed there more or less three or four months. From there we went to Finsbury Park. We stayed for five, six months in Finsbury Park. After that I stayed in Haringey for one-and-a-half years. I got married and stayed in Haringey. In one room, there wasn't a kitchen. In one room Fezile Abla used to stay, in other room a woman from Galatya used to stay. They were husband and wife with four kids, their father used to take refuge in the guest room and in the room they have their meal downstairs. That is to say, how many people! There was no kitchen. The hob was in the corridor, we used to cook food there. We used to go three steps down and wash the dishes there. There was my bed in the room, the bed was like that, my cupboard was like that, there was a kitchen cupboard here, my table here, kitchen table, and your sister in law's bed here. All of them were in one room.

Friends and sometimes middle-aged women who didn't work, used to take care of the children. She used to earn her living from that. They were Turkish. I gave Şensal to a childminder for a couple of years. I gave Bayar for six months. After six months when we bought a house, I started to sew at home.

MELEK KAZIM: My first son is Dean, because of Dean Martin, I used to love Dean Martin. My second one is Robert James, James Dean again. Samantha Grey, Samantha is my daughter, because Samantha I used to love the film, I used to want to be a movie star. All English names.

I had my first child in 1963. I got married in '62 and year after my first son. '63, Robert was born '65 and Sam '68.

My mum was very beautiful, I used to say to her: "Mum you should have been a film star instead of getting married." She was very beautiful. I have got beautiful pictures of my mum.

EMINE AHMET: I stayed in the hospital for 40 days. The birth was difficult. The baby came as breach. After I left the hospital I had a real difficulty while I was a tenant, we didn't own a house. After I got married I stayed in the same house in Highbury. Husband and wife we stayed in the same house again. We used to rent a small room. It used to have a kitchen upstairs. There used to be kitchen cabinets in the kitchen. They give two shelves from the kitchen cabinets. I could put six cups and my pan. Four people used to share the cooker. I suffered like that. There is no bathroom to have a bath. The landlord let the third floor to Indians and Pakistanians. The house had a bathroom but they used to wash their dishes in the bath tub. While they were sleeping, I used to heat up some water in the pan, go upstairs in the morning, clean inside the bathroom and have my bath and go downstairs. I suffered like that for 11 months. There is not space for bathing. We were eating, drinking, washing our clothes in one same bedroom.

Nobody was using it as a bathroom. He let the rooms to Pakistanians, they used wash their cups in the bathroom. That is how I was a lodger. I used to have a bath in that and my husband he used to have a shower at work. He used to have a shower everyday because he was working in a restaurant. We could stand it there for only a month. There was no telephone, nothing. We had someone called Remzi from our village, he is deceased now, God rests his soul on this holy day; he said "Come and stay in my flat." We went there without seeing the room. It was on the third floor. We used to stay there. My room was very large but there is neither a kitchen nor anything else. You would climb 20 steps up to a dark attic where there was a small cooker in the passageway. A sink and the pan doesn't fit on the cooker. To cook food you would wait in the queue with the Arabs. Every time I was going to wash the clothes I would have to bring the water 20 steps down, wash the kid's nappies in the room and take the dirty water upstairs again.

GÜLSEN LARKINS: My first child in1963. Girl. She is very pretty girl. Lovely girl. One year 11 months. In 1965 I have a boy.

HATICE FETTI: As my husband was working I didn't care about spending my money. We used to live on his money. Well, after that I bought nice coats, suits for my kids, everything. From somewhere else, Aldgate, I went and I bought a nice coat for myself, bought dresses. I got ready to go and pick up my kids [from Cyprus].

I returned alone by plane. It was something like £35 for the plane ticket in those days. I went by plane. When I went there, I was going to go before but it didn't suit me, I couldn't go. I missed my flight. I didn't go, I went the next day. The next day I went to the airport again. When I came to our home, my child Ahmet was five years old, he was playing over there. There was a sand heap, the child was playing there. I said, "Ahmet, come, I am your mum." "No, you are not my mother, my mum is in London," he said! The child didn't come near me. Later on when other kids came, they cuddle me, he said, "You are my mum too."

He didn't recognise. I think I stayed there [in Cyprus] for three months. I sold all of my furniture, I rented the house. My tenant is still in it. My house is still there. I mean Greeks repaired it for me. I received rent until 1974. I couldn't get it after that. The same people stayed there. They respect me, but I don't know if the things will settle down. I haven't done anything about it. I didn't persist with it. I took my kids, we came by ship. That time we returned by *Konetra* ship, with my children. That one was Italian as well. It was nice, there was a cinema inside. I couldn't handle one of kids on the boat. He wanted to see the fish; he was rushing around to see the fish. We had a nice journey. We got off in Paris. I wanted to walk about. They were crying because they thought I was going to lose them. From there we went to Italy, we stopped over in Italy. We walked about in Italy as well like that. My eldest one was eight and my youngest one, the youngest daughter was one year old, I came with five children. The one-year-old was in my arms and the others were walking.

They liked London because around the place where we lived there were many Turks. They liked it, but our flat was so high up that when the ice-cream man was passing, they used to call me, "Mum, I want ice cream." I used to put the money inside a paper for them, throw it from the window; they used to pick it up. And then, "Mum, we want a sandwich or something." I had a basket, I used to lower it down for them, they used to take it, they were fed up of climbing up the stairs.

The schools were opposite us, like this. A road was separating us. When you opened your window, the school was opposite. They used to go. They learned the language somehow. They had some difficulty, sometimes when they wanted to go to the toilet, they used tell their friends who knew [how to speak English]. Because there were people here before us. Our neighbours, we used to get on with them. That is to say, before there wasn't any fear. It would be seven, children used to come from park you didn't mind at all. Oh! Something happened to my child, never. The children used to say, "They only bother the rich kids." So I used to think "Well, we are not rich, So I don't have to be worried."

They liked school. I didn't go to see the teachers, I didn't know you could or that people did. I used to work, whenever I came home, I didn't know it was necessary that I should be interested in my kid's lessons, I never knew. "What can I do?" I used to say. As a matter of fact, I didn't know the language, either. I have never gone.

As soon as we bought the house that day, at night we rented. It was in a very nice location. It was by the bus stop. We rented, we used to stay on one floor, we rented one floor. We stayed there for three years. After three years, we bought this and came to this one [in Palmers Green]. We wanted to sell that one, we didn't want the tenants. The children were grown up. I didn't want it anymore. We bought this house since 1963. And also when I went to my first house, I gave birth to my son there. Afterwards when he turned six years old, we bought this house. At that time we bought it for £6,000. It wasn't that much money. But I liked my house a lot. I used to sew, I started sewing at home.

During school holidays, first my mum used to look after them. Then they were grown-up. When I came here the second time with my children, my mum and my sister came in the same year. They used to stay with me, look after my kids. Afterwards, my mum left. My sister got married. She went with her. My mother-in-law used to look after them. Well, later on I sat at home, worked at home.

GÜLSEN LARKINS: My mum was very kind-hearted, my dad was the same. But then again my dad would not mix with just anybody, my mum too. First my mum would say, "Hello, how are you?" The people she knew were good people, gentlemen and ladies, her door was open to those. Relatives would come, neighbours, acquaintances would come.

We used to go to the weddings with my brother because we didn't know [the way]. My elder brother would take us. He would be responsible for us.

IBRAHIM DERVIŞ: In 1951 I said I was going to return to my motherland. My mother had died and we met the funeral costs. We buried my mother here. Osman Ürek and the likes helped us – of course they knew the area much more. The funeral was organised by the funeral parlour in Commercial Road, they were there even back then.

We were all very happy living together and I found a job again. But we departed from there soon after my wife came, because my sister made a fuss. In truth we were crowded. My big sister got married for the second time and she too departed from the house. We were now lodgers in Camden Town again, opposite the Zoo. My wife was working, I was working and we would have picnics in the evening. We had three children, one in 1954, one in '55, one boy, one girl – and then six years later another girl.

LALAGE FAIZ: What I was saying, our children are now 47 and 51, and they had an entirely an English upbringing really. The elder one just can remember Cyprus. And the younger one can't remember it at all. But it does mean a lot to them to go to the house in Zeytinlik and I think they feel quite emotional when they go in to Cyprus, even though they don't know any Turkish. There is something about the land and the fact that part of them belongs there that is quite important for them.

The elder one started as Murat, he found it difficult in England, How do you spell it? Where does it come from? and in the end, he uses his other name, which is Hugo, and my daughter Nesrin to start with, but it has moved into Rosemary. So she will, they will answer to either. Mostly they use their English names.

They mostly go back once a year. They like to do that. Partly because they love that place, partly to their uncle who is still alive and other relations as well.

Being Turkish, Turkish identity, is something they are always aware of. At the back their minds, being Turkish, Turkish identity, is I think something they had get used to it – is same for any person whose parents from different races. They are thrilled when they meet someone Turkish, but then they just hope they like them – perhaps they do, perhaps they don't.

And yes, then you have to start explaining yourself, "Why aren't you speaking in Turkish?" But the person who was very important in their lives was Süha's mother, Şifa Hanım, because she was the only living grandparent. And so she was always *nene*. My mother-in-law, she is dead now, she used to speak quite good English, got a bit in England, not perfect, but pretty good, and that was great help to me coming as a new bride, you can imagine.

I don't think she missed Cyprus, I think she had such a miserable time in the last years, before she left that she was quite glad to be away. She adored the children anyway.

We had different flats, she had the ground basement flat, she was cooking separately for Sedat my brother-in-law, so we ended up in this house with different generations. So I was cooking upstairs, she was cooking [Turkish] downstairs. Ye, she could be quite a bossy mother-in-law! She spoiled us for restaurant food, because home cooking in Turkish is much much better than restaurant.

HATICE ISMAIL: The good things are my children. When it comes to my marriage life, I am satisfied with my marriage life. We brought up our children, married them slowly slowly. The best of my life is this, my children. They were born and bred here. They didn't have any difficulty. They used to go to school here. They didn't have any difficulty. My first child was born in 1959. My mother-in law-used to look after them. She used to look after my two daughters. I was working outside.

Sometimes teachers used to tell us, send us a letter. We shouldn't talk in our own language, we should speak in English and help them and so on, as English was a little bit difficult for our kids. We were still speaking in our own language, we didn't want to forget our language. When they first started, as you know, I used to want to learn English a little bit so I used to speak a little bit in English to them, but their father never spoke. He never liked it. He didn't like them to speak English at home, they should speak in Turkish. They used sent us a letter, they were saying, "Talk to your children in English. This country is English. English is valid. You came here, you have to talk to your kids in English." They used to make it compulsory for us.

Now they know. It is compulsory for them to know their mother tongue. My youngest grandchild went to Turkish school as well. There was a Turkish school in Edmonton, he/she went there for a couple of years.

The children used to speak in English to each other. They used to find it easier, that is why. They were born and brought up here. But at the same time they know Turkish like me. Amongst us we still speak in Turkish. Because we didn't get angry with them, didn't stop them. Because they spent most of their time at school with English, that is why we didn't prevent them. We used to know three language Turkish, English and Greek. It's not a shame to know languages.

MEHMET ALI BEKIR: I came in 1960. My father, mother and sister – the eldest sister, Hatice – came six months to a year later. We heard by correspondence with letters, in those days letters used to come much more easily. Nowadays it is more difficult.

My father and sister are coming. I picked them up from Victoria. I picked them up and I found a house for them in Newington Green before they arrived. One room, my father and my sister would stay there. I was staying in my place. And if I am not wrong, after six months my mum came. Or was it less than six months? I've forgotten. My other two sisters and my mum came. Slowly the whole family is here. I bought a big flat in Newton Green, we rented. I don't know if there were council houses, because we didn't rent them. For instance, if I know you for years, you might have a place, I would come and rent it from you. After my family had come, we rented a house.

When [my first wife and I] got married, I used to stay in Newington Green. A year later I bought a house in Stoke Newington. I was a painter at that time, I used to get paid £21 a week. 1963 – 64. I got married in '63. We had a child in 1964. I bought a house before the child was born, for £3,700. My wife continued to work as a secretary, until the child was born. After the child was born she gave up.

Three children were born in that house. From there I moved to Southend. Because my children started smoking in London. At a very early age, and to save them, we moved outside of London. This was the 70s. I went to Southend, I sold the house here for £9,500 and I bought the house in Southend for £11,700. I set up my own painting business with an English partner in Southend. I stayed there for 10, 11 years, until 1980.

HATICE IBRAHIM: My brother put his foot down and said, "I do not want my sister in this house, it has no bath." At the end of 1955 my brother made [my husband] buy 88 Hither Road. It was a beautiful five-bedroom house in Brixton Hill.

I gave birth to my daughter in this house in 1956. Her name is Gülten. She has changed it to Rachel now, because my child's husband is in the airforce. There was lots of difficulties. I am so glad that all my children are married to Americans.

My son is married to an American girl too. Ibrahim my son was born in 1958. In 1959, another girl was born, Narin. Those two are very close. She is unmarried. She is left, she is at home. My child is big, she is 45 years old but didn't get married. I have a son Ahmet born in 1961. He too is married to an American. He has three children. He has been over there for ages.

I have two children in Georgia and one in California. I have been to California three times, once to Colorado. I really liked Colorado. Narin lives in London. My youngest daughter Esra Sema was born in 1970, and lives in Hemel Hempstead. Her husband is English.

After three children, my husband bought two houses and started to fill the houses with lodgers. I did not count my house as my home. In any case, my brother helped and a third house was bought near the really nice house. This happened when my Ahmet, my fourth child was four, in 1965.

He wouldn't give me any money. I wanted to buy food to cook for my children. Nothing nothing. I suffered such sadness.

"I will divorce," I said. Not with four children, but even if I had 14 I would divorce. I started, I found a solicitor to divorce. But they did not divorce me because I had been married for 15 years and had four children. "Why did I want to divorce," they questioned. There was no belief, they did not divorce me. The English. This went on for seven years. I started to hate him in 1969 and wanted to divorce. In this period he gave me another child.

I used to sleep separately, but he caught me when I was isolated, one more child happened, Sema. In other words nine years after me last child. Nine years after Ahmet I gave birth to my little Sema. He thought that I would not divorce him if I had five children. He sold the houses.

I worked so much that I was not involved in going to see the teachers at their school. But later I learned that it would have been a really good thing for the children if I had gone to the school more often.

Although I said the government would not divorce me, they did eventually – but we were staying in the same house. I had a small child, my husband would torture me in private, he was angry. I was to wake in the morning, feed the children, four children, have breakfast. They were sitting – one boy one girl, one boy one girl – like that, at the table. And I was holding my baby. These children were fighting with each other with their hands under the table. I think it was Narin and Ibrahim fighting. Narin spat in my son's face. I was holding my baby ready to breastfeed and put to sleep. When I saw the spit, I got the butter knife – which wasn't sharp – and threw it. To stop them fighting. Not to spit. I don't know how it happened, but the knife caught her arm. There was blood pouring between her little fingers. I was in shock when I saw this, and was unable to do a thing. My married brother was there. He took her to Kings' College Hospital.

I was back at home, breastfeeding and washing the baby. I have no idea of what's happening. I put the baby to sleep. I started to fry courgettes, for the afternoon, for lunch. Two policemen arrive. Detectives. How was I to know who they were? They go looking round the house. One of them took a courgette and ate it and told the other one, "Take one as well."

"No!" he says to him. Two nice youngsters. I still have no idea about anything. "Come on," one said, "get ready."

"Get ready for what? What's going on?" I said. However it happened, I left and they put me in the car and took me to the police station. Prison. Key after key after key. Doctors had asked what happened when they took my daughter to hospital to get have some stitches. They said her mother threw a knife. That's why the police came.

I am sitting on a piece of wood. Not knowing what to do. A woman comes and opens the small hole, looks at me and asks "Are you alright?" And then shuts the little hole.

"Excuse me!" I shouted

"What?" she said.

"Bring me my baby," I said. "I have to breastfeed her. It's her feeding time."

"Oh my dear!" the woman said. I had breastfed my baby and put her to sleep. There were people at home but how did I know they were going imprison me?

They came quickly, the police let me out. They took me back home. They started to have a go at the police – why hadn't they do any questioning? After that the case was heard. We went to court. They read my case in court. I was going to divorce. The police apologised to me and my solicitor. The court hearing finished and the two young police and the solicitor said, "Come with us to a restaurant."

"I have got a baby," I said.

I raised my children all on my own. I never remarried. There were people who wanted to marry me but I wouldn't. I had three daughters and two sons. Who was going to take me?

Hatice Ibrahim standing outside her house in Brixton, London, 1955

NEVCIVAN JEVAN: As matter of fact I used to work in the factory. I gave the children to the child-minder. I was working. I can't remember how I used to do it.

GÜLSEN LARKINS: In 1957, I wasn't married. He was supposed to have a life prison. He had a girlfriend who fell in love with another Turk. She prepared her suitcase. She put all her clothes in a suitcase. Her shoes were left to pack and he stabbed her. They took one of her kidneys. He loved the girl. She was Irish. She didn't die, it was execution if she had died.

I didn't know this before I married. How would have I known? No I didn't know. He was very good to me. He loved me. He got out of prison in 1961. He has just been released but I didn't know. My brother saw it in the newspaper. I was very well, I was happy. My husband was good then. He didn't do a bad thing to me.

I wasn't stupid when I came. And he loved me then. We used to go out in secret, and then my mum heard about it. We went to the cinema a few times, but he wouldn't touch me. He was an honourable man. We went to Trafalgar Square, to dinner. My brother heard about it too. I got two slaps from my older brother. Not my mum and dad. My dad said leave her, she's not a child is she?

Leave her. He asked for me later and my dad gave me. My mum didn't want him.

My brothers didn't want him. My dad didn't want to break my heart. He said she is a 21-year-old girl, she isn't a child. In truth he was happy. But he was good [the husband], very good towards the family. But look, anything different would be ungratefulness. But he loved and respected the family a lot. He had respect for all my family, all my friends. He was a polite man, very polite.

ŞABAN LEFKARIDI: I didn't go to my kid's school, but later on when our other child was born, the teacher used to come home. For one to one-and-a-half years I used to pay a teacher, from Ankara came here, for my son to learn a language. We agreed, and he used to come home and used to give lesson to our son Turkish lessons, because he was born here.

When my wife went in to give birth to Hüseyin, we knew very little English. We had some difficulty at that time because there weren't many who knew English. That is to say, we half understand one another. People were good, the doctors. They would help us. Hüseyin was born in Lambeth Hospital.

I'll tell you, in 1960 we bought a house here on Queens Road, in 1960, from here. We got divorced in 1963. We went to court, we had two kids. Court gave the kids to me. They didn't give anything to the woman, anything to her. She didn't have any rights, because I think they probably found her guilty. They gave the kids to me as well, and as she didn't have any rights over the house.

I was a single father in 1963. One of the children was seven, the other one was nine then. In 1963 when there was conflict in Cyprus, I had my mum called, via the Red Cross. I went to Red Cross here and they helped me. I paid for her ticket. She used to stay with me in Elephant and Castle, later on she went. When we got divorced my mum was with me. I brought her mum and dad here. They used to stay all together with me. When we got divorced, her mum and dad were staying with me. My mum used to stay with me as well. For six, seven months, nearly for a year I was the only one who was working. Looking after six people. They [mother-in-law and father-in-law] had both their son and daughter here. I told them, "Find a place and go, because I'm finding it difficult." Looking after six people, isn't it? First they said they were going to go, later on their daughter encouraged them so they wouldn't go.

My wife was staying somewhere else. My mum used to look after the kids. They used to go school. After the divorce in 1963, I had my mum. She wanted to look after them anyway, but later on I had a girlfriend. We used to stay together and English person. My last child is from her. Afterwards we got married, 17 years later. For 17 years I was alone with my mum. Before I divorced my wife, this woman came and stayed in my house, let's say the English woman, and she gave birth to the child before I married her. But I still gave my surname to that child.

The school was close by. They used to go and come back, they used to call me in sometimes, but they were good at school. My son, even when he went to secondary school, afterwards when he went to the third, he had to sit an exam, he was about to start to work. That is to say, for one of the government offices. The headmaster wrote me a letter to see me. I didn't know of course. When I went there, the headmaster and two teachers, I took Hüseyin with me. He said, "If you want, leave this kid at school. He should stay here for longer, because his future is very bright. His head is good."

But the Turkish teacher told me this as well. The teacher that used to come and give him lessons, he said, "If you don't have money, sell your houses to educate this child."

I swear like this. I'll never forget it.

When we went to talk with the headmaster, he said, "Do you want to talk or should we?"

I said, " I don't know why I have come here," I said.

He said, "Leave this child in school because his future is bright."

I said, "OK, he can stay as long as he wants. I would do my best to help him." So he stayed and studied. I think he stayed until 25 years old, he was still studying.

Then there were exams for Telecom. 1,200 people entered and 160 passed. And I think our one was second.

The kids learn English at school. I would talk in Turkish; outside they would talk in English. They went to Cyprus quite often; I used to take them to Cyprus every year. The big one can read and write in Turkish, he can speak like I do, but the youngest one has forgot, because he couldn't go to Cyprus that often. He knew some but he forgot them as well.

NEVCIVAN JEVAN: I stayed in our relatives' house. As a matter of fact they used to cook at the beginning. I used pay my rent, stay in that room. It was more comfortable in that sense. But they didn't have a bathroom and their toilet was outside.

Yes, of course, of course we used rent rooms from relatives or other Turkish people. Your relative would send an invitation, through your relative you would come here. Well, my relatives invited. As a matter of fact I came with my uncle, I didn't have any difficulty. Only it took very long time on the ship. I became sick, vomited, because I wasn't used to it. I don't know, I think we stayed in Italy for a couple of days, after that we took a train again, from train to ship, something like that.

EMINE AHMED: At hospital I didn't know the language, but when I became pregnant, I had a nephew, his wife, my uncle's son's wife, had been here for a considerable amount of time. She used to come with me to do interpretation. She used to interpret at first. Afterwards I used go to the doctor on my own if there was something. If the doctor wanted to say something, the doctor would write it on a paper and I used to go and have it read at home. If you got sick, you would take someone with you who knew English to the doctor, he/she would talk to the doctor and translate it to you, you would tell your problem. It was a bit difficult then of course. Later on kids started bringing letters when they started going to school. Let's say letters from the government, from this and that would come, and of course I can't read. It was a necessity to give them to your kids' friends. He/she would read and explain the issue in Turkish, of course if he/she would understand Turkish. I had a big difficulty because of that.

I felt settled in this country when I bought a house in Turnpike Lane. Before that I used live on third floor in a house on Whiteman Road. I used to have Şensal [her daughter] sit on the chair and I used to put Bayar [her son], he wasn't two years old yet, in bed, because if he'd run inside the home, the tenant below us would come and say, "There are people downstairs, keep them quiet!" So I used to have Şensal sit on the chair and put Bayar in bed not to disturb them. But they were kids.

When I bought the house I felt relieved. Nobody can kick me outside. When I was living in Whiteman Road, my landlady came and gave notice to leave the house when I was due for to give birth to Bayar very shortly. I would say, "My doctor knows this place, the midwife knows here and so on. Now how can I pack up my things? I became 12 kilos when I was due for Bayar. She said that I should gather my stuff and leave there. I was packing my things when I was pregnant. I found another place so I would leave. Later on she came to me and said, "Emine, it is difficult for you". She was from village as well. "It is difficult for you, don't pack up yet, give birth, you can go after you give birth," she said to me. We said "OK!". The following week she came again and gave me notice to leave again. Whenever she has a fight with her daughter she would come and give us notice so I would leave. "What did I do?" I said. I said, "Whether you believe or not, whether you kick me out of here or not, I am staying." I said to herself. "I will not leave this house without giving birth. If I give birth to this child to day, I will leave bleeding," I said to myself. I gave birth to Bayar, the following week I left and moved to another house. I said, "Oh God help, I would buy a house and leave, oh God help I would buy a house and leave." Oh, I had to bear with a lot of things.

Emine Ahmed at home, London, 1962

EMINE MEHMET: I have only two daughters. The first one was born in Cyprus in 1951, and I gave birth to the second, Gonca, in Lambeth Hospital in 1956.

I wish [the English girl] Margaret had married my brother. They didn't marry. He took a Turkish wife, and then they divorced. That brother of mine died from worry. Margaret really loved him. And she was such a special girl. Blue eyes, he would take her by the arm, and she would take him by the arm. He died of a heart attack aged 57. That brother of mine died. He left five children.

IBRAHIM DERVIŞ: I had a good wage. Though we of course had living difficulties, we had a more comfortable life, in terms of materialism, we had no difficulties here. A comfortable life.

Gokmen Mehmet and family, London, 1954

7. CULTURAL LIFE

MUSTAFA HÜSEYIN: When I first came here, I used to go mostly to the West End. Our entertainment was cinema then, we used to go to English cinemas and the dancehall. We used to go dances. In the 60s there were dancehalls, there was the Lyceum in the Strand. There is Astoria, on Charing Cross Road, it was a dancehall then. It is a club now, drinking club. There was Hammersmith Palace, Streatham Palace. There was in North London, in Finsbury Park as well. The owner of all these was Top Rank. They were not casinos' just dancehalls.

There was one [dance] after three o'clock. They used call it the tea dance. And also there was Café de Paris nearby in West End, in Leicester Square. We used to go inside there because the restaurants used to be closed from 3 till 6 pm. Where would you spend that time? Either we used to go cartoon films, or to dance, to pass the time. At night it used to open it again from 6pm till 12.

I used to ask the English girls to dance. Some of them used to say yes, some no. There were friends there as well. There were so many friends from Cyprus around my age.

Mustafa Hüseyin and his friends in West End, London, 1956/7

KEMAL AHMET DAVRANDI: He [My cousin in Manchester] went to work. He used to work in Wimpy. He came back in the evening. "Are you hungry?"

"To be honest, I could even eat you," I said. I was dying of starvation all day in this house, I told him.

"Come, let's go," he said. He took me to a fish and chip shop. Did I know what fish and chips were? My first meal! They put a fish in front of me and a load of chips – and that tomato ketchup on top. I took one mouthful, it was as if my intestines were going to come out. "Why did you put that stuff on top!?" I said.

"Hey cousin, eat it, it nice"

I said I was full. I was unable to eat even a single bite. From that time I have a loathing of tomato ketchup. I don't know if it because I was hungry at the time. That's just how it felt.

I said, "Cousin, I did not come here to sit, there is no money in my pocket. I have £1 10 shillings. I have had one fish all day, I bought some cigarettes and all I have is £1 10 shillings now."

"OK, my cousin," he said. "I'll find you a job. I'll talk to the boss and find you a job."

He come and goes [to work].

"Well? What's happening, cousin?" I ask. It was a Friday.

"Cousin," he said, "let's go out tonight," he said.

"Cousin I want a job!" I said to him.

"No, I have sorted out two girls, one for me and one for you!"

"Give up! For the love of God!" I said to him. "I am unemployed, I have no money, I want a job and you have sorted out some girls! I'm not going!" I said. In short I didn't go. He went. I have no idea if the girls were English, Italian, I don't know. Of course I didn't see them. He came back on Saturday.

I said, "Cousin, what's happening? Work boss? Work?"

"I swear," he said. "I asked and the boss said no."

"Look, I will wash dishes, whatever," I said.

But he said "No, cousin," he said.

"What am I going to do, cousin?" I said.

"I swear I don't know either, cousin," he said.

"I mean, two people staying in a tiny room together!" I said.

"I swear, you think about that," he said.

I said to him, "Son, write a letter to Cyprus and ask them to buy a ticket to return, so I can leave."

He said, "OK." That was one week after I had arrived in England. Well what else could I do? No work, no money, dying of starvation. My cousin wrote a letter to Cyprus. But he didn't write the address correctly. We waited a week.

We are waiting and waiting and waiting, no money is arriving from Cyprus. "What am I going to do?" The money had not arrived.

"I don't know either," he said to me. "I don't have any money either or I would give you some if I did. I get £4 10 shillings a week and I give 10 shillings for the rent, give some here and there – the money finishes."

I said, "Cousin, you take me to London. Leave me there and I will find some friends there," I said.

"I swear, but cousin, I can't take you to London," he said.

"So what will I do now?" I said.

"Come," he said to me. We got up Sunday morning. He took me to the train station. "Look cousin," he said: "This train," he said, "goes straight to London, to Victoria Station," he said.

"So how will I know where Victoria Station is?" I said.

"When everyone gets off the train, you get off too," he said.

We bought the ticket from there. We gave 10 shillings there for the ticket. I was left with 10 shillings in my pocket. I got on the train. *Tak tak tak tak.*

EMINE AHMED: Sultan Abla, my nephew's wife, took me to Madame Tussaud's once. We went to a museum only with her. She came here in the 50s. Madame Tussaud's did exist in the 60s. She didn't take us any more once we left. After that my brother took us to the zoo once. There was London Zoo then. He took us there, I don't remember anywhere else that we went to. When the kids grew up, I bought a car, once I bought the car, we started going to the closest resort places, seaside such as Brighton. In Madame Tussaud's there was a girl [*kızcağız*], I took interest in that a lot. It was a girl that had a battery in her heart. That was what I showed the most interest in. I think it was Sleeping Beauty. She has died while she was sleeping. I looked at that a lot, she was sleeping like that and her heart was beating. I took interest in that. Maybe it is still there but I don't know. There weren't many things in Madame Tussaud's then. There are lots of things now. You could only see five, six things in that. We went there with Bayar four, four years ago, there are quite a lot of things in Madame Tussaud's. There was nothing then.

The early years, I always work. It passed with work. Don't say anything. I got married, I have never gone to a restaurant and had meal there in my life. Even one day. If you ask me whether I went to a restaurant to have meal, I haven't. Never gone to a restaurant and had meal in private. Never. Not even to the cinema. Turkish cinema was launched, I couldn't even go to that, because I didn't have anyone to look after the kids.

I didn't travel at all. Not all, not at all. You would go out, have a dinner in private, never. In Cyprus, everyone would go out and have dinner in private once a week. No, we have never done. We didn't have the opportunity. It is not we didn't have the opportunity but how would I know, some people don't do it. Of course I wanted to. Why shouldn't I want to go out with your kids and husband and have meal outside once a week, once a month? Of course you want, but we have never done that. It is something nice of course, it is a change. When you keep working you get utterly bored. You can't find any time because of work.

HULUSI MAHMUD: I went to the cinema in Upper Street in Islington. It used to be [the Rex] but there was one further on, where the petrol station is, if you went up there used to be a police station before the town hall — there was a cinema there as well. And plus there was a cinema just before Essex Road, in Upper Street, that was a very good one. I remember. Very good.

The films. It was all foreign to me, you know. Because you know what happened, my brother would go up front to get the tickets. And I didn't know at that time it was two bob. The tickets and the two and six, half-a-crown*. They just laughed at me, because I didn't know how to say the ticket. This brings back too many memories you know.

I went to see films together with my brother, *The Ten Commandments*, *Psycho* – an Alfred Hitchcock film. Very scary. I didn't understand too much. But *The Ten Commandments* was a very good film, you know.

They used show Turkish films. It used to be in Turnpike Lane, showing Turkish films there. That was afterwards. Sometime in the mid-60s. They used to show Turkish films there.

I used to go to the museum and so on, but not outside London. Sometimes, we were involved, too much work, you know. Only do work, work and work and work.

ALI HASSAN: There was other Turks there. Like I said there was a few from Köfünye village and there was Cemal from Nicosia. We started to slowly slowly get to meet these people. We used to go to the parks. We used to play a bit of football, that time we was young. We used to play football. There was nothing to do with drinking alcohol upon us at all. We used to go to cinemas. No, there was no Turkish films at that time. There was no Turkish at that time. Turkish films started quite a while after, the 60s. No. In 1960. I'm not going to be able to remember the year exactly, but the Turkish films came about quite a while after we came here. Let me not lie. I can't remember the exact year. Yes we mixed with the Turks at the parks. It was all the close people any way, we all used to meet up there. We used to go to the park together. I'm not the type of person to go out to the cafés. I go from home to work, work to home. I don't go to cafés to drink coffee, play cards and gamble.

EMINE AHMET: We used to meet Turkish people at weekends. We used to go to the corner shop to see a Turk and meet up. There was Kemal, in Upper Street. His wife's name was Emine.

That was in the 60s, because I moved to the last place in 1960 and I used to go that place. At weekends, on Saturday afternoons, you couldn't even buy a lemon, everywhere was closed. When I was buying a lemon from Mrs Emine, I asked for some sugar as well. She hid it in a packet behind her as it was Saturday and

---

* An old-money coin worth 2s 6d, or 12.5p in 'new' money. See text note on currency on page 79

everywhere was closed in the afternoon. It was like that those days. Everywhere was closed, whether it was Sunday or not.

HÜSEYIN YUSUF: We used to socialise in Trafalgar Square, Lyon's Corner House which was in Strand. Lyon's Corner House was like a big café. Big room, tea room. Men and women went there. Single Turkish guys, there was no Turkish girls in those days anyway.

To be honest with you I don't what is there now. There was another one in Tottenham Court Road. There was same style, sort of thing. And also we used to go to Dominion Cinema in Tottenham Court Road. We watched all films, cowboys and things like that. All type of movies, you know.

Lyon's Corner House, date unknown. Image courtesy of London Metropolitan Archives

I stayed in Upper Street for about six months. Then he sold the restaurant and we all moved to Brighton. Altogether, my uncle, my cousin, his family, his partner. We moved to Brighton. They bought a restaurant down there. Oh, it was a different thing down there. It was much better. Beach was there. We used to go swimming and all that. It was quite good in Brighton.

The people were quite friendly, actually. Nice people. In the first six months I started missing my family. Because after a while the excitement went off. You start wondering what is happening back home. And then I had a bit of misfortune, I had an accident. I hurt my leg. I spent a few months in hospital in Brighton. And when I got better, I went, I used to go to a dance hall there. There was a Greek guy who was in Merchant Navy. He used to always come home with lots of money in his pocket, he used to tell all his adventures. He used to go to various countries. Various islands, Caribbean. It was exciting, you know. I was excited about it, I wanted to do the same thing. I want to see the world, because and I did. In 1956 I joined the Merchant Navy. I was British you see at that time. Cyprus was British Colony. I was in the Merchant Navy from 1956 to 1975.

I was a single man. During that time I got to meet an English girlfriend. In the early 60s. I got married. I also with her until 1972. And then I got divorced because it didn't work out.

CELAL HASSAN: Usually when I found a friend I used to go to cinema. English cinema. After few years a few friends came from the village, because the trouble started there, you know, and people were scared, they started to run away to come here to have a better life, you know. So I mixed up with them, we used to go to the park there and here, make friends.

MELEK KAZIM: Our house, my house was like a club. There was no café, no nothing, and so every Saturday, Friday and Saturday, mum and dad used have all the friends coming over, eat drink, be merry. It was an open house. Whoever heard, the Turkish friends would come. They would immediately ring the door and go in.

EMINE AHMET: When we came bread was fourpenny. I bought a lot of English food in those days.

My husband used to work in a restaurant, so he knew. We used to buy, I didn't have any difficulty, that is to say. When I went to the corner shop I used to buy whatever I wanted.

I used to go the shops that were close by. I have never gone to the far ones. I have never gone to West End on my own. I used to go to work. The times when he was working, I used to do shopping from the local corner shop. When he had a day off, we used to go to my nephew in Peckham at night. We went to the seaside a lot.

MEHMET ALI BEKIR: In England, we had a real difficulty in terms of food. Especially from meat, from the butcher or whenever you go to a restaurant. We couldn't eat meat. Because its taste was very different for us. For example there was someone called Kara Bina and he had a restaurant, we used to eat meat there and we could never enjoy the meat. Especially we had difficulty with meat. We use to eat there. Our food problem.

With friends we used to gather in Kara Bina's café and after that to the cinema of course, in Angel, the one in Upper Street. There were three cinemas there, on the right- and left-hand side by the third traffic lights, and another one up by the park.

When we were young, for example, there was a Turkish café called 'Lefkosa'li Ozkan in West End'. Around Tottenham Court Road, there was a Turkish café in those days, and we used to go there, meet up there. My friends Halil and Tezel had a car in those days, Tezel's brother Halil's car, a Vauxhall Victor. In those days not many people could afford to buy a car. It was £200, or something like that, but it was new.

Another entertainment was, at weekends for instance in the summer, we used to go to Brighton, or South End. We used to go to the seaside at night and sleep inside the car.

EMINE MEHMET: There were no neighbours. For years there were no Turkish neighbours where I was. Because I came here married. I lived in Kennington, in

Peckham, in Lewisham. My husband would buy and sell, buy and sell. He would buy houses and repair the insides. He kept buy and selling houses, and we would move somewhere else. We bought our first house one or two years after we arrived, but not a freehold. There were very few Turks around then. We used to meet mostly on Saturdays and Sundays. We used to talk with friends. We used to meet in their houses. We would find their addresses and go. They used to come to our house. Then the weddings started. We used to go to weddings when people increased. I mean we used to help each other. There would be a bride and we would pin money, for this person and that person. Like this.

The weddings started five or six years after I came. They started lightly. But my sister was married here. There was a pub on the way to Lewisham. My sister got married in there in 1954 or 1955.

I was the first from my family to come here. They all came after me. We brought them over one by one. My mother and father came. My father had land, they telephoned him from Cyprus to say that it had been left unkept. My father went back out there. My father worked at the Savoy. All the English ladies were after him. The man was young at the time. He came to see his children and got a job in the Savoy. The man was bored sitting at home. He stayed two or three months and then got a job. He would come and go. There were lots of Turks working there. He would come and come and go.

Later my husband bought another house and would sometime rent the rooms upstairs. We used to have their rations* [i.e. ration cards] and go shopping everyday. They used to work at the Savoy, so they would take their rations and give them to us and we would do shopping. We used to buy eggs, buy bread.

Our lodgers were Turkish. They would arrive, they had no one, no home, they would leave their wives and come. Later years passed and my deceased [husband] helped people in this country. Only a few men can be found like that. He helped lots of people. The husbands, the wives, would be in pain, and he would put them in the car and take them to hospital. If anyone need anything doing, Mustafa *bey* would do it.

MUSTAFA HÜSEYIN: There was the Cyprus Turkish Association in that Richmond Building, near Dean Street. It moved to D'Arblay Street later. It was Richmond Building.

Yes. We used to go because you hear news from Turkey, Cyprus. You couldn't get the news anywhere else. Turkish newspaper used to be delivered there. They had a radio. Well, we used to go there for news. We used to go there almost every day. Because food, they used to cook Turkish food in there. There was an office upstairs, women used to go there as well. There was such a thing; a wife would come to the West End to meet her husband after work. There wasn't badness or

---

* In order to deal with the extreme shortages of food during and after World War Two the Ministry of Food instituted a system of rationing. Each household was given a ration book containing coupons allowing them to purchase a certain amount of some kinds of food each week. Foods that were rationed included sugar, eggs and milk. Rationing did not end in Britain until 1954.

anything. Everyone would know everyone's wife, so there was no coming on to them, and there are so many English women, girls, it would be a disgrace an embarrassment, it wouldn't happen

We used to go there, sit, have our meal; we used to give 5 shillings, 10 shillings. Then it was like that.

HÜSEYIN YUSUF: Our meeting place was Trafalgar Square where the pigeons are. We used to go down there one or two other old timers, like myself. We used to congregate down there, we used to go to Lyon's Corner House, have a cup of tea. That was our meeting. It was too cold out there. And you know tell each other stories, whether we liked it or not, our jobs. things like that.

IBRAHIM DERVİŞ: When we came there was no Association. We thought about forming one – for our culture, the future of our children, to help with our sorrows, the yearning we had for each others' company, and out of the desire to be together. We were given a place in Dean Street by Nevar Abi. But our first meeting was on top of Hasan Cağlayan's restaurant in Greek Street, an English restaurant. Osman Ürek, Necati Sayar and people like this attended the meeting. Osman Ürek and Mithat Berberoğlu were studying to be lawyers at the time – Denktaş had finished and went back [to Cyprus]

Regulations for the Association were prepared at Hasan Bey's restaurant. I think it was Osman Ürek and so on that prepared them.

This place became a meeting point because we had let friends and relatives in Cyprus know about it. So then family, friends, relatives and acquaintances from Cyprus began gradually turning up with the address in their hand. We used to meet and hold votes. The first Chair was Necati Sayar. I worked with him. But I was always supportive from a distance or I would get friends to become interested, to become members. We had about 100 – 150 members at the most – later on I think it rose to up to 400. But it went quiet later also. We then changed our building, and moved over to D'Arblay Street.

At this time we, Necati Sayar, asked the Turkish Embassy for a teacher, to give lessons in Turkish to our children. This was in 1952. They said no: "You are English citizens – why do you need a Turkish teacher?" He then wrote a letter to I think it was Güner Alp, the Minister for Education [from Turkey]. Then came Fahri Bey, Abdullah Bey with his wife, and someone from the south. We had to find a building for the children's lessons. The Turkish Embassy – who had been in communication with the Ministry of Education in Turkey – provided a teacher.

IBRAHIM MUSTAFA: I used to go out with mates, not my wife. My social life with my wife was visiting families. We never did any sightseeing. No, no, no. I am not in those kind of things. Even up to now, I haven't been to Madame Tussaud's in 44 years. Never been to museums or anywhere. But I really like London. I don't know why. I might go back [to Cyprus] when I retire but the other half don't wanna come.

MEHMET ŞEREF ALI: In 1955 or '56 there was a snack bar called Blue Kettle – it was a very large place. It was open until morning. When you come to Angel from Upper Street, huge like this, turns left or right, before you turn there on the left hand side there was a dance hall on top of a tailor's. A little bit further down there was this snack bar called Blue Kettle and there was a cinema over there. And we used to drink tea until one, two at night. There was a kettle and this steam used to come out of it. They used to call it Blue Kettle. I previously argued with this Greek boy in a Greek café in Upper Street. We used to go there every now and again. There is Halil Basri, opposite his café. Now it is not there, it is not a café. I don't know it has been destroyed. At that time, there was Ibo, but from time to time, sometimes at the weekends. He used cook 'kebab in the oven'. There was Uncle Ali. He was really from old times, possibly from the war. He used to work there some Sundays. We used to go there. There were five, six Turkish, one or two Greeks. The owner of the café was actually a Greek but the chef was Turkish. Possibly they were from the same village, if I am not wrong.

HÜSEYIN YUSUF: We came here, I got business with my brother. Osman his name is. Osman Yusuf. Next door. I made a kebab house. It was the first kebab house in London. In 1975, towards the end of '75. We were there together almost 15 years with my brother.

SÜHA FAIZ: [I have written] two [books] that are published. But the Yunus Emre one is a kind of a determining event, because the origin of it was when we were on holiday in Turkey*. We used to go on holiday in Turkey and a chap gave me a book. I was still working then, I wasn't retired then. In retirement I tried to translate this book. The book itself is a big book, but in it there is 157 of the divana, which is highly disputed now, how much is Yunus, how much is not Yunus, etc. In translating that book, in particularly then when I retired and [was] putting the actual work into verse, this gave me a perception of not only being a Turk – that doesn't necessarily apply to everybody for myself what being a Turk is – which is something which I wasn't aware of before. I would turn the question back, and ask a Turk what being a Turk means, there are some aspects of it which I don't like and there are aspects which are common not to us but to Greeks, we and the Greeks resemble each other in very, very, very many ways – and we don't like it, and I will give you an example of it what I don't like. In Cyprus at the end of Mehmet Akif Caddesi towards the city, before you turned left because the barricades there – I don't know if it is still there – there is a sort of barrier what is written on it is *"Bir Türk dünyaya bedel"* – now my feeling is if anybody thinks Turkish are all allies, think that one of me is the equivalent of the whole world, he is either a liar or he is so lacking in self-confidence that he has to say that. The mere fact of saying it you shows that you don't really feel it. So we are untrue to ourselves. Yunus Emre is beyond that. I don't think the word 'Turk' appears in the whole of Yunus Emre. So I would say, not my success, but what I am pleased to have done, is produced that book.

GÖKMEN MEHMET: I learned the English language because I never mixed with Turks. I always worked with English people. Even when I worked in the shirt factory with the Turkish girls I still had English friends. Because I like to learn English, that's why.

---

* The City of the Heart, Yunus Emre's Sufi Verses of Wisdom and Love, Süha Faiz, Near East University Press, 2004.

In my time there was no *davul zurna*, no hall. People was very poor in them days. You couldn't afford it to go in the halls. We had a party in his brother-in-law's restaurant. I got my outfit before I got married. I can't remember where I got it from. I was single when I bought it. I didn't plan to wear it on my wedding day! I bought that suit a couple of years before I got married! I always wore the suit before I got married.

EMINE AHMET: Our sea [over here] wasn't clean. It can't even come close to our seas in Cyprus.

ÇETIN KAYA MUSTAFA: No, no, we didn't go out with anyone. We used to go straight away home, take a bus. For example you get on the bus, you go to work, when you come back from work to your neighbourhood. We had friends in our neighbourhood, and we used to go to the swimming pool, every day. There were Turks and an English, Irish, we used to call him Johnny. We were friends with people at work but, well, only at work. We didn't do anything like going out and so on.

In those days my brother-in-law took that house on himself. There were agents. From an agent he took a book, his own name is written on top of that, it had "rent book" or something like that written on it. And my brother-in-law used to pay for everything. And we didn't use to pay to my brother-in-law. Because he used to always pay for it as we were his brother-in-law. I think my brother didn't either. But what I remember is in those days, no matter how much food and bread we buy, it used to finish within a minute. Bread used to be consumed very quickly then. We used to eat like that, I don't know is it because of the cold. And my brother-in-law, my sister, her child, my brother and I, all of us used to stay in the same building. Later on when my brother-in-law was gonna go back to Cyprus, my brother and I stayed here. And we then were gonna let the house out to some other Turkish people, those people were about to kick us out of the house. They wanted to be cunning, throw us out so the house would be left to them. This time my brother-in-law had this thingy, the rent book to us. In short we wanted to do good, we were about to experience badness.

In the end, they couldn't do anything and we stayed there. They stayed as well. They stayed in the big room, we stayed in the back room.

We went to learn English. I think around 1963.

It was a night school in Princess Lane. All of them were foreigners. There were at least 15 – 20 people. All different people: Indian, Pakistan. And I used to learn English.

Music, I also went to learn guitar. I used to like playing guitar, I wanted to learn how to play. But when you press the strings with your fingers for example, it used to hurt a lot. I left it. But my children, both my sons play the guitar very nice. But I don't keep things up if something is very difficult. I don't like it. My fingers were hurting a lot so I gave up.

It is more different here. Here, I mean how should I explain to you. Roads are wide, pavements are big, lots of shops. I mean it is a very different kind of place. But young people like it here. Because there are so many different things. There were pools, a lot of cinemas. For example I used to go the cinema here. I was so interested in the films that the film used to finish in one cinema, I used to go the other cinema. It was cheap as well, one or two shillings, I had money as well.

I used to like king films. I am talking about the English ones. Or Hercules. I used to like cowboy films a lot, or pirate films on the ships for example. As a matter of fact, I used to see outside the cinema you know, there are photos in front of the cinema. As you see the photos you make a decision for example. You see the photos of the daily programme and you would say, "Ah, this film must be nice." and you go immediately go in. But in those days, I remember the first Turkish film came to that cinema – which is Aziziye Mosque. It was a film called *Taş Bebek*, starring Gönül Yazar in it, and I liked it a lot too. That is to say when a Turkish film came we used to go from time to time. Once Göksel Arsoy came, he used to sing songs, he came to Classic Cinema – I can't really remember the name, the one before you go to Dalston, it is still a cinema on the right-hand side. On the corner. On the left-hand side it is Argos. Yeah, OK! That was Classic Cinema.

I went to a concert. The cinema was full. Later on he gave us his autograph. He gave us autograph. That photo is at home.

There were Turkish Baths and we used to go there for example, with friends. Opposite the pub. There were baths and when you went into there, for example, in those days, there wasn't a bathroom in most people's house. It is not easy. In some of them there is a bath, there is a bath in the kitchen for example, and that bath, there was wood on top of that. It was used as a table. This time you put that down, have a bath, close it again. It was very different. Loos were all outside in the garden, in the streets. You feel cold, it is very different. Outdoors. It was very, very different.

My first success was when I learnt English. I learnt photography mostly here. It is my job. I can colour black-and-white photos. I can do thousands of tricks in both of them. I love photography very much. That is to say, the best thing I love in my life is photography. I like gardening as well. I like working in the garden a lot. I like swimming a lot but – because of laziness we don't go. A person shouldn't just say they should do it.

ALI HASSAN: There was times when we worked six days a week, times when we worked five days, there was never seven days a week. There was no Sunday. In fact in those times even the Sunday grocery stores could not sell dry foods, because by law it was not allowed. Absolutely no grocer could sell dried beans. If there was cooked food, it had to be in tins or cartons, they could sell that. They could sell bread, they could sell ready-cooked foods, but they could not sell dried foods. They could sell things like dried nuts, but they couldn't sell foods that would take long to cook, because our people would not make it to church to go and cook. If people stayed at home to make food that took too long to cook, they would not make it to church.

They couldn't go to church. We had nothing to do with the church, but for religious reasons in those times it was like that in England. Many foods like dried beans would take long to cook, these were not allowed to be sold. You could buy cooked beans in a tin, but if you bought a whole load of beans and it was seen in your bag while you was shopping, they'd shut the groceries. Yes we used to find

Turkish foods. In Aldgate there was a Turkish grocer store, we used to call it 'Salih *Dayı*'. That's where we used to go. There was also an Italian one. There was also Salih Dede, Fat, his wife was Jewish. And there was one Italian. 'Salih *Dayı*' was there even before 1957, a long time before. Yes, he came here way before us lot.

The last we heard he got ill, they sold the shop. Baflı Emine Hanım's husband used to do the best, what was his name? He had a thing in Angel as well. I can't think of his name at the moment. He used to bring in everything. In Angel in a place called Cross Street or something. There, Emine Hanım with her husband, what was her husband's name? In fact Emine Hanım later became our in-laws. She used to run the shop together with her husband.

They were from [...], let me not give the wrong name. Emine, her family lived in Famagusta. I don't know where they were from. However her family were in Famagusta, Emine Hanım's brother married my father's daughter later on. They had Turkish foods as well. Everything, they had everything. Yes they had olives and white cheese, those times we could buy them from tins. We used get olive oil in tins.

GÜLSEN LARKINS: I learnt to speak English from the neighbours, and when I started to work.

The food here didn't even bother me, I'm not posh. We used to leave work and go for a meal. We used to eat everything. Forgive me, but no pork. I still don't eat it. They used to bring *molahiya* and *kolakas* from Cyprus. There was a man, my brother's friend, he used to bring things in a van and sell it, he had a shop. He had a shop the same year he came. He had a restaurant in Cyprus, in Nicosia. His shop was in Angel but he used to come [to South London]. He was a fellow villager. No, first for a month there was a man from Aytotoro in Elephant and Castle. My late mum (god rest her soul), my dad and husband used to shop there. He was called Kaba *Dayı* Arif, Radiye. But he has passed away, that man.

SEYIT MEHMET: I was a member at the Richmond Building [i.e. The Cyprus Turkish Association] . They had a lot of members. There was a lot of, full of people at that time. Every time I used to go there up there in the afternoon, it was a restaurant down there and upstairs you know it was a club. There was a lot of people, full up. Well, in there it was a gathering with people, you see your own people. Don't forget in 1953, especially in 1949, when I came here you couldn't have had more than a 100 Turkish people, Cypriot people there. That is about all. And if you see somebody, and he standing in there, it is like you see your family, you know. I mean we were so close, I mean even with the Greeks we were close. They had one café, a Greek café, it was, and we used meet there as well. It was before you go to Camden Town on left-hand side, in Goodge Street.

I don't know what happened to the place [Richmond Building] now. That time there, all I knew was that it was up there you see after, I didn't go any more there. In the beginning when I came over here in 1949, the first club we made was in Greek Street. There was a Santa Romana restaurant over there. On top of there, it was just for the Turkish people. There were 10 of us, we get together and made it a club up there. We used to go up there before the Richmond Building. It was called the Turkish Club. Türk Kulubu. It was a restaurant down below there, the owner was a Turkish Cypriot, and the flat up there they gave us to make a club up there. We used to play backgammon and gather like people there, you know.

We used to dance, Astoria dancing every day. Pay half-a-crown*, we used to go from 3 to 6. I remember the Harry Louis Orchestra. They used to play all this. Do you know about Glenn Miller? It was all his music that time there. He died during the war, you know.

Ohhhh, the girls. It was easy to chat them up. Oh, ye, the girls used to come and ask me if I would come and ask, "Would you like to dance with me?" Because I was very good at dancing, you know. I was a young man. I was a young man. I was very different then, you know. We used to go dancing, I was good at tango, quick waltz, the waltz, the foxtrot. Everything. The cha cha cha, the samba, ye.

Of course we went to the cinema, the club, to have dinner for two. I mean I used to take my girlfriend out in 1953, and for seven-and-six pence, I used to have a three-course meal. Seven-and-six in the old money, seven-and-six, Do you know how much is it today? 35 and a half pence. My girlfriends were English, Italian, Danish, Swedish. I had a Turkish girl as well. A Turkish Cypriot in the 1950s. I used to meet her in the park. Of course, her family didn't know.

Before I got married there was that place in Piccadilly near Hyde park Corner. They use to call it Pigalle, it was one of the best nightclubs in London there. And I had relations that came over here and I took them there one night, that was before I got married. And I remember I wanted to take them somewhere nice place. There used to be cocktail club called the Gay Compton Club. It used to belong to Mr Hikmet, a very rich man he was. Neval Bey. He was here before the war. I booked the table for two [at Pigalle] from the Gay Compton Club up there. When I went there, the head waiter put us somewhere in the corner. I went there to see the Pink Champagne Show – they used to call it Pink Champagne – and you couldn't see nothing, it was too far away. I said to him, "Listen, can't you do anything better than that?" He said, "I'm fully booked." I said, "Look, I'll give you a pound – " – and them days, you're talking about 1956, it was. I give him £1, and said, "We are going up there for a drink, and see what you can do for us," and by the time when we went up there to have a drink, I ordered one manhattan and one dry martini, something like that. So by the time the barman bring us the drinks, he came up there and said, "Mr Mehmet, the table is ready." And guess what? They gave us one of the best tables on the floorshow. The cabaret there, and us in the centre on a table for two. Honestly, I never forget that. I spent £16 on that night for two of us. People used to earn £5 a week. In today's terms, you might say £1,500. In one night, drinks, wine, brandy, smoke salmon to start, main course fillet steak, this and this and this. We had a lovely time. That was me. Once a year I was living like a millionaire.

My uncle [who I took to the club] was so impressed. I would always go into restaurants and have a good meal. Order a bottle of wine. Best wine. I used to order it with my steak you know, every week.

---

* An old-money coin worth 2s 6d, or 75p in the 'new' money.

I took her [my wife] once to the show in Leicester Square: before we booked a table, and we ordered nice lunch and everything, and she was pretending that time that she was drinking, and she had a glass of wine or something like that, and she was sick and wanted to go the toilet. And we left everything there and took the taxi and paid the meal and we came back home. Because she wasn't used to drinking.

HULUS IBRAHIM: Life in those times of course, ahh, the women, the girls, in other words in this country there was five to every one man. Foreign men were suited and booted, and money was a problem because it never ended with just entertainment. You had to show generosity, going out for a meal and buying drinks. The English have a custom to do with men and women and money. The women would sometimes take out their money and pay. Sometimes a woman would even meet most of the financial needs of a man. And because of this, the girls living in England liked foreign men. We would never allow the girls to pay and we earned another kind of value.

The situation was that when you went for example to a dance, in my time the Astoria was an important place. That big building on Tottenham Court Road, on the right. We used to go to the dance, but the girls went free, they didn't pay. Single people, widowed, or those who wanted to spend their night there, or form a relationship with a man, would go. But for example this wasn't the situation for men and women in Cyprus and Turkey. There, if a girl was to go somewhere like that, people would say the girl has become bad, or she has no future – her father or mother would come and take her away. There's nothing like that here. Sometimes English families would bring their 15-16-year-old daughters, and wait for them. The daughters would cuddle, kiss and so on with the men, and then say goodbye and go. In other words it is not seen as wrong. Boyfriends for example. At 14 or 15 they have boyfriends.

There was the rumba, samba and later the cha cha cha. I knew these dances when I was in Cyprus. A lot of the women and girls didn't know how to dance. I taught them how to dance.

MEHMET MUSTAFA: When we first came there wasn't any entertainment. My brother-in-law Hasan also came after a certain time of period, he came three months later. My elder sister came as well. No, my brother-in-law was here; he brought my elder sister as well. We bought a big flat this time in Stoke Newington. As a whole family we used to stay in that flat. As I was working hard, I used to go to bed even without watching television towards the evening, to get up early in the morning and go. There wasn't any joy. Our joy started after my elder sister and so on went away for nine months, nearly for a year. We stayed in the flat with Çetin. That flat was in our hands. We started living youth life. It started a year later. Well, then we went to the war and so on. I started, because my brother-in-law left with my sister in 1961. He left the whole flat and everything to us. We used to pay, but not everyone had a big flat like us.

Now, after my elder sister and brother-in-law left, we had freedom. We could do what we want. We didn't have to work until the morning for four shillings, any more. This time things changed, as a matter of fact, became nicer. You earn more money. We used to go for a dance every Saturday and Sunday. There used to be very important dance styles, there isn't that many now. And Turks, English used to go. One of them was in Holborn, the Lyceum Dance Hall. The Locarno Dance Hall in Streatham. There was one in Hammersmith.

We used to go about them, ye. We used to walk until morning. Until the morning in the snow.

We haven't seen snow in Limassol. When I first came everywhere was covered with snow. That was my biggest enjoyment then. Now we have got rheumatism, which is another issue! We used to walk in snow up to here from West End to Stoke Newington until the morning. No problem. As a matter of fact, there weren't any buses at that time, at two or three. The music was very nice music. There was Elvis, he just died I think. No it was somebody else. I remember it had been two years when Kennedy died. I was in thingy when I heard the news about John Kennedy. I heard it in the very middle of the town. But London was more beautiful in those days. Do you remember Deli Orden, Hasan Behçet etc.? All of these, all together we used to go to Piccadilly Circus. There were specific places. They used to put your head like in a cut out, on your own, and the whole Piccadilly Circus was all around you. Very nice.

Now, there is something very important. They are still talk about it in Tottenham. There was a group in Tottenham, it was an elderly group. Now and then the English talk about it. It is very famous. It doesn't come to my mind. It was a jazz group. The one I talk about was very famous. Their albums were famous as well. They are still today. All this rock'n'roll and so on, all sorts of music is from our time. Well, they say "the music from 60s."

We learned the dances and music from Cyprus, we used to mix with English people in Cyprus.

DUDU HAKKI: I used to go to the cinema once a week. There used to be a Turkish cinema* in Hackney, Kingsland Road, in 1963. Oh, the cinemas used to become full and in truth they were very good. Everyone used to go every week to the cinema and meet our locals and relatives. There was one in Elephant and Castle and then later one in Wood Green. Everyone would go. There was a showing at night, going on till three in the morning. They used to show really good films. Week after week we would go. They showed very good films. Then when these videos came out, everyone used to hire films and watch them at home. That was after the 70s. Everyone watched at home and no one went to the cinemas and they closed down. But it was better when there was Turkish cinemas. We all used to meet up; it was a day out of the house. Husbands, wives, and we would take the children.

We could find some of the Turkish ingredients we needed but not all like now. We couldn't find *molohiya*. There was one Turkish grocery in Stoke Newington, and everyone used to go there. You could get *hellim*, olives and olive oil – there wasn't much import and export then. They used to bring things once a week, or once every 15 days. Buses used to go and come. That's how they bought things over. But there was very little that you could find.

---

* Now the Rio Cinema

HATICE ISMAIL: My brother, my nephews and nieces, all of them, would come at night to see me [in hospital]. I was young then. People used to come, they used to feel pity towards me, including young nurses, they used to come and talk to me for a fair amount of time. There was a foreign nurse, she used to sing songs to me. As you sing a lullaby, sing a song for a child, like that. She says to me, "Come, I shall teach you my own language." It was Welsh – and while she was telling me, I used to write down a few of them.

When I was leaving they were both happy and sad. In there, they took my blood, on one hand they were taking my blood, on the other hand they were giving me blood. They were also injecting penicillin so it will be clean, 86 injections. I recovered. Thanks to God.

Later on when I started getting better, I used to write these little bit. I gave it to my friends. One day, someone was asking about me, and also my neighbour, she was like a sister, "Here it is. Take this and read my memoirs." I said to her. "I was going to write a book." I said to her. I was going to publish but I gave up. One day she was absorbed in my memoirs – while reading them, she was also crying. "Oh!" she says to me, "What things you suffered!"

A letter written by Hatice Ismail while in hospital

A grief without hope, a long reminiscence, 13 April 1957

I stopped but before I stopped from my job, but two days before I stopped work my shoes cut my toes. I went to the doctor, doctor gave me medicine but it became worse. While I was using the medicine, my toes infected . At last, I started walking slowly, slowly. Even though the doctor again gave me another medicine and said that they would come and see me at home. Anyway, after seeing me at home for a week, as it didn't get any better it required to go to hospital. As it required, after doctor called another doctor who is a friend of mine, the head doctor came and saw me. As soon as he saw me he advised me to go to a hospital. Anyway, the hospital taxi came and pick me up from home and I went to the hospital. They took me in immediately. They put my feet into medicated water. After they washed them for a fair amount of time, they medicated them. The next day they did the same treatment again. They took my blood, they did injection and they started cutting the skin off my feet because underneath was hard. They started cutting the skin off my feet, anyway they cut it for a week. First, second, when the third week arrived they started cutting the skin of my hands. Even if I wanted to get up and walk a bit on the third week, unfortunately I couldn't succeed. I walked slowly, slowly, nurse took me in the arms and put me in bed. Anyway, as the underneath of my feet were bleeding and crying; I went into my poison sleep. The next day, when I woke up I felt as if the whole hospital was spinning in my head. My whole body was in pain. At 9:30 o'clock I went to the bathroom. Only the skin on my heels was left on my feet. They peeled and finished all over my hands, palms. But I was in so much pain, so much distress that I became like someone shot through the heart. I can't bear this pain, if only I could see my family once before I die. I felt as if my heart veins were broke off. I immediately lost consciousness and passed away and collapsed in nurses' arms. After a certain amount of time passed, I came around by crying. The moment I came around I found myself in a bed and five doctors were at the bedside. I couldn't help crying again. Doctor did an injection and I went to sleep. After a certain amount of sleeping I managed to control myself. Anyway, two days later they examined me, put me in the x-ray, took my blood, injected penicillin again. As I didn't eat anything for four days, they gave me serum.

Suffering those three months. It is not a joke. Anyway, as a matter of fact it was those first weeks that were hard. During the first weeks they didn't know it either, where it came from, what it is. For my blood to be poisoned this much. They thought it may be a contagious disease and so they used to do tests on me. They cut a piece of skin and send it inside to do the tests, you know.

What can we do? It is terribly difficult when you are away from home. Especially when you are alone. It is very difficult.

A poem written in hospital
By Hatice Ismail

There are many people in the hospital, there is no patient like me.
Now my temperature is high, my pain is a lot.
Crying, I don't have the cure.

My feet had been cut with scissors
A flame glows in my heart
Come my mum, I shall see you.
My grave has been prepared.

Another poem written in hospital
By Hatice Ismail

The door of the hospital looks over trees
The hurt of my pains burns my heart.
Today my illness is a danger
Five doctors look after me.

I cry in the hospital.
I burn with my fire.
I am destitute in this place of far exile
I don't know what my sin is.

White along the beds,
Crying, they are going to give injection
I want to get up and run away
They will grab and not let go.

My flowers are wilted
My heart is sorrowful
My neck twisted, I am praying.
I don't know, I don't have a remedy now.

The wounds on my feet
They wrapped up my hands.
I have been in the hospital for a month
They haven't found my cure.

The pain of my hurt pierces my heart
Tell my mother, not stay, to come
Here I am dying in the hospital
All of my relatives should come to my funeral.

Crying yana yana, my eyes smeared with blood
This grief all through my exile is worse than death to me
I read my books, keep brooding, preoccupied
Being this much ill, I don't know what is my fault?

I took my medicines, as I take I lose consciousness
I am sorrowful in this place, my grief increases
The birds perched opposite me; my eyes have become full of tears.
Until I recovered from this illness
My lungs became white

That is to say it has ended.

ŞABAN LEFKARIDI: Jock Ritchie [or Richie] was the Scottish manager that put me on the machines, and we used to go out together. There was a club in Elephant and Castle. There were two, one of them was Bedi's Club, I forgot the other one. Bedi's Club belonged to a Turk from Aytotoro. It used to have both restaurant and club. He used to be my best friend. This was before the 60s.

The owner's name was Bedi, it was Mehmet Ahmet but they used to call him Bedi. When he was away, I used to look after that place. I used to help him but he was my mate, I didn't get any money. There was eating and drinking, there was music. Families used to go as well.

They played Turkish music. We used to go there together with Jock, he liked it a lot. Sometimes he used to dance. He used to mingle, mix sometimes. He would dance along with Çiftetelli.

Not everyone would go to English clubs. Let's say we used to go to Greekish clubs! There was one in West End. Then there is that John Aziz. He opened a club in the city. Probably it was in Greek Street, it's gone out of my mind, I can't remember. He was our friend as well; we used to always spend our time in Elephant and Castle together. He used to have a house in Vauxhall; we used to go to his house, play *gonga*, play cards. Later on they bought that club, we used to go there for him to have some work as he was our friend.

My wife didn't use to go to the club but other people's wives would go.

NEVCIVAN JEVAN: When we first came we sometimes used to go to the cinema, the park. I wonder if it was in Battersea Park? I remember we used to there at weekends quite often. I didn't like nowhere of England. Now I have got used to it. Even if I go to another country, this place attracts me. Here feels like my own country. Since the age of 18 I have been here.

Did men go dancing in West End in those days? I don't remember something like that. The women and the men weren't the same.

ALI HASSAN: We used to go to the Turkish films in cinemas, we used to go sometimes when they first started, but not often. We used to go to the parks in Plaistow, to the family parks, we used to go and play ball there, we'd sunbathe. We'd bring our children to play there.

HATICE FETTI: I worked for seven months in Elephant and Castle and then I went on to wedding dresses. I worked in wedding dresses for two, three years in West End. I used to bring [work] home on Saturday, Sunday as well. I used to sew two wedding dresses for eight shillings each at home. I stopped doing that, I went to a coat factory right nearby our house, and that was men's coats. I used to sew coats there. I also worked there for a couple of years. After that we came back, we bought our house. When we left we put tenants in the house, it was necessary for me to stay at home. I found a boss and I used to sew skirt, I used to sew at home. I started to sewing at home in Holloway, in 1963 when I came here, I still continued sewing at home. One evening we were going out with my son, with my third son, but my daughter was grown up as well. I didn't use to mix my girl with other people, nobody. We used to go to a place, my son used to take us, we used to wait for him to come and collect us after he had finished daytrips. We used to go to my mum, we used to sit down, fall asleep, wake up and still he was gonna come and pick us up. I said, "Wait, you will see. I am going to become a driver as well." Like that. One day my son took us, we went for a long day out. When we were coming, I said, "Oh God, I also want to become a driver so much." I used to daydream. He said, "Mum, do you want to?" "I want to," I said. We went and bought a driving licence for £3. A learner's licence. They used to work at the dry cleaner, every day at four o'clock my sons used to come, "Mum, come on, let's go to drive." We would get into the car and they used to take me. Every day, when it was Sunday, "Come on, mum, get up, we will go." they would say. We used to go to the forest for quite a long time. I used to always go to them, every day. They taught me. Later on I took my 90 lira rent money, they sent it to me from Cyprus. I went and bought a car for £90. It was an Anglia. It was a small car. Here, I used to take it to the front, backwards, to the corner. This was in 1963. I used to drive it around here without a driving licence. That is to say, I was brave, I used to take it and drive the car, take my daughter, we used to come to go on outings, nothing happened.

After that, I wanted to go on the test. But a couple of times I went with somebody else. I am gonna go for a test. I went, I went to this Limassol school. He said to me, "I know, you drive well. You need some lessons." I took lessons as well, twice a day. But why did I hurry up so much? Because one day I was going, driving without a driving licence and I didn't put my L-plates onto my car. I went to do shopping. I came out exactly when the police saw me. They followed me. I stopped and I went into a corner shop. I went into the corner shop, they came into the shop. They said, "A woman came in here. She was driving this car." I came out, I said to them, "My child has become ill so I came to buy medicine urgently." He said "Where is the medicine?" I said, "I am going to buy it, I haven't bought it yet." I said. They booked me because I was driving without a licence. Within one month, I had to go to court because I was driving without a licence. When that happened I found that Limassol School. I went, and I started taking lessons twice a day. I went, I passed it first time, on the very day of court. I went to the court, the police called me "Mrs Fetti." I said to him, "I am a good driver," I said to him. "Because first time I passed the test," I said to him. They fined me £25.

But seriously I used to buy a nice car every five years. I used to keep it for five years. After five years I used to work myself, I worked well. I would go fill up my car [with work], bring it to home, I used to sew at home. That is to say, I wouldn't neglect my job either. I would look after my visitors as well. After 15 years, I went to Cyprus. After 15 years, sometimes I used to go twice a year. I used to go every year, take my youngest son, my daughter, and go. The older ones didn't want to go. They didn't. Well, because he was small I used to take him and go.

Later on we made some friends and we used to go to wedding, after the wedding either in my house we used to cook soup, or in other friend's house. It used to be nice. Very nice. We used to go the cinema on Sundays. There was a cinema in Caledonia [Road], we used to go there.

We used to take the kids on Sunday evenings when there was a cinema. They used to show two films and they started late. Barely to the first one, until the second one all of them used to sleep. I used to say, "Why did we come?" We used to pay for them as well. "Why did you come?" I used to say to them. All of them used to sleep. When it finished we used to wake them up.

People were very good before. When I first came here. We used to make friends. Now, now, people are different, indeed. Still I have my permanent friends. My environment is very big. Because, if you are my friend, I phone you, they phone me. I would never disconnect. I would come. For example I have my days and I would call you. You would cross you from my mind and I would say I am going to go to such and such. They would come to me, that is why I continuously have friends. My environment is big. My friends are Turkish, my own religion. I get on well with English as well. With black people. A black person came to our neighbourhood, two days later an ambulance came. They put two kids in to the ambulance, they went. That is to say, as soon as they came to our neighbourhood. The next day in the morning I went and knock on their door. I said, "I saw the ambulance in the evening. They took your kids and went. What did they have?"

The man said, "I couldn't believe," he said, "[that] someone would come to me, knock on my door!" I said "Why? It is because your colour is different?" I said "For me every human being is the same." They are very good friends with me. I made friends with everyone.

They are still in the neighbourhood . Every day they inquire after my health. They come to drink tea. Here my friend gave birth, I bought her a present. If the one on this side buys a flower for her house, she would buy one for me too. This is a foreign girl as well, an English teacher. She is educated, she is nice. I like friends.

There was a Turkish shop at the bottom, going towards Wood Green. We used to buy from there. We used to do our shopping and they used to bring it to our house. When you go to an English shop, you would look and buy what you want.

SEYIT MEHMET: The first holiday we had was in Herne Bay in 19-something, it was the train robbery, those brothers. It was in Herne Bay in 1962 or 63. We had a holiday there, and every year we used to go somewhere in the car. I had a Zodiac. We used to go everywhere. Herne Bay, Isle of Wight, Worthing, Hastings. In them days Cypriot people didn't have holidays. But I used to take them.

EMINE MEHMET: We used to go and eat fish and chips. There used to be English fish and chip shop on every corner. Sometimes they would make these pies, these pie things. They made [something] with curry on top, and they put some mash near it. My husband used to like that a lot. I don't know, I can't remember the names. It's been some time.

We used to go out and eat. My husband had the business and we would go out to eat for lunch. We would eat out together and return. Listen, my husband used to eat these Indian and Pakistani foods. He would telephone them and they would bring the food to the shop. That meat, that rice cooked in oil. It carried him off.

"Don't eat them, Mustafa!" I would say.

"Emine, if I die, my stomach will be full," he would say.

ALI HASSAN: The hooter of my car becomes a donkey, becomes Tarzan, whistles at people. Life doesn't go if you do not joke.

8. COURTSHIP

HULUSI MAHMUD: I got married in 1962. Through relations. I had the wedding here. We got married in Blackfriars. It was a special hall there off Blackfriars Road. Just before the bridge.

MEHMET ALI BEKIR: [Where I used to work], we were neighbours with this English lady, nearby the house. With friends we used to go to Newington Green Park. We met there, from there we started going out. For a year we went out.

In those days English people didn't like foreigners, because my wife wasn't from London. She was from Buxton in Derbyshire, she was a private secretary. Because at that time a craftsman's secretary would only belong to him, and we got engaged.

I concluded a marriage agreement with a Turkish girl. It had been arranged by an acquaintance from Cyprus, and I felt the girl was more open than I was, much more precocious than I was. About life I mean. She was already married, she got married and got divorced. Since I knew her and fancied her I didn't mind about her former marriage.

After the conclusion of our marriage agreement, I realised that she was more open than I was and we had a quarrel. We had an argument, I left her and I went back to my ex-girlfriend. To the English girl – and we got married.

I had a row with my dad. We rented the whole house. From Dalston Market towards Shoreditch, somewhere near Metropolitan Hospital, we rented a house. In those days there was lease house. We rented, for example, one room is mine, upstairs two bedrooms, my dad's, bathrooms, we used to rent it flat by flat. We were there, they were Jewish-owned houses.

One day, somehow, I asked my sister to iron my suit. My sister Hatice said, "If you want, go and employ a servant for yourself." We had a quarrel with her. My dad held her side, of course, my sister's side. I packed all of my things, left the house, ran away, went straight to my girlfriend.

When I was getting engaged to her, my wife told her parents in Derbyshire that she was getting engaged with a foreigner. In those days, they were truly English-originated. They didn't want foreigners. Eventually they accepted to see me. It was over the New Year time. We went by train.

We would be introduced. They picked me up. Her dad had a farm. I saw oxes, pigs, chickens. I took my clothes off very quickly, her sisters' boyfriends, husbands were there as well. At home by the fire – in winter the weather was very cold, in those days the weather was cold. I mean it was the highest region in England. Not in the whole of Britain, only in England. I don't mean Scotland, only in England. Anyway, I went very quickly, they used to milk the cows; I put the boots on very quickly to help them. For example my deceased father-in-law, Eric was his name, had never given a party before. And that night, that New Year night he gave a party for us. For the first time in his life he gave a party, and that man liked me a lot. That man loved me so much. God rest his soul! Him, my mother-in-law, all of my sister-in-laws, including my brother-in-law, loved me a lot.

And I stayed married with that wife for 21 years. we had three kids, their names are Turhan, Aydin, and my daughter Meral. We divorced because of a problem. Two years after we split up, I got married to a lady from Limassol in Cyprus. I have been married to her for 20 years. I am married to her for the time being.

When I went to my father in law's farm, I looked at the tree, it was full of birds. I asked my father-in-law if he had a gun. He told me that he has one, we call it forten. He gave it to me, bullets too. I went, I fired the gun twice under the tree, all the ground had become full of sparrows. Or starlings, not sparrows, because they were big. I picked them up, cleaned them up, of course coal was on fire. I started to heat up the coal, then broil the sparrows. None of them ate them. That first night I ate sparrow all the time, all on my own. They had never had any other food than English food. My wife cooked rice with black-eyed beans. At the beginning she used to learn cooking Turkish food.

EMINE AHMET: We had the wedding party in a restaurant called Chicken Grill in Upper Street. It was Halil Basri's restaurant who was from Sinde. There was about 70 – 80 people. When you don't have anyone who do you invite?

MUSTAFA HÜSEYIN: I got married to my first wife in 1963. She was Turkish. I have two sons. One of them is 41 years old, the other one is 39 years old now. I have got grandchildren. I have two from my first wife. From the second marriage there are six. It will be eight, our bride is expecting.

I got married here in 1963, in Bermondsey, in Sparrow Road. Then it was in the town hall.

In those days most people didn't have weddings. No, they didn't use to. It wasn't that much popular and there was the financial situation as well. And also we suddenly got married for example. My deceased wife had gone to somebody else as in-laws to get married. She didn't want him. They let me know via my sister-in-law. She said [to the sister-in-law], "I'll run away with him because I don't want that one. Tell your brother-in-law, he should come and take me. I like him. I see him at the weddings, I fancy him." That's what happened. She ran away and we got married.

The weddings started in the 1960s. They used to do it in Shoreditch, Stoke Newington, Hackney, Holborn. They used to do it almost everywhere they found a hall.

SEYIT MEHMET: I got married in 1957. I saw her in Bermondsey. They used to live in Bermondsey. I saw her once and I fancied her. I went to their home and I said I like this girl there. I told her brother, and things like that. My father came with me too. He just came when I was trying to propose to her, he was over here. He was demobbed from the Police Force, you see. He was in the Police Force.

Gökmen Mehmet in her sister's garden in Bermondsey, London, 1954

GÜLSEN LARKINS: 1961 I got married. I was working with his sister. I got arranged. I got married in Elephant and Castle. Town Hall. Not a wedding , a registry. I lived with my husband's family in Liverpool Road.

[After I was married] I used to go to visit my mum. I wasn't allowed to. She didn't know where I lived. My brother didn't know where I lived but he found out.

Ye. My first husband was Turkish , I got married for the first time. It was all right. It was as good as gold. I was very happy marriage. Ye. He was good to me. We supposed to buy a house. Them days supposed to be cheap house. £50 used to put down for the deposit, used to buy house. It was about £3,000. Not even £3,000, it was about £2,000 them days. The best house was £4,000. Very, very good house.

My dad is sensitive. "Don't you dare," he said to me, "buy house with him. One day he is gonna leave you. I can see," he said to me.

KEMAL AHMET DAVRANDI: When my sister came [to London] we went to stay at who they used to call Ahmet the Barber. When my sister came I found a bigger room. We put two beds in the room. I was staying with my sister. My sister came, we had a cousin Mueccel living in Newington Green. "Let's go see my cousin, let's go see my cousin," she would say. So we went and saw our cousin. It was a Saturday.

We went and sat down. My cousin said, "Don't go. I making dinner. We'll eat lunch, this and that." We sat and ate, we drank and it became night time.

"Let's go on a trip," my cousin said.

"What trip, hey?" I said. Apparently my cousin had asked my [future] wife, "Do you like this boy?" And she said, "I like him."

"All right," my cousin said to her: "He will come and ask for you tonight". I had no idea what was going on. So they left, my [future] wife with her brother. They used to live in Haringey in Kimberley Garden, in someone's house who was from Galatya. It became night time and we got on the bus, Fezile my sister, my cousin, her husband and children. *Tak Tak*, we knocked on the door. They opened the door. We went upstairs. She [my future wife] lived in a room with her brother. "Why have we come here?" I said.

After my [future] wife left [my cousin's house] with her brother, my cousin said, "So how do you find the girl? Do you like her?"

"She's not bad," I said.

"They are very rich. Wealthy!" they told me.

I said, "Look now cousin, leave the richness out, for God's sake!" I tell no lie, I said, "Does she have a brain in her head? That's the kind of wife I want," I told my cousin.

"They are very good people," she said.

"All right then," I said.

"Well, let's go then," my cousin said.

"Where to? And this can't happen with just the one viewing!"

"But I have already said something. I have even asked for her. We are going to go," she said. "I have said that we will."

So we went and asked for her. She said, "I have to ask my brother." She had a big brother with the name of Mehmet. In short we made an agreement and got married. Şensal was born in that house. I mean we were still lodgers when Şensal was born, in 1963.

Kemal Davrandi's wedding in their friend's house, Kimberley Gardens, London, 1961

IBRAHIM AHMET: [Marriage was] old-style. We had the wedding between the two families. I was here. When my wife came here I had been here almost for five years.

HATICE ISMAIL: On New Year's Night party, my nephew invited me to go over Christmas. We used to go to each other every ye, as a matter of fact. As I was a single, I went to my niece. My husband's sister used to stay as a tenant at my niece's and she already saw me and liked me. She said, "I have a brother who is single. Let's see, let's do something," she said this to my cousin. My cousin invited me, I didn't know. She invited her brother as well. Well, we met over Christmas dinner. He saw me and liked me. I like him. They asked me, well it was destiny. He was from Lurijina. Afterwards they come to me as ask for my hand in marriage. I used to stay at my cousin's, my uncle's son. It was a destiny, it happened. I got engaged, after that I got married but I didn't have a wedding. We had a small party just amongst ourselves. We got registered [married] in Islington. There was a registry office in Islington.

MEHMET MUSTAFA: My marriage, it is again a long story, you know. After I came from Cyprus in 1964, I was looking for a job again. Our Ibrahim, he said, "Let's work on the buses." He found a job as bus conductor. After him I went as well. I left the waiter job, I became a bus conductor in Tottenham Garage. The 73. For years, I worked on the buses, more or less for four and a half years. But there was only us two Turks. There wasn't anyone else. I started in 1964. After I came from Cyprus, I didn't go to West End any more. As a matter of fact, it was a thingy lifestyle, there was a casino, we used to gamble. When I came back, through my friend I went back to Manor House, had an examination and passed test. To think there were even bribes in there. You would give a packet of cigarettes and they would say, "You shouldn't," and put it [the pack of cigarettes] into his pocket, and you pass. Ibrahim and I were the only Turkish bus conductors. There was a policeman from Lefkosa. His name doesn't come to my mind now. We took him with us as well. We were altogether. We became three, four after that. First, only two of us. After I worked for a certain period of time, I found another friend from Lefkosa. There was a course in television. He said, "Like a mother and father I will look after you, give you money, I will educate you."

I became a bus conductor in 1964, I wanted to become a driver but I could never pass. Because either you go fast or slow. I am glad I couldn't pass. I stayed as a bus conductor. Ibrahim, our friend, said, "Let's go, my brother-in-law is coming from Cyprus, again on a ship. Let's pick him up." I had a Volkswagen with a steering wheel on the left-hand side. But I didn't have a licence. The steering wheel on the left-hand side. It was from 1953. When I used to put my uniform on, nobody would touch me. Bus conductor uniform. It looks like a sailor in the navy. The buttons are like a police, like that. I used to wear it: captain. I used to put that on, go in the Volkswagen, neither a licence nor nothing. We are going to pick his brother-in-law from Dover. My wife was a neighbour of this boy.

We went to the port to pick him up. My wife was a beautiful girl then. Very, very beautiful, that is to say, the whole country wanted to get married to her. Of course it was my luck!

"Oh, welcome brother-in-law," and so on. "Let's give a lift to this poor girl as well, you came together, we picked you up, we are going to pick her up as well." It was especially prepared before hand for my wife to be able to work in Prince of Wales Hospital. And now Prince of Wales Hospital is closed now.

We picked them up and came. Then little Mehmet, I and the girlfriend, Çetin Kaya, Little Mehmet and a girl called Sultan from Magosa. "Let's go out, youngsters." I without stopping change my car. Two cars, I left Volkswagen, bought a Vauxhall. We used to go about.

Anyway, we decided to get marry. It was heard there [in Cyprus]. By the way, there was a gambling house as well. I used to work on the buses, I went and found a place in Stoke Newington. I opened a gambling house. I used to run that place in the evenings. There was an Erol from Piskobu, he was a handsome boy. There was Tailor Ayhan. I employed him, I said, "You don't work. Take this £5, and a packet of cards. Set the table and everything upstairs. Run the gambling." When I finish work in the evenings I would come and share the money. That is to say, we used to do like that. Anyway, when I proposed her, it was heard on that side [Cyprus] that I was a gambler. They didn't want to know But whether they liked it or not we got married.

There was this Arab Derviş, a carpenter, his wife is my wife's aunt. It was only him in our wedding. He came with another chap. We had a hall, somewhere like a council housing. We rented it for £8. We had music. There was Mevlut. He opened a new place called Üsküdar, before you go to Newington Green, in Green Lanes. When I was young he used to play music at the hotels, restaurants. When it comes to money he was flashy – he used to play music. I know him from that time. When I was gonna get married he said, "I'll come." and he brought his band as well. There was this famous man, he arranges all of the music. Perry. He took me in his Jaguar, took me to Hackney, he booked me this hall in Hackney. The guys, in fact, they charge about £50, when all money I gathered was £80. I paid them with the money we collected [at the wedding]. But I was happier.

HATICE IBRAHIM: I was bored, depressed and ill. I didn't like it, not the place, not them [my sisters-in-law], nothing. It was winter.

My brother and his wife would come round every day and ask, "When is there going to be a small party for them?" My sister-in-laws asked why I didn't bring a wedding dress when I knew I was going to get married. I thought, these people pleaded and pleaded, caught me, brought me to London! Apparently my brother had a £200 debt to my sister-in-law Remziye that he had to pay. "So get him to do what's needed and to forget about marriage!" I of course knew I was finished. I gave up hope from everything. We went to the Registry Office and were registered. The Registrar knew from my face that I didn't know very good English.

The Registrar said, "I am going to allow this girl seven days, and she should come and see me if she wants to change her mind." He then said, "Put the rings on." None. They did not give me a ring. My older brother had a ring and they gave me that one. The Registrar was shaken. That's what happened and I was married.

MELEK KAZIM: My mother and father arranged my marriage without telling me. From my newly appointed job, I received by pay packet with excitement. I got £1 10 shillings per week. It was a lot of money. Rent at that time was £1. From the excitement I ran home and I found the house full of people. At that time I was very shy. I thought what was going on. As soon as I walked in they gave me a ring. They said, "You are engaged." With who? I had never seen him before.

It was my father's barber friend, with his barber friend. He knew this boy. They arranged this for me. He was 28 years old. He was a lot older than me. My uncle [mother's brother] was here at the time. He stayed with us. I was very scared of my uncle. My father and uncle were very strict. I was not as scared of my father, but I was very scared of my uncle. There's was nothing I could not say until Monday when I am going to go to work. I told my friend that I am going to run away from home because they are marrying [selling] me off. This friend of mine was English and we use to work together. I said that they have sold me off to this man. I have forgotten his name, but I think it was Mahmut. Mahmut the mechanic from Haringey. Anyway I ran away from home. I went and stayed with my girl friend for 1 week. She hid me under her bed.

They couldn't come to look for me because they didn't know where I was. The police did come. One morning, on my way to work, my friend's father saw me, "Where have you been? They have been looking for you for since one week."

"Oh leave me," I said. "Don't bring me back."
My friend had hidden me under her bed, anyway her father got hold of me and took me to the police station. I told the police, "I grew up here, but they have sold me off." At that time you had to be 21 years old to get married in this country.

The policeman replied, "You are living in this country, you should follow this country's rules."

I said, "They don't allow me to go out to my friends." At that time I use to really like music and dancing. Then I told them [my parents] that I do not want to marry this boy. "I don't like you." My mother then said, "It can't be by force. She does not want him," and we separated.

DUDU HAKKI: I got married in 1961. I came here on 14 September. My [future] husband and his friend came to visit us in January 1961. I didn't even have any idea why they had come. "Go and dress up, we are going to go out," said Mehmet Emin *Abi* to me.

So I went and dressed up. I wore a skirt, fanella* and brushed my hair. Then I hear the doorbell go. When I look, I see that guests have arrived. I don't know them or anything. They go and sit in the front room. Later Mehmet Emin *Abi* called me into the other room. He came to me and said, "I'm going to ask you something."

"What?" I said

He said "See that *Uşak*?" They used to say *Uşak* in those days. "That *Uşak* has come to me and said that he wants you to marry you."

"How has that *Uşak* come to us for me? I don't know him nor does he know me..."

"Yeah well, they have told him about you and he has come to see you and for you to see him. And if you like each other... why go back?"

Mehmet Emin *Abi* knew this was going to happen. He knew the *Uşak*. They had told him but they didn't tell me. Mehmet Emin *Abi* said, "Come and have a look at him." So then I went to the door and looked in. I looked and there was two men sitting in there. I turned and left the room. "How am I to know which one he is?" I said.

"Watch," Mehmet *Abi* said: "I'm going to go back and sit in there. I am going to touch his knee. I'm going to put my hand on his leg and then you can have a look and see if you like him." This is how it happened. So I looked at him, but how can you know what you are looking at with just one look, or decide if you like them? So then I went in the other room.

Mehmet Emin *Abi* came over to me again and asked, "What's going to happen? Do you like him?"

"*Vallahi* – I didn't really see. I don't know, I don't know who these people are at all, but if you know that they are good, that he is a good person, if you think it important," I said to him. On the same day, the same minute, they made us shake hands [as a form of acceptance of the engagement]. The rings were bought a week later. We got registered one month later. One month after that our wedding happened. The wedding was in a restaurant in Holborn – there was quite a lot of people. 100 people. All acquaintances, all fellow villagers. Our relatives, my husband's relatives, all my fellow villagers came. My [future] husband had been here for five years already. He used to work in a factory, he used to pack cow tongues.

---

* A Cypriot word for a jumper.

Dudu and Zekayi Hakki's wedding, Holborn, 1961

MELEK KAZIM: I saw my second husband in the dancehall. He was English. We got married three days after we met. Yes, in three days! I told my mum when she came home. He was an English man. He asked me to dance. We danced. "Do you wanna something to drink?" We sat on the other side and drank our drinks. He then said he wanted to marry me and that was it. He proposed from the first day, the first hour. He had not seen me before. I said, "No, I don't want to get married." Anyway, one day we went to see a film. Saturday he came to ask my mother and father for their permission to marry me. He came alone. I said that I wanted to get married. I said come and meet my mother and father. He was living in Edmonton. He had a very good job in Asphalt. Construction. Houses.

We got married in a registry office. The reception was in my house, just neighbours, friends. I did not want a big one. I did not want a big one. My mum just made everything. His family came too. They came. His family were very nice too. His family were very nice. It was just like a birthday party. They brought presents. The Turkish pin money, but they all brought presents. We were married for seven years.

We had three children and we moved to Berkshire. He bought a house there. At that time, my mother and father had opened a restaurant, and they had asked me to help out for one to two weeks until they would find staff. I went to help them. It was at that time that I started to want to mix with Turks. For the first time I realised how Turks were. I didn't know at all. I married an Englishman, but my life before that was spent mixing with the English, as there were not many Turks.

But my mother, father still cooked and ate Turkish food and we spoke Turkish.

HULUS IBRAHIM: I have been married twice. I met three or five girls. When I met my first wife I was very suspicious of everyone, because as a political person, I wonder if she was a policewoman, a detective, a this or a that. I was very cautious of this kind of thing when I talked. And I was looking for closeness, but I had to be certain. Because they tried hard to assassinate me in Cyprus. So I preferred to marry one of the girls, ladies, foreigners, that I met than a Turk.

A friend's family did take me to show me a girl [a Turkish girl to marry]. I didn't fancy the girl. She came and sat in front of me with a whole load of make up on her face. "What's this?" I thought: "Is this Mickey Mouse?" Of course we didn't say anything to them. "We'll think about it," we said, and left.

I met an English woman and fell in love with her when I was ill. This was in 1958. I was seeing two or three women at the time, but I was keener on one of them. She was a nurse. She said, "Come and meet my mother and my father," of course this was after a few months. We were going well, so in any case we went to see her mother and her father.

They started to question me: "Are you married? Are you single? Do you have any children?" Her father was middle-class. And his daughter was adopted. They had adopted her after World War Two. Her mother and father had died, and they took her and raised her. Anyway at Christmas they didn't want us to marry. They wanted her to marry someone English, and her father had a friend whose son would come and go from their house. She told her mother and father that she was going to marry this foreigner. When we got registered she didn't tell her father, she told her mother. She told him after. They were wealthy but I wasn't interested in her inheritance.

GÖKMEN MEHMET: My husband's sister was a neighbour and she found me job, but I didn't know him [the husband]. I only know his sister. I think my husband's niece introduced us. I was married in two weeks, I never see him before. Arranged wedding anyway. When I was told that he [my husband] fancied me, I said, "I got family, come and meet them if you want." I wasn't ready to get married. I was going back to Cyprus. I stayed two years with my sister and then I got married. It just happened. My brother said you're going to marry. I was registered straight away. He came with his dad and asked for me. Like the Turkish Tradition, I made him a Turkish coffee. I wasn't shy or nervous because I been modern in my country. I was 20 when I got married. Of course I was glad I got married.

In them days there was no pinning the money on, just presents. Plates, tea sets…

My husband used to have a nice job in Grosvenor House. I used to go once a year to a party there. It was beautiful. We had lovely times. When you're young you enjoy your life.

I was looking for a man like him anyway. He was smart and different to Cypriot people. He was very modern and used to love life and all that, parties. We used to go everywhere. He tried to make me smoke. I'm glad I never did.

Seyit and Gökmen Mehmet with friends at new year in the Empire Club, Leicester Square, 1958

SEYIT MEHMET: I got married in a registry office in Camberwell. Of course we had a wedding. It wasn't a big wedding. I got married in '57, I was living in Jamaica Road, my sister had a restaurant there. We had our wedding on the top, there was about 40 people. I am still married to the same woman. Today they have gone to Eastbourne. She is 70 now. She is from Nicosia. We have been married 49 years.

MEHMET ŞEREF ALI: I got married in 1963. I went back in 1959, after I left the army, to visit. Ye, for the second time. In Tahtakale, my wife's grandmother used to stay. I was there too, I saw her. I asked my elder sister who this girl was and so on.

She says, "Why? Want us to [get] her for you? You know, her brothers and sisters."

"Take her if they will give her," I said. She asked for her hand in marriage, my Afet Abla. She stays somewhere around here. They went, asked for her hand in marriage. I don't even know that they asked for her hand in marriage. She was given. But as she was going to go to London, they regretted it and they didn't give. I didn't have 100% desire for marriage either. I came back, in 1962. You know Yaşar Halim, he is my *bacanak*. We went to their house. Now, Yaşar Halim is a cousin, that is to say our grandfathers were brothers. In short, we went, was it the New Year's Day or a birthday party? A party, there is something? When I looked I saw that Yaşar's sister-in-law Tülin was next to her aunt. I said, "Who is this girl?"

He said the same thing: "Let's marry you to her, she is single."

Oh, I asked who it is. Then I recognised her. I remembered.

Yaşar said, "She is my sister-in-law." But I didn't know she was his relative. I am from Cyprus but I didn't even know who she was from. "As it is like that, ask for her hand in marriage," I said. They supported this idea there. Let's say three sisters-in-laws, Yaşar, his wife, Özdemir's wife, Yaşar's brother's wife, the children and so on.

"She is a dress-maker," they said

"That's good, she sews as well." I thought. Now, the important thing is of course they asked her hand in marriage from these. Now there's a saying: "In 40 days the gossip comes out." One said he is married, one said he has got five kids. Some of them said that he has English girls. Things like that. People said things after me for a while. They said that, "He is married, he's divorced." That is to say, they said, "He is not auspicious," and so on.

Now, if I said, I had no girlfriends, I would be lying. A single man that doesn't go on dates? But I will say something; seriously, I lived as single for how many years, only once I stayed with a woman for six months, to try. In order to find out whether I could stay if I got married. If I was going to be able to stay married. She was a very good person, too. Forgive me but in those days [10 girls were £10]. So I used to go to dances and so on. I didn't have a girlfriend continuously. I wouldn't keep them continuously. I have this kind of habit. I realised this [marriage to Tülin] was not gonna happen. I wrote a letter. I said, "I came to this country at the age of 20 – 21. In the house I stay in there is a bed, a chair as well as a cupboard. I would leave work at four, five, six," I said: "Sometimes the sun would be in the sky. At three, four, five o'clock, where will I go? Should I stay at home, in my room? Of course I would go to dance," I said. "That is to say," I said, "He who enters the Turkish bath, will sweat before coming out," I said. "When I go to dance, I don't come out empty-handed." I said. "I gambled now and then." That is to say, I told the things I did. "But," I said, "neither did I marry, neither was I engaged." I wrote this letter to my now-deceased father-in-law. "By God," I said, "If you don't let me marry to your daughter, I don't care." I concluded the letter like this. I was fed up. Every single day I would hear something. My deceased father- and mother-in-law had read it and said, "This boy is a *delikanlı*, I will give my daughter to him," he said. Because of the letter I wrote.

I told the truth. I said, "Believe whoever you want." I said, "I have gambled. But neither I have been engaged to anyone's daughter nor I asked her hand in marriage, nor I promised, nor I lived with an English woman." I said. "But during the time I have been single, think whatever you want, whichever way you think." I said. In short, they let me marry her. That's what happened, we came here and got married. She came in 1963, we got married in August 1963.

We were fine. She is a very nice woman. I didn't make her work anyway, I've never made her work. She is always at home. Only in a very nearby factory, in our neighbourhood. I mean you could walk there within two minutes. She only worked in that factory, she didn't do anything anywhere else, she didn't work.

Anyway she has such a character that she can't walk off to go to work, she wouldn't get on a bus like that. She was a real village girl. We are still together, we are not married, we got divorced but we are still like together. We have two children. One daughter, one son. Three grandchildren from one of them, three grandchildren from the other.

My achievement, as I said, I have two kids at home. Both of them have got their own places, we married both of them. They have kids. Their situation, *maşallah* I am very satisfied with my life. That is to say, I had indeed, a very good family life.

None of my kids have never, ever experienced any suffering, anything in anywhere. Both of them have turned out more intelligent than me.

My daughter is married in Turkey. I wouldn't change him for one million Turkish Cypriots; my son-in-law would be number one, by God. He is from Adana. When they got married he was 18, still a child. I raised him as well. They have house both here and there. That is to say, they are well off. If I had 10 daughters, I would give them to 10 son-in laws like him.

IBRAHIM DERVIŞ: I was single. We used to have girlfriends. They used to ask us out from across the room. They would make gestures and say, "Let's go out together, darling!" and so on. I wasn't single for long. But I used to tell my girlfriends that we were going out but there will be no marriage. "Because this is how we are." When we went out they would even offer to share the cost. "This does not happen in our culture," we would tell them.

I missed my motherland and friends – and also I was thinking of marriage – so I went back to Cyprus by boat. My family were now settled in London, I said *selamett* to them – in other words they were no longer my responsibility. So I thought, "I can go back to my country." At the same time one or two families wanted to send presents back to their families in Cyprus.

I saw my future wife there. We were neighbours, I mean from the same neighbourhood. I saw her when I went to deliver the presents. Her name was Jale. They asked her if she would go to London. She had a cousin and her mum's sister here in London. They were very close. I had someone ask for her on my behalf. Her mother knew me like her sons anyway. There was trust because we were neighbours.

She accepted and agreed to come to England. They said we cannot afford any of the costs. We said we don't want anything. That's how it happened. We got married.

9. LONDON

HÜSEYIN YUSUF: Ye, I liked it. It was new. I thought it was a new world. Where we came from in Cyprus, it was a small village, hardly any excitement there. Suddenly you are coming to a big city. You catch a bus to go to Trafalgar Square. It is a big thing, you know. I had some experiences down there, believe me. They used to kid me, you know. They used to kid me about how easy it was to pick up a girl. They used say to me, wink at her, and just give her a little pat on the back, if you like her.

I tried it only once. I did, and I had a really bad dirty look. In fact she was going to hit me with her handbag. So I thought that was wrong and that was the end of that. And that was the first experience I had about girls. How did we meet girls? We didn't really.

Hüseyin Yusuf with friends, London, 1953/4

MUSTAFA HÜSEYIN: No. I didn't get lost in London, or anything like that. The places and which way the bus was going to follow was written on the buses anyway. In the trains, again on the maps, which line goes where, where you are going, where you need to change, all this was written. I first got on the tube with a fellow villager. That is to say, it was different for me, a train underground, people walking under the ground, or the buses that were two floors, that was a difference. The trams used to sometimes come off the rails and the tram would get stuck until someone came to put it back on. It used to leave Aldgate and go till Warren Street, all on electric. From the bus station, there was electrical thingies [wires overhead].

Trams, London 1952. Image courtesy of Science and Society Archive

MEHMET ŞEREF ALI: They had their son-in-law on Fulham Road at that time. It was close to West End, too. Their relatives from Cyprus came to stay with them. He said, "If you want I can take you to our son-in-law's house on Fulham Road. I went, I stayed there probably for three, four months. Suddenly, one day there was a football match. When I came out of the station, I used to turn left, always to the side which I knew. I said, "This time I should go to right." I walked a little bit, when I looked, Fulham Broadway station and a huge crowd apparently, they were going to a football match but I had no idea. Inside the crowd, a boy called Mustafa from Tatlısu, – during wartime, they used to send people from the towns to the villages – this one went to Tatlısu. Anyway, I bump into this boy in that crowd. I asked "Mustafa, what is this crowd?"

He said, "Football!"

I asked, "Where is it?"

He answered, "There! Where do you stay?"

"I stay in Laurence Avenue," I said.

I said, "Is that the football pitch?"

He said, "Yes, let's go, come on."

I asked, "Who's playing?"

He said, "Arsenal versus Chelsea." We went to football match for the first time. Since then I have become addicted to Chelsea. Since I came, I loved Chelsea. Well I stayed there for a year.

HULUSI MAHMUD: I felt like England was my home when my kids were born there and so on, and then I fell in love. I used to live in North London for 18 years. I stayed there longer, because we had a shop, then we moved after 18 years. Every time funnily enough I crossed the river, the other side towards North, I feel at home. I don't know why. Because that is where you set your home.

EMINE AHMED: I don't remember at all what my knowledge of London was at the time. How would I know? That is to say, then nothing like [it wasn't like] I was gonna be afraid. I was going to work, that came to my mind as I came here. I came as if I was coming for a holiday. That is to say, a purpose doesn't come to my mind. I was 18, 19 years old when I came. I don't remember at all. That is to say, then I came as if I came for holiday. "Go, you also help your brothers," my dad said. They sent me. For how long are you gonna stay at home? You want job, don't you? So you work.

MEHMET ŞEREF ALI: Angel, when I close my eyes, I see a different world when I look at the place now. What was it like and what has it become? I could never explain what kind of place it was, to someone without them seeing it. Right where the traffic lights are at Angel, there used to be a drinking fountain and toilets, right in the middle. Near Chapel Market.

KEMAL AHMET DAVRANDI: In short we arrive at Victoria. I show the address. I had the address. Caledonian Road it said. I had the address of Topcu. I gave the address to the taxi driver and he took me there. "This is it," he said to me.

I gave five shillings, he took it and went. I knock and knock on the door. But there was no one there. I wait and I wait and I wait. It was where he worked not lived. I wait and I wait and I wait. There was nobody there. "*Gavelle*," I said. "What am I going to do?" I left. There was a bridge, I went and put the suitcase [on a bench], and it was cold, and the rain, it was pouring and pouring. In October you understand. I lay down and slept. I woke in the morning at nine. At nine I woke up. I wouldn't move away from the house. I got up, wiped my face and brushed my hair. Grabbed my suitcase and went. To the same place again. *Tak tak* I knock on the door. A girl from upstairs opens the window and says "What do you want?" In Turkish. I take one look at her. She's from Kyrenia. I know the girl.

I say, "Hey, Gülsun, what are you doing? When did you come?" I say.

"Oh, Kemal is it you?" she says

"Yes, me," I say.

"I came recently," I say. Of course I didn't tell that I'd been here for weeks. "I came last night and knocked on the door, but you didn't open it."

"I was out at dinner," she said.

"Well, isn't this the address of Topcu, my girl?"

"It is," she said, "but he has rented it to me. He has another place," she said.

"What am I going to do, my girl?"

"Take this road and in front of the prison you will see a café. There are tomatoes planted in front of it. Don't be scared at all and go in that café." It didn't even take five minutes to walk. I got my suitcase and walked. I sat in the café. The coffee man came.

"What would you like to drink?" he asked. I have five shillings left in my pocket. I don't have much money. Who knows what a cup of coffee costs here?

"Make a coffee, no sugar," I say. He made the coffee. We were talking in Turkish. There was a man sitting looking at me attentively. I recognised him. He was from Kyrenia.

He got up and came near me: "Hey Kemal is it you?"

"Yes it's me, Hüseyin," I said.

"When did you come?"

"Just now," I said. Wouldn't say that I went to Manchester, here and there, now, would I? We shook hands: "Where are you staying?" he asked.

"Look, I've only just arrived, I have nowhere," I said.

"Don't you worry at all, your fellow villagers will be coming here soon. There will certainly be a solution, I will take you stay at ours tonight if there isn't. You can come here again tomorrow morning, to the café."

"OK," I said. And sat there in the café. It was all Turks that went in there. All Cypriots. It became afternoon, and not one fellow villager came.

"Come on, Kemal," he said. He grabbed my suitcase and went to his home.

She [his mum] made dinner for us. We went and sat there, ate there, but my eyes were straining. He said to his mum, "Fix up the bed for Kemal *Dayı*. He is going to stay with us tonight. Until we find his fellow villagers. Maybe they will come tomorrow," he said.

"All right, my son," his mum said. I went and fell on the bed. What time was it? Was it three? It was winter. Was it four? I have no idea. I slept. The next day at 11, I was still sleeping. He came and woke me.

"Hey Kemal! Are you dead? Let's go the café and sort something out," he said.

"If it doesn't happen, then you will stay at mine until you find a place."

"Well, that's good," I said. But there's no money in my pocket, just five shillings, I'm thinking.

We left and went to the café and sat down. God rest his soul, may he rest in piece, there was one Salih *Dayı*. He was from our village but I didn't know him. He got married in July, left the village and never ever came back to the village. I got to know him here. Hüseyin said to him, "Look! Salih *Dayı*, your fellow villager has come."

"Whose son are you?" he asked me. "Are you Davrandı's son?"

"Yeah," I say.

"Welcome, my son!" he says. He hugged and kissed me. We shook hands. "Where are you staying, my son?" he asked

"See I came yesterday, last night I stayed at Hüseyin's house."

"Don't worry at all, I'll find you a place alright," he said.

He found me a place, thank goodness. "Come my son," he said and took me to Abdi Mehmet's place in Caledonia Road. 28 Belitha Villas. I'll never forget the address. We went there. He wanted 10 shillings a week, one room and something like a kitchen.

Salih *Dayı* said "No way! It's too much. He still has no job." We agreed on nine shillings. "Go on then pay the money," he says to me.

"Did I tell you that I had money?" I said

"Alright alright alright." He turned and said, "I'm going to pay his rent," to the landlord. "I'll pay for as long as he stays here." I put the suitcase down and gave us the key.

"Hey Salih *Dayı*," I say. He used to come to the café on a Friday, and if not, definitely on the Sunday, to give me the money [for the rent]. He used to work with batteries. In other words that was close by to Caledonian Road.

Kemal Davrandi with friends in café, Angel, Islington, 1961

IBRAHIM AHMET: There isn't touristic places here. What would a shepherd in a village know about London? It wasn't touristic then.

EMINE AHMET: We came with English passport. We used to travel before. I used to travel a lot. We went to the places we could. Around Queen's house and so on. I didn't know anything about London before I came because I didn't have anyone here. We used to always hear that it was cold. We didn't come to make money. I came here to get married.

ALI HASSAN: The train and bus routes, after you'd been once with someone you'd learn yourself anyway. Maps and stuff, everything was with maps. Yes, this brave. Even if you got lost, you'd say, "Excuse me, I want to go to so-and-so place." We learnt the basics, "excuse me" and stuff in the first few days. We'd say, "Excuse me I wanna go this address." And they'd say, "Get on Central Line, or District Line, you know, get on so-and-so bus," they'd answer. The first time we went on the underground, it felt weird to us, it'd go like this through the darkness like this *chucka chucka chuk.*

Noisy, they used to make a lot of *chucka chuck* noise. Now smaller. But we had a brother-in-law, he used to stay here, and because we used to go with them they'd teach us. Because they already knew though. They already had a house at the least when we got here. He came here three to five years before us.

Yes, he knew the streets. And he learnt the language. We was curious about the language as well. There was an elderly lady and he was staying at her house. Her husband died in the army. The man loved her a lot, and because she was the house owner. And she kind of used to just sit and talk to herself, for hours she would sit and explain things he didn't know about, but he'd learn. You know like this that and the other. What I mean is that she'd teach him English.

We learnt English by speaking to the people in the factory. I could say that now our English is conversational. By speaking more and more to people we learnt English. We don't really have correct grammar English or the ability to write well. Yes, our English, it's understandable, sometimes we get it wrong.

HULUS IBRAHIM: Well, I said, "Am I going to sit at home?" So I take a road and start walking. At first I go to Angel Station. I look and see lots of people going in and out like bees. I thought, "Where are they going?" I went down, and saw one train going one way and another train going another way. I went into one of the carriages. People got off at each station. So I thought I'd go five or six stations, and then get out. I had heard about the trains and people going in and out of them. I thought I would go and see where it takes me to. I remember that I got out at what must have been Trafalgar Square. There was the Queen's palace and something like a bridge, so I went looking around. It became night and I had to ask how to go back to the train station. I didn't know how to get back. I got to the station and trains were going this way and that way – I ask for help, I'm told, "Go this way, go that way." Anyway at last I found my way and went back home. The next morning the door bell rings. It was Ferit. They did not allow Ferit to stay in Paris because he didn't have a visa. They wanted a visa.

GÜLSEN LARKINS: I didn't go to any tourist attractions when I was unmarried. I used to hear that London was very good before I came here. We used to hear a bit about the weather. That it rains, is cold. We would here because we had a fellow villager here. She came back to Cyprus for a holiday and would explain it to us. When my brothers came here in 1954 they stayed at that woman's house. They said the people were good but the weather was bad. Sometimes bad and sometimes good.

IBRAHIM DERVIŞ: I came across a map. I said, "Let me go and explore for the first time. The Zoo is nearby," I said to myself. I left home and went. To London Zoo I went, in Camden Town. I went alone, looked around and returned home again. I had never seen a lion, an elephant and so on, so of course I watched them with interest, their movements, the monkeys' movements. And then there were the unfamiliar beasts – for example some of the birds, such as Humming Birds. They really interested me – when they flap their wings and stayed in the same place.

I returned, that is to say I found my way home. For example, to go by tube, with the underground, it goes in two directions – one to Edgware Road. I noticed that. It was the first time. Curiosity. I wasn't afraid.

FEZILE AHMET: My brother took me to work for the first three days on the bus. After three days he said, "You can now go on your own."

"Will I find my way?" I asked him.

"You'll find it," he said. "Take the number 29, and it goes directly to Camden Town." From there I would get another bus to Kentish Town.

I went on my own for three days, after three days I got off the bus, and I was looking for the street next to the shop with the cake in the window. I was going to turn down the street next to the shop with the cake in the window. "Oh my God!" I said, "There's no cake!" I walked up and down the street looking for the cake in the shop window! I can't tell which road to turn down without the cake. I started to cry, what was I going to do? I can't find the street, so I can't find the house, so I'm going to have to stay in the street. The cake had been sold. It was gone! Just then the landlord was walking up the street. I didn't tell him what had happened but I followed him home. When I got home I told [him and my brother] what had happened – they were wetting themselves laughing. I was ill from worry.

I swear to God. It was a long time before things got easier here.

ÇETIN KAYA MUSTAFA: *Vallahi* by God, before you come you are curious, what kind place is it? We came and saw for example. First, before I came to London, we used to hear that London was very cold, they put the newly born babies in snow so they would get used to it. And then, we used to hear that there was so much dirt [adultery/sex] in London streets, with women and men. And even if you see them, you would pass straight away, you can't look, it is shameful. When I came here I didn't see anything like that! But even if I see, I wouldn't look at it. It is shameful. We would pass straight away. Because in Cyprus we don't think of looking at it. What else did we see? When I first came to London, first I came and left home to go to the corner shop. I went, I saw olive, I saw that, I saw this. "Oh," I say, "There is such and such here as well." That is to say, I thought the things which are in Cyprus are not in London, but there was everything here as well. But here it is more different: for example two or three kinds of olives. I don't know what you are going to buy, and then there was pig that we didn't know what it was. In fact we learnt pigs in London. Bacon, sausage.

When we were in Cyprus, there was green olives or black olives. I mean Cyprus things. But here there weren't many Cyprus things here. For example there wasn't *helva melva* here in our time. Later on slowly, slowly. There was *hellim*, but all of them used to bring *hellim*.

But after I came to London and went back it was easier. When someone came, we used to speak with a pose. London is nice. For the time being there's no intention of going back, there isn't anything like that. For a person to go back to Cyprus they have to see their kids are comfortable. Everything is going right, then you can leave.

It didn't take any time at all for me to accept London. As soon as I came to England I felt myself English. Everything is plentiful here.

And in Cyprus, no one says, "See you"! But I don't see them as wrong, because here is different, that place is different. That is to say, they were happy to see you, most of them used to ask me help them to come to London. Most of them did want it. You can easily obtain. I mean, you are gonna buy something, there is money as well. Opportunity. There are things here.

I used to stay in Cyprus for example, my father used to give me food and drink, but I couldn't put a lot of money into my pocket. Because he used buy everything I wanted. But here if there is no one you always do it yourself, you are more comfortable. London, as I said there isn't a place like your own place. Tell the truth but we say, "Not the place you were born, the place you are fed." Because if you are fed, you're living, everything is fine. If I go there, what am I going to eat there? Am I going to live on air? Isn't it true? You want to earn something. It is necessary that you can live, stay somewhere. We go there for holiday. We love it, because we especially go for a holiday. But if you stay there more than holiday, nobody will want you. When I go like a Cypriot. I mean like it's my place that I go to see my family.

DUDU HAKKI: Once I fell off the bus. I was going to work. It was dark and it started raining. There was so much rain and fog that you couldn't see where to get off the bus. I was going to go to my Nahide *Aba's* house. But I noticed that the bus went past my stop. I jumped off the bus from fear of getting lost. I fell flat and smashed my elbows and knees. The bus immediately stopped and then people got down to look at what had happened. They picked me up. I didn't know what to say to them. I didn't say anything. I went home. If I had continued on the bus I would have got lost. I only knew how to go to work and back to Nahide *Aba's* house. I had identified the exact bus stop I needed. Right outside Hackney baths, then I would walk to Nahide *Aba's* house. On this occasion the bus was going past it, I didn't realise and then it turned the corner and I jumped off.

I went home and Nahide *aba* said, "What's happened to you girl?"

I said "Well, the bus past [went] my stop, and as I wasn't going to recognise how to come back, I jumped off the bus."

"You could have broken your arms and legs. You should have asked someone." I always carried my address on me in case I got lost. I never had to show the address to anyone. I never got lost.

10. FAR AWAY

EMINE MEHMET: In Cyprus, my father had land in Anafodiya – vineyards, grapes and tomatoes this big. My father would bring us some, so I had seen well. When I came here I was bewildered, they used to sell small bunches of grapes. I found it very strange. We suffered torture here!

We were on rations*. They used to give us one egg a week. One egg per person each week! A tiny piece of meat per person. The country had just come out of war at that time. And that's how we lived. I saved my child. I used to take him to the park, I used go home and wait for my husband. I mean it was another kind of life.

I used to miss Cyprus, its greenery, its fields, the food. I really missed the food. There was very little food here back then. Not like now. If you were to talk about grocers, there was a Zahariye in the West End. We used to look for things like olives and yoghurt. There were no yoghurts like now. These yoghurts increased later on. The English didn't know how to make plain yoghurt in the time that I came here. Zahariye would bring everything and we would go and buy it. Later there were Turkish grocers everywhere, Everywhere filled with Turks and Greeks, and so there was no need to go to the West End.

ÇETIN KAYA MUSTAFA: *Vallahi*, my brother-in-law didn't like here that much. Because my brother-in-law said, "London is a civilised prison." That is why he didn't like it that much. As a matter of fact, my brother-in-law came here to learn some craft. See something different and go back to Cyprus and do it there. For example he used to make iron chairs. He learnt for example how to make a iron chair here. He went to Cyprus; however the Greeks were already doing that job. They learnt it much earlier.

Vallahi, I stayed. I said that I should see a different place. I liked it as well. I was also young. There were lots of girls for example. I would look around. I liked here. That is to say, in Cyprus you can't look at somebody's daughter, it is disgraceful, and if her brother sees you, you would be in trouble. There isn't any freedom there.

IBRAHIM MUSTAFA: When I was back home, I never used to go to the beach. Only when I was working in Larnaka we went to the beach. Apart from that we

---

* See footnote on page 131

never used to get time to go. We were all based in the fields. In Cyprus it was work work work.

KEMAL AHMET DAVRANDI: I didn't go anywhere. I used to cook my dinner at home, once I got that job in the cake factory. I used to stay home. Saturday and Sunday I would eat out at the restaurant. I used to miss Cyprus, but I couldn't go there because of my money situation. I used to miss my village mostly. To climb the mountains, pick mushrooms, asparagus. I used to go fishing. These were my things. I didn't like anything of London, I tell you.

CELAL HASSAN: England was different. To live in the village and to live in the town is completely different. Before I came I knew it was going to be different, but it was still a surprise to me because in Cyprus I didn't see cities and towns. The weather was different, it was very bad in those days. One day I walked from Haringey to here, because you couldn't get a bus or anything. So much foggy this and that. Cold and all that. We never had that in Cyprus.

GÜLSEN LARKINS: I didn't really miss Cyprus when I first came here. I like it here. I don't know why. Because we didn't go outdoors in Cyprus. I wasn't allowed to go out. What I am saying is, in Cyprus you were not allowed to go out. When I came here, I stayed with my uncle. My mum's brother. He asked me stay there. I stayed with my aunt.

GÖKMEN MEHMET: It was of course different here to what I expected. To me it was terrible. I wasn't working in Cyprus. Of course in the beginning my life was better in Cyprus. Because I got luxury life in Cyprus, no work, no worries.

SÜHA FAIZ: I wanted to be in Cyprus, because it is my country. And obviously I had missed it. Well, had I? I liked it. I saw Cyprus and I liked it. I mean I knew nothing about the people, part from the fact of not knowing Turkish – and incidentally in that eight months that I was in Cyprus, from July 1946 to whenever, I learned a lot, I mean I could speak Turkish again as far as I could speak it. Because I had cousins I went around with.

But being back there, compared to being regarded as English when you were in England, I didn't feel as much Turkish as I felt Turkish later. It comes in waves this kind of business whether you are Turkish or English, and eventually if you are lucky, you find a sort of balance. At that stage it just didn't arise to me.

DUDU HAKKI: When I first got married I stayed in Muswell Hill, a very nice place. My husband used to stay there when he was single. It was one big house with five families living in it. He lived in one of the flats. When we got married we lived in the flat for four years. It was really nice around there. The owner of the property died all of a sudden. They said as you live in the house you could buy it for £4,000 if you want. The house was so big but was un-repaired. It needed a lot of repairs done. And anyway my husband was very afraid. He was a very scared man. "Oh it's going to collapse, oh it's going to collapse," he would say. So we didn't buy it.

So I went to the estate agent to find a home. And he took us to Walthamstow. From Muswell Hill he took us to Walthamstow at night. We saw a house that was repaired and decorated. It was a very nice. But after I didn't like it, I asked my husband to sell it, but he didn't want to leave once he was in there. I started to warm to the area after my niece Rahmeli and my nephews Kamil and Şakir came over. That was when I felt that I had someone, family, around me, and my confidence started to come back. Otherwise I used to cry every day and day and night, until they came. I wanted to leave and return into the war. My husband used to say, "Let's go if you want to, we'll go back, but there is war." We would have gone back if there wasn't war. I had a child at the time but I loved my family a lot because we grew up together. My nephew Şakir was born when I was nine. I helped look after my nephews and niece – Şakir, Kamil and Rahmeli. That's why I was very devoted to them and would cry for them night and day.

There weren't many foreigners around, the odd one or two. I used to live in Muswell Hill, and if I heard Turkish I would go and stand near the person speaking to listen, just to hear Turkish or Greek. I used to go and talk to them. There was the odd one here and there. But now *peeeeeeee* – there are lots. You hear Turkish and you leave, the Turks have increased everywhere. That's why London is finished, it doesn't even resemble London. Those years were good. The people were very friendly. They used to help a lot, the English.

EMINE AHMET: I missed Cyprus when I first came here. Can you get used to here easily? I didn't accept it here at all as my country. I have never accepted. Oh if I didn't have grandchildren here. Oh, I have been here for 30 years, it [London] has never warmed to me once within these 30 years. Whatever you do you are alone. You can't warm up to anywhere.

MELEK KAZIM: I have been very influenced. I try, I didn't want religion to get into it, because once religion get into any kind of friendship or relationship it wouldn't last long. Both my sons have been circumcised, but in hospital. For health reason and Muslim thing. Ye. I understand that a mother and father for example would want his child to grow up like a Turk, like a Turkish Cypriot, but also to speak English, but not to be English. My children were under my direction only. I wanted them to be both English and Turkish. I would speak to them in English. I also forgot Turkish as there were no Turks living in the area that I lived. I would cook them Turkish food. My children still eat Turkish food. They don't eat English food. He [the husband] also liked Turkish food. He loved stuffed vine leaves. He never made any fuss when it came to food.

In Berkshire, I was living in a square. Every week neighbours and friends from London would come to see us or we would go to see them. We would make food, drink, talk, it was like a party. We used make our own bread, things everything like that. This time it was not like the time in Tottenham, at school where I felt like a stranger. They [guests from London] felt like strangers.

I suppose because I speak very good English and I was clean, homely. I don't know. I was accepted for who I am. There was no sign you are a foreign. There is nothing like that. They thought it was a good thing being Turkish, because my mum used to drive two times a week all the way from London bringing me shopping and things. Because nearest shop was six miles away. She would bring anything, anything I couldn't get over there. My neighbours thought that it was good. They used to say, "My mum wouldn't do it for me." Do you know what I mean? My mum used to do everything. All I have to do is lift the phone, she will send it by next post or bring it over.

I come back to London to hell, my mum and dad. I had three children, my daughter was six weeks. When I came back to London to hell, then I realise, I used to be here from Turkish neighbours in Tottenham – that Turkish men, all they want is sex. If you go with a Turkish men. The first thing they saw you do and you have got bad name. So I used to keep away from Turkish men. But then I had realised they were human beings.

ALI GASBAR: Who doesn't miss their family, the place they were born, grew up, the place they lived? You miss your country. The unfinishing Greek-Turk affair has become the reason for missing my country a lot.

SEYIT MEHMET: In the beginning it took me five, six months to recover. Once you get used to it is all right here. No, no, not recover from leaving the army or Cyprus. You recover because at that time you are far away from your family, you are in a strange country. It takes you time to settle down. I still love it here.

FEZILE AHMET: So I arrived here, by asking this person, that person, hitting against this stone and that stone, we entered this land slowly. I lived in Caledonian Road when I first came. I worked for the Jewish in Kentish Town, the lady that I lived in the same house with took me with her to where she worked. When I came here I had no idea about any Turkish Associations or organisations. There were very few Turks here then. Not like now. You would sit on the bus and listen out to hear if anyone was speaking Turkish. There weren't many then.

NEVCIVAN JEVAN: They told me London was a big city, it has a nice life. Our life was nicer in Cyprus. It might be different for today's youngsters. I was very comfortable in my parents' house. I became a dressmaker, I used to work at home, go out. Turkish films used to come to town. We used to go to see Turkish film every other week. There used to be a sandy beach at the shore, we used to walk up and down. There was a nicer life for us there. We came here, what did we find? Nothing.

Of course I prefer it there. I still prefer there. There isn't a Turk like me. I don't go anymore. In fact when you have kids here you don't want to go back. You can't leave them and go. When you go *gözün arkada kalır*. For ten years I have been having chemotherapy. Treatment after treatment. That is why I can't go to Cyprus at all now. I can go for holiday but I can't stay there permanently. Because everything is expensive there. Where can I find chemotherapy treatment? Now cancer treatment is so expensive. Even if you sell your house you can't have a treatment. Because every tablet given is very very expensive. How can you pay for that?

EMINE AHMED: As a matter of fact I started not to like here. I didn't like here. When my first child was born, for me to work again was a necessity. Is it easy to pushing a pushchair in snow and crowd? You don't have a car, you don't have anything. You are going to push the chair and take it to the child-minder, you are going to come from the child-minder and take a bus back again and go, you are going to come out of work, pick up the child from the child-minder and come back. I didn't have anyone, I had a great difficulty until I raised the children. When I bought a house in Turnpike Lane I felt relieved. When we bought the house Bayar was one year old, in 1967. We were tenants when I had Şensal. We were in Turnpike Lane, on Rally Road.

I used to send letters to Cyprus. At that time there wasn't telephones at all. There was only one phone in the village which was in the *muhtar's* shop in Sinde and that was for emergency. Greek Cypriots used to cut it off. That is to say, those Greek Cypriots used to cut it off continuously to prevent us to send any news abroad.

GÜLSEN LARKINS: My children were born here. They looked after me well but I don't want my husband. I didn't miss Cyprus because all my family was here. My mum, my dad, my elder brothers were here.

HATICE FETTI: Well I learnt to speak English somehow. When I go to doctor, I go on my own. I can tell my problem. Even if I have a court case for something, I would go, wouldn't need anyone else. I can understand. I used to sit in front of the television, I used to hear English, I used to write it down. When the kids come home, I used to ask them, "What is this, kids?" Slowly, slowly, like that you get used to it in a long time. After five or six years I felt comfortable here. As I said I went back to Cyprus 11 years later. When the kids grew up, they never talked in Turkish among themselves. As I heard them speak I learnt as well. Now I am OK. I speak, my everything, when I go to a doctor I go on my own. If I am gonna buy something, myself, I don't need anyone else.

Before my sister's husband who studied here, he used to read our letters. When I was going to go to the doctor, I used to go with someone who knows. I didn't have difficulty because I gave myself to work. I wanted to do all of my things. I did all of my things normally. I am so satisfied with my life. I made it. I sew on the machine. Until the age of 71 I sew.

ALI HASSAN: I used to miss our own country. I used to miss everything about it. Everything, the family. We wrote letters, letters from here used to take ages to come and go. We used to miss our country. Do you not think that we miss it still? We still miss it.

MELEK KAZIM: I came back [from Berkshire], I got mixed up with Turks, ye. I started learning Turkish, then I met my second husband. I suppose I can say that we fell in love. Because I didn't love my first husband. It was just, I had my freedom. I can go out. My first husband was my escape. Yes, I found a way to escape and I got married.

HULUSI MAHMUD: At that time I didn't miss much [about Cyprus], because in Cyprus you suffer a lot. It is hard work. The living is very hard. To earn a living. Here it's more comfortable in that sense. So you don't miss much. Only I missed the weather at that time. Because you can't really beat the nice weather. That's what I missed. I don't know anything else.

They [his brothers] didn't mind the weather in London, because they get used to it themselves. They got a good life, that is the main thing. But only one thing though, six months after I came, they abolished the army services. You know you had to do three years army service. I missed that as well, if I really wanted to go to army. If they'd asked me, I could have done. But I missed it, just abolished it. I wanted to do it in the first place. But after I came here I didn't, after six months gone. So, no way. Because my brother had to change his name, and so on, not to go to army.

He changed his name because they wanted him to go to national army service, so he didn't want to. He came over here as a British citizen, so you had to do it, whether you want or not. You must. If it was me, I wouldn't miss it. I would just go straight into it. Some men are different. I didn't want to do it voluntarily. Well, there were a lot people who had done it [national service]. I didn't do it in Cyprus either.

MEHMET ŞEREF ALI: During first years, until 60s, I used to miss them [mother's dishes]. After the 60s, corner shops opened, people who came here brought some; beans, black eye beans, pasta, *molohiya*, leek, that is to say the variety increased. Of course, after getting married, within the family, that is why I didn't have any difficulty.

HATICE IBRAHIM: Let's say my life was good, but I found it very hard, I had a child, a husband and breastfeeding to keep up with. For five years I cried and wanted Cyprus. Every now and then I would write to my mother. I was very dedicated to writing. I had this work to do, that work to do. Cypriots were not really educated. We found it hard to write. I used to miss the weather and things like that.

[Later] I went to the Post Office. I couldn't communicate. I gave the paper to the Post Office but it was supposed to be given into the bank. I was resentful. Why didn't they educate me? They should have left me in my village. There would have been no need for embarrassment me in my village, would there? For a grown married woman, you don't know what can be done in a Post Office and what can not be done. However if I hadn't been bought up in Nicosia and had I been left in my village, I may have been taught to read and write.

A lot of the time I used to curse when I worked in the cloakroom. Because rich rich ladies put on an attitude and walk past. They would throw three or five pence into the plate and go. And I used to feel like nothing near them. I can't bring the past back. The time when I was nine and they took me from my village to Nicosia. I would not be sorrowful if I had stayed in the village with my fellow villagers and lived and got by with them.

Of course by growing up with others and being left uneducated in a big places is a big blow. I could have lived comfortably in my small village suited for my education.

MEHMET ALI BEKIR: I never thought to return in those six months. Nothing attached me to here, but when it comes to going back, I couldn't go. Not because there wasn't money, because I had a job here, I couldn't go.

Going back never came to my mind, yet I never liked here. Since the day I came to England, I never liked it. I accepted [things]. There was nothing in Cyprus which attracted me. Apart from my family, of course. At that time we were longing, of course. What I missed the most was our music, cinema, public [people]. As we are a minority here, for example our cinema is once a week. Our music, if we heard a Turkish music while walking, that used to give us so much heartache, I mean at that time we used to feel a sense of longing.

HÜSEYIN HASSAN MEMOUR: I don't really miss Cyprus. I miss the countryside, because I am a country man and I love the countryside. In a big city you can have nervous breakdown, tension. I did, I did partly. I got used to now, you see. I had three nervous breakdowns, I was in hospital several times.

DUDU HAKKI: All my family was over there. I had no one. My nan, my mum, my sisters, their children, everyone was there. My sister's children were young, I had helped look after them. I missed them a lot, oh but a lot. Whatever child I saw here would remind me of one over there. I would be walking down the street with Nahide *Aba,* and I would say, "Ah! He looks like Şakir, he looks like Kamil, she looks like Rahmeli." I used to always cry.

11. THE ENGLISH

HULUSI MAHMUD: The English people treated you the way you treat them yourself. They couldn't pronounce my name, they called me George. In fact when I was in the Italian restaurant a woman named Carla, probably she passed away by now, she was about 32, 33 then. I told her this. I tell you what she says to me, "I call you George."

I said, "I agree". They started calling me George, I used the name ever since.

They say, "Why, your name Mahmud, Hulusi? Why are they calling you George?"

"I don't know, you tell me. What is the difference, it won't kill you." So they called me George. They still call me George. With my work surrounding, they call me George. But my children's names are Turkish of course: Suzan, Caner, Hazen.

FEZILE AHMET: There were lots of English people working in the factory. I learnt some of my English from them. The English were not ill-tempered. Nothing like your Turkish. No, no, nothing like that. They had nothing against us.

MEHMET ALI BEKIR: English youngsters used to make improper remarks to us. During that time there were Teddy boys, and we had a fight with the Teddy boys once or twice. Our last fight was in an Armenian café in Newington Green. The Turks were always mixed with the English. You know, we would run after girls more, because in those days, before 60s, English people used to be more interested in sports, and they wouldn't show that much interest in girls. When we, foreigners, arrived and paid more attention to girls, then English youngsters started being jealous, and they fixed a plan to beat us. One day for instance, we, seven Turks, were in the café, they sent the girls inside, we started chatting with the girls, and after them 20 people attacked us. A big fight erupted. Because they were so frightened, they got in their car within two minutes. We cut the tyres of their cars. They ran away while the tyres were cut. Within two minutes the police came. The girls told the police that we were not at fault. In result of this the police didn't do anything to us and after that incident, that fight [the English] became very good friends with us.

ALI HASSAN: [On marches] the people around us used to respond to us positively. They would never give bad looks. The English loved the Turks anyway. It wasn't like now, how they don't get pleasure from seeing foreigners, because the foreigners have started to do a lot of things to the English. Foreigners don't even do one good thing for the English. Don't look at what others say, from one point of view the English are actually good people. Being Turkish Cypriots we came here a bit modern. The English knew that we came here for work. Now everyone sees all Turks, they come for the mafia. Of course the English don't like it. If it was you, you wouldn't either. Neither do I like it.

There was nothing like that. Not from the English. In fact a while before I opened my shop, there was a door sergeant, he did English military service. He was born here. Before I opened my shop, when I was working for the Jewish. At the door there used to be guards and these were generally people who were withdrawn from the military service circulation. This Turk was in war aged 14, in war aged 20 lost his leg. The man says, "I lost my leg in Turkey. But I love the Turks because we were the ones at fault. We went there to take their land and homes, and they did this to us," he says. He used to love us. When he'd see us coming into work, he'd sign us in straight away. The man used to do that many things. What I mean is he'd never hold the fact that he lost his leg in Turkey against us. Never. We, I used to work in there. Hüseyin from Köfünye, a friend, used to work in there. Our boy, us three worked there. And there was a Rifat, he was in there too. And when he used to see us [the man who lost his leg] he'd come over and hug us. Always over the moon to see us in the Jewish factory.

There was foreigners that used to take part in the walks, Pakistanis and so on. There was even English with us. Some of the Turks were married to English, some had English girlfriends, they'd take part. The English used to take part in things like that.

The knowledge I had about things in England before I came here was not different once I arrived here. It was just the language problems at first. When we started and learnt the language, then it all got easier. We heard that if you work there [in England] a lot of money comes from it. We used to make money because we worked. We didn't struggle for money or anything. The struggle was the house situation, and to buy a house. Yes of course this was because we had a child and they wouldn't accept that children make a racket naturally.

Yes, we used to get on with our neighbours really well. We used to get on really well. They were English. In fact every day in the mornings when they used to clean the dust from their door windows, they used to come and clean over ours as well. Everyday, every single day they'd do this for us. When my daughter started school and she'd come come, my neighbour would take her into her house, make her tea, give her some cake until we came home. They used to call me Hasan here. Some people would call me by my first name but Hasan especially, Hasan, by my second name. No, they [the English people] didn't change my name. No, no, there was no John, Jack or anything like that with us. For example, I had an uncle, his name was Celal, and they used to call him Jackie. He was a bit of a show-off with girls, he was single and with all different girls so they called him Jackie.

HÜSEYIN YUSUF: In the Merchant Navy, the others [sailors and workers] didn't know I was Turkish. They know me as Joe, they didn't sort of, we didn't go around saying am Turkish and that. I come from Cyprus, we used to tell him [other sailors and workers] we are from Cyprus. Cypriots.

In the early years, when we worked in the Merchant Navy, we used to go to South Africa. All the way down to South Africa, on the way we used to call at Maderia, Las Palmas, a couple of islands, and then we came to Cape Town and then all round Durban. Once your job is done, once your service is finished, lunch or dinner, we used to go out and see these places. I was in the catering. All the time. Yes, I enjoyed it. I used to meet a lot of people. I actually used to end up being good friends. Because we were there for a while. It is quite good actually. I enjoyed it. I have quite a lot of photographs.

As you go along you become adapted to the life here. You forget your past. I mean you don't forget it, but just get used to the idea of being here and the way of people living here, you just follow so.

Hüseyin Yusuf at work on cruise ship, 1963

DUDU HAKKI: The English people were very kind, very very smart, and nice *boylu poslu*: handsome boys and the girls were tall and slender, like young trees. There was lots of discipline in this country. When going to work, you would stand in the queue at the bus stop and no one would take your place. Everyone would wait in a queue. You would go, there was a conductor, buy a ticket and go and sit down. A young person would immediately stand up and give up their seat when an elderly person got on, if the bus was full. They used to think I was English as well. They were very welcoming. They didn't realise that I was a foreigner. At first I didn't know English. I couldn't speak in English, just yes or no.

EMINE AHMED: I got used to the English people here. How should I tell you? You are going to accept her as your sister, your friend, that is to say, even if it is your neighbour or your colleague it is necessary for you to get on well. There is no end for a fight. I have never had an argument with my neighbour. But when I was working with those *Cıras* they didn't want us among them. They used to always bring up the troubles in Cyprus. As a result our foreman sent the *Cıras* upstairs and he left us on the second floor.

MELEK KAZIM: We had no choice but to attend Princess May school. It was there that they taught me English. I learned to speak English in three months. When I first walked into class, it felt very different. They were all English. In Cyprus they were all Turkish. I felt I had to attend. I wanted to. I wanted to go to school because it meant I was going outside, outside of the house, outside of the prison. I was scared on my first day at school. My teacher was English, and the children all strangers. At nine years old, I was shy, and at that time I could not speak in English. In a foreign place, I remember I was shaking when a lady put her arm around me. It was my teacher. She said, "The child has arrived from Cyprus," and they [the other children] didn't even know where Cyprus was. They thought I came from the air. This blonde little girl. They pronounced my name Melek, easily. In three months my teacher taught me to say, "I used to live in Cyprus." It has stayed in my brain. "I use to live in Cyprus." They were my first words. This is what I learnt. It was my teacher that I first got used to in school.

NEVCIVAN JEVAN: I was single when I came, but I wanted to leave, I didn't like it. Terrible. Everything has changed now. We didn't have a bathroom at home. You had to put some water in a tin to wash yourself in the same water. The toilet was outside. You would get up and go outside in the morning in ice, snow. And also you would go to bathroom if you want. The bathrooms were outside. You had to queue until it is your turn. All the English people, old people, you know where in the queue. Everyone used to have a bath outside. There used to be public baths. And then the water, the staff who worked there used to turn on the tap on for you from the inside. You would go inside the water when it was warm. There is no more water. You would have a bath with that water, wash your hair and body in that water and then get out of that water. That is it.

I don't remember about the towels and soap. I wonder if they used to give them? There was no central heating, no electric. There used to be gas lamps on the walls. They used to light the gas lamps when it is evening. Everything was with rations*. You couldn't eat as many as eggs, chocolate, biscuits as you wanted. Every person had a book, coupon in their hands. We used to use those coupons. You couldn't buy meat as much as you want. They used to give, let's say two eggs, or one egg if you were allowed to. They wouldn't give you more than that. It was really different. The people who are coming now are very lucky. Everything is perfect, bathrooms, central heating, washing machine. There wasn't any in those days.

These things were not in Cyprus either but the difference in this country was the dark. Cold, rain. For example you wouldn't leave your home and go to a factory or to have a bath in Cyprus. You would heat up the water in a tin at home. You would go to one corner of the kitchen, pour the water from top of your head, you would clean yourself. It was different. Here you would go into the same water and come out of the same water. It was like that in old days. My life there was cleaner. Cleaner, nicer. For example the weather is nice at weekend, you would go out with your friends or your parents. You would go for a walk, sit down somewhere,

---

* See footnote on page 131

drink coca-cola, have some desert, drink tea, walk up and down. No, we didn't do that here. You wouldn't know streets, how could you go somewhere else?

It used to take 15 – 20 minutes to have a wash in the public baths. My mother came here once, stayed for nine months. She said, "*Uyuz oldum be*, I should have a bath." I would wash her at home but she didn't like it. I said, "I will take you to the baths." I took her to the baths. My mum went into the water. We went there with my mum. She went into the water. While I am here, I decided to go into the water. She says, "But it is not even enough for me. No my dear, I am going to leave, I will go back my motherland," she said. She left and went back to Cyprus.

Ye, we paid money for it, so I thought while I am here I might as well go into it as well. The water was jet black. These baths were near to the Angel market in Islington. It was so expensive.

There were Turkish Baths a little bit further down Holborn. Someone used to wash you, scrub you. After we got used to it, we started going there. My mum came in 1954. After that I got used to these Turkish Baths. I think there are still Turkish Baths, but I don't go anymore. These people from Turkey do everything, they haven't done Turkish Baths. It would be great if they could do it for only women.

EMINE AHMET: That is how my kid turned six months old. My husband's wages was very little, they used to pay £9 per week in the restaurant. He used to get tips. We couldn't buy a house, we stayed in one room. That is how I suffered. I had to bring the washing from the third floor to downstairs, lay them on a towel and go upstairs again. I had to heat up water on the stove. By chance there was a retired old English man living in the other room. He said to my husband, "I feel sorry for her, if she likes my room – in other words if she is not disgusted with it – she can come to my room if you allow it. If it's OK?" he said. His room was upstairs to ours. I used to stay in the big room and he used to stay in the small room. When we had a baby, he took her in his arms. He sent her to sleep in his arms in his bedroom that was with my oldest daughter. He was like a father to me, God blesses his soul. I have two daughters, they used to know him as granddad and call him "Granddad, granddad." He stayed with us for 13 years. Afterwards we stayed in all sorts of places but we couldn't buy a house. We had a real difficulty. He was English. That old man liked us like his children. When we wanted to buy a house, he endeavoured with us, ran around everywhere. My husband was working at nights, he used to help me to look after my kids, change their napkins, clean them, make them drink their milk. He helped me a lot. He stayed with us for 13 years. I was absolutely delighted with himself. What shall I say, may he sleep in peace.

Emine and Ibrahim Mehmet, their daughters and "Granddad", c.1950

ALI GASBAR: In England at that time there were the Teddy boys and we would frequently fight with them in Piccadilly and Angel. They didn't like us because we were foreigners. They would be racists. Even in the 1950s, we would not talk in Turkish amongst ourselves in public. They would react badly towards us and would make us do the dirtiest jobs. There were also those on the mopeds and they would raid some of the Turkish cafés and cause fights.

ÇETIN KAYA MUSTAFA: We never cared what other foreigners thought of us. That is to say we strove to get on well, as a matter of fact they were foreigners, we were foreigners. Everyone used to mind their own jobs.

There was no discrimination from the English. There wasn't anything like that. No, in those days, in my time, the time when we came here there were Teddy boys, in those days there was something like that. Apparently, they would put a razor blade inside a potato, they would throw it your face, they would cut your face with a razor blade. There was something like that in those days. They used to do it. They did it to a friend of mine. But a Turk did it to him. They were not on good terms.

Turks used to handle the English tactfully in coffee bars. We used to get on. But sometimes some people who you don't know used to start a fight – but I haven't been into such a thing.

Çetin Kaya Mustafa with friends in café, Angel, Islington, 1961

HATICE IBRAHIM: We used to go out with other friends. There was Aydin's family, the Hasan family. We used to go out. To the seaside. I later got used to it here. I used to like the hospitals. I used to go in them a lot. There was a lot of respect. I gave birth to those children in them, the spotless beds, the nurses were very kind. There's nothing like that now. Oh the nurses, the doctors, I can't explain it. You're virtually in heaven. The compliments you would hear, the beauty you would see. Nurses would come to you in pairs, they would look to see if the bed was straight, if the sheet were clean, if you needed anything.

I had learned English by then, I could communicate. Some nights I couldn't sleep and the nurse would come and say, "What is the matter, darling? Shall I make you a cup of tea, I'll have one too." When I used to say "No," so as to not disturb the nurse, she would say, "No, not at all. I want to." She used to make me tea because I couldn't sleep. I used to like the respect you got on the buses.

CELAL HASSAN: The people in England in those days were very polite, people were very, very nice in those days. When you go to the bus to get a bus, you have to wait in the queue, nicely you go in, if you can't get that bus you have to wait for another bus. It is not like now, they are pushing you, they are dragging you in the road. I was not happy in those days, because I felt lonely. I had no family, no nothing, you know and then I went there [Cyprus] in 1960. I tried to get a job in the English camp, English places. But they said they give you the same money you know as what I was getting in England. It didn't work out.

I didn't understand English at all. If I have to do something, if you buy something in the shop you showing that and give him the money and then slowly slowly slowly. Because when you are young you pick up English. It didn't take me ten years, it took me two, three years.

IBRAHIM MUSTAFA: I learned English from the other people who I was working with. I socialised with the English. I used to go to cinema with my brother at weekends.

After work I used to socialise with them, my English work friends. In Stoke Newington there was about five or six cinemas, English cinemas. One night we would go to one, another night the other one. That is how I learned English as well. I would go on my own sometimes. So there was nothing to do, so I would go to the cinema for a couple of hours, watch the film, come back. There was nowhere else to go. Except when we used to go to Hulusi's [a café].

A Turkish picnic – it is very different from when English people go on a picnic. The difference is, we know how to make barbecue. They don't!

MELEK KAZIM: Yes, this English girlfriend for 50 years, we have known each other since school, we are still friends. There was a dance place near us... and then they pulled this down. They called it Dove Royal. It was only dancing there. For Saturday nights, for 14-15 year olds. It was opposite the Tottenham police station. They have pulled this down now. There was a school. Then it was Mayfair, but first it was Royal, then Mayfair.

Anyway, on Saturday nights, there was dancing for teenagers. I use to tell my mum that I was going shopping with my friend, but we use to go dancing. The dancing was at lunch times, during the day. From 2pm to 5pm. We use to put in a bag, high heels, make up. You couldn't see what we were wearing under the trousers. We would go to the dance, we would dance. At that time it was rock-and-roll. It was beautiful. It was 1961, as I got married in 1962. In 1960 – 61, Elvis was so big then.

Once a youth club had opened at the Bruce café. The first youth club at Bruce café. My brother and I had planned that when our mother and father went to bed to sleep, we would slowly creep out. My brother is four years younger than me. There was no television at the time. My father would tell us a story. Then they would sleep, because my father would get up early, they would sleep early, at 7pm. We would wait until he would fall asleep, then we would slowly go out. We would for exactly one hour. Exactly one hour to see how it was there. When we came back and we opened the door, my dad was sitting there. My heart stopped. It was the first and last time my father smacked me. Anyway, we got scared at that time and did not go back.

SEYIT MEHMET: I left from Holloway Road after about six months, something like that. I went to Maidenhead. Ye, because when the King died in 1952, I was in Maidenhead. Yes I remember that, because they were going to bury him down in Windsor Castle. All the flags were half way down. Because you see Maidenhead and Windsor is not too far away, about a couple of miles. And then the Queen at that time, either she was in Australia, or New Zealand, and she has to come back, or she did come back when he died. And then in 1953 the Coronation officially. Of course I remember that.

The Coronation in 1953 was I think in June, something like that, I am not sure, it was summertime and I used to work in a hotel called Nivera in South Kensington. We used to do breakfast, lunch, dinner there. Lunch was until three o'clock, so we used to go out and go back six o'clock. One day before the Coronation, we used to take every day the bus to come down, there was a Turkish Club. There was a Turkish Club in Dean Street and so we used to go there for a couple of hours. But that day particularly the traffic was so slow because there was over 100,000 people in the park, you couldn't walk. So we just go out and walked and I was living in Romford at that time. And then it was an order that we had to stay in the hotel during night, because they wouldn't let anybody from outside to come in. So we get up next morning five o'clock in the morning, full of Americans, we served them breakfast and everything and then they go down to the ceremony. But when they left by eight o'clock, nine o'clock there was a lot of other people in Trafalgar Square, lots of people and they came over there two or three days ago and they were sleeping there just to see the Coronation. But fortunately we have been lucky, in our hotel there was a television set and they put it there and we saw everything on television, you see. And all the Indian troops, and it was raining that day. And one day before it so hot, like today. And the next day it was raining, and all these people are staying in Trafalgar Square must have got wet.

When we were watching it on the television there wasn't [just] Turkish people there. It was all different nationalities. English, Polish, Italians. Obviously, of course we were excited. It was a young Queen. She was married just a couple of years ago, she was princess and she became Queen. Yes.

MEHMET MUSTAFA: There used to be Teddy boys in those times. They were not that many in reality. They were about to finish. Now you hear and go to a café and so on in the same way, and a couple of years ago, it wasn't that long ago, before we came, they used to come and break the windows and so on. A man even made a complaint according to what he says and police. He said, "This time I am going to sort it out." And he had bought a knife, he butchered whoever came. Now, here is a pretty mess. "I did what I could do," but this was a little bit earlier than us.

MELEK KAZIM: Yes, there was a cultural difference. I found it really hard. It was all English. Well, I was in the middle. That was the worst part of my life. Because I used to go to English school with the English people. You had to do what they did to be in with them, or you get beaten up. You try to make yourself like them acceptable, and then you come home you have got your parents saying you can't do this, you can't do that, you can't go out with that, you can't go out with men, you can't go out with boys. You are so mixed up.

GÜLSEN LARKINS: Oh my god! Good that you asked. You'll laugh. Because in Cyprus we used to go to Nicosia. Our mum would sit in the automobile, our dad, our family would sit.

When I first came, an English person would sit near me and it would annoy me. I didn't want anyone to sit near me. My uncle would always bring and take me. When he didn't have space, sometimes someone else would come and sit near me and the man would stare. "Why's he looking at me?"

"Speak quietly," my uncle would say to me. God rest his soul.

"Why didn't you come and sit near me?" I would say, "and now he has sat?"

"Ssh Ssh," he would say, "Sit! It's OK. He won't do anything to you," he would say to me.

But I wasn't used to it [sitting near strangers] and my uncle knew. Later I learned but I was shy. I was scared. I used to pull back. Everyone would look at me. My uncle used to say, "Forgive us, I apologise but this is her first time on a bus." My uncle used to tell them it was my first time and explain.

It was the same on the trains. Don't tell me about escalators, I'm still scared of them. Someone needs to hold me before I step on them. One day they didn't believe me [that I was scared]. My older brother knew me. He used to hold me tight. "Come come hold me," he would say. He would hold me. "Don't be scared, don't be scared come here. Come and nothing will happen to you."

"No, I won't come," So we were forced to leave from there.

MEHMET ŞEREF ALI: I didn't know anyone, so that when I was looking, I would see a useless crowd. From my left and right. I wasn't excited. No, I didn't have anything like that.

I said to Mustafa, "How are they like this? These people are like sheep." Yet in fact people were civilised. They wouldn't hit, touch you. "Sorry sorry, excuse me, excuse me," always like that, until we got to the pitch, about a quarter of a mile. That day is the moment I felt, "They are people." In truth they were humane. That is what I know. If you ask me, give me English, I would slaughter five of them. That is another issue. But when it comes to truth, they were humane. That is to say, there are some racist ones, there is every shit – excuse my language – but they have this humane side of them as well.

In short, that friend asked me, "Where are you gonna go this evening?" I said "I don't go anywhere, I go to the cinema sometimes." I didn't use to go anywhere else.

He said, "Let's go to a pub to dance. Do you know?"

I said, "I know," but in Cyprus, I went to a cabaret for a couple of times at the age of 18. I said, "I could even do this dance in my dream." There was the School of Dancing around Lambeth Bridge. We went there. It's rude to say, but there was 500 girls and five guys inside there.

I said, "What is this?" There weren't any men at all! He said, "Whichever one takes your fancy!"

It's rude to say, but it was heaven. I was a young boy then of course.

IBRAHIM DERVIŞ: I have never felt left out of society here. In the early times, yes, you are foreigners. For example, at work an elderly English man came to repair the electrics, and we were chatting away in Turkish among ourselves.

"By the way, where do you come from?" asked the Englishman.

"We are Turkish," we said.

"Ooooooh! You beat the British in the Dardanelles," he said.

"But what were you doing there?" we asked. "What was your business there?"

"Yes you are right," he said.

12. WEATHER

Until the Clean Air Act of 1956, the fogs of London – affectionately termed "pea-soupers" for their thickness – had not only been a byword for centuries, but a shocking health hazard. The output of millions of coal fires and thousands of factory chimneys combined with local conditions to produce a smog that – at its worst in 1952 – killed 4,000 people, at the minimum official estimate. Two very hard, long winters also fall into the era covered by this book: snow lay for three months or more in 1947 and 1962 – 63 across most of the UK, the latter being the coldest winter since 1740.

DUDU HAKKI: There was lots of fog. In those years you would be walking, and if you walked into a post box, you would think it was a person. You couldn't see. You couldn't see the red post box. It was pitch black. The ground and the sky was one in winter. I was in the dark for six months.

People used to burn coal in the houses, factories, and everyone used to think the smoke was the country's weather. People used to think this country's weather is no good. But look now: it wasn't the weather, it was the coal. But it was winter. Winter was really bad. There was snow for six months.

But there was no fear. I wasn't afraid. You weren't scared to walk around in the streets until morning, because people were very friendly.

MELEK KAZIM: When I first went out of the door to go to the shop I was ohhh! very scared! Very scared! I remember focusing on this smell – there was this really bad smell. The smell was not due to coal, but due to these white plants, they smelt a lot. They were in the hedges of houses. When they flowered, they would really smell. There are none left now. I could not eat. For six months I would cry, I did not want to stay there. I didn't like it here. My mother used to tie a rope to us, because the weather was misty and for her not to lose us, because you could not see who was near you. It was misty.

I would pass time at home well, feeding two children, changing nappies, their tea, then we would play games…

NEVCIVAN JEVAN: In those days there was so much fog. I am not used to frost, ice. I used to get up in the mornings, I was 18 years old. I used to get up in the morning, go to bus stop, wait for an hour in that ice. It was dark, pitch black. I was taking bus to Wardour Street. I went there to work. Firstly we used to do pleating, afterwards we went on to machine.

KEMAL AHMET DAVRANDI: We got married in 1962, she was pregnant with Şensal, she was due any day. I worked in the cake factory, and she worked in Newington Green, dressmaking. It was foggy, and I didn't know what fog was at the time. The boss said we could leave early. I left and went out on the street to get the bus home. I wait, and every bus that comes is full. I thought I should walk to a another bus stop, and I walked. Full again. Walked to another bus stop, full again. I got to Holloway Road. I came from Kentish Town to Holloway Road by walking. I looked and Finsbury Park was full as well. There was smoke. "Oh, a fire must have broken out," I thought. I walked into that darkness and got lost. It was fog! I didn't know what fog was.

You couldn't see a thing. You walk onto a lamp post and say "Sorry!" You walk into someone and don't realise. The railings of Finsbury Park came to my mind. I held onto the railings and walked to Manor Park. The buses couldn't be seen anymore. The lights outside were faint. I went to Manor Park, and was now just standing there. This road goes to Newington Green, I said, this road goes to Tottenham. "And if I turn left, I get to Haringey," I said.

A lady was crying, in Turkish she was saying, "Oh my dear children I am going to die, save me!" while bawling and bawling.

"What should I do?" I thought. I went over to where she was crying, to where the scream was coming from. I look and see the woman. "What's wrong auntie?" I asked.

"Oh my son, you are a godsend," she said.

"What's wrong, auntie?" I say.

"I'm lost. I need to go to Newington Green, but I don't how," she says.

"Take this road, auntie," I say to her. "No right no left – it will take you straight to Newington Green."

"For the love of God, son, come and take me there. I'll give you £100 to take me there."

"But auntie, I'll get lost," I say. "I'm going to Haringey," I say to her. "My wife was at work, I need to go home – she is due to give birth any day now. How can I take you?"

She wrapped herself around me pleading and wouldn't let me go. "Go on leave me" I said-"Go on, go your way!"

At last I said, "I'll get lost if I take you." I left the woman there shouting, "You can't go." I turned and went home. I open the door and look in. No one there. No Fezile [my sister], no Emine [my wife]. See my son. I couldn't stand it in there, so I turned and went back out. I went all the way to Newington Green and found the factory that my wife was working in. I knocked and knocked, the lights were off. The factory was closed. I went back home. Fezile was home, Emine was home. She came home along the same road as me but I was unable to see. How could I have? Fezile had walked from Camden Town. I got up in the morning coughing. Jet black was coming from my mouth. From my mouth, from my nose.

EMINE AHMET: Afterwards we bought this three-storey house on Balfour Road in Highbury Park. We came to the house. Where are you going to sleep? Sit down? There were still tenants, Turkish tenants in the house. Plastic bags were hung on the windows. Neither a glass nor a shutter, and that year there was snow for six months. We bought the house.

FEZILE AHMET: London is not like I hoped. I'll tell you what I expected and you'll laugh. In Cyprus we don't cover up when we are harvesting, while working because of the heat. I even packed my headscarf because I thought I would be working in the fields.

It seems like a lie to you but I swear to God that's the truth. The aeroplane flies on top of the clouds, but I didn't know this at the time. As we were flying over, "Oh my God, how are we going to work over here with this much snow?" I said. Clouds looked like piles and piles of snow. I swear to God.

When I came it was covered in snow here. There was snow, lots of snow. One night, I'll tell you this too, as it will make you laugh. It was foggy. There used to be lots of fog. Apparently they telephoned the Jewish man and told him to send all his workers home early as it was going to be really really foggy. The pimp didn't tell us about the warning! I come to Camden Town and was standing around, people are coming and going around me. I'm standing there and I don't know English to ask for directions. Then a Greek woman came up to me and asked me if I knew any Greek. I told her that I did.

She asked, "What are you waiting for?"

"I'm waiting for the bus to go home," I said.

"There are no buses," she said. "Haven't you heard? The buses have stopped and are not going anywhere, there is too much fog. People are going to walk home." What was I going to do? I was stranded. I had walked from Kentish Town to Camden, and then walked with the Greek woman from Camden Town to Holloway Road. *Allah inandirsin seni, Vallahi!*

I don't know if we left work at five or six, but by the time we got to Holloway Road there was so much fog that the police had tied cloths to their sticks, to show people the way to go. I swear to God. Well, anyway. The Greek woman asked me if I could find my way home from here. How could I? She could speak English. She then said, "Come, come and stay at our place and you can leave in the morning."

Yes, but I didn't want to stay with them, I then took a road and started walking but where was I heading? If they were to stick a finger in your eye you wouldn't see them. All you could hear was *tik tik* the footsteps.

I said, "Excuse me," to a man.

"Yes?" he said.

"I want Finsbury Park Station, please," I said.

"You go wrong way, you come with me." he said. So where was he going to taking me now, I thought? Who would understand? I'm going off with a man. Where could I go?

"I have had it now," I said to myself. Anyway, my God this may seem a lie to you but the young man took me to the station. We went inside the station. He looked tall to me.

"What language do you speak?" he asked me.

"Turkish," I said.

"Come with me," he said. He took me to where the people were coming out of the station and asked, "Anybody speak Turkish? Anybody speak Turkish? Anybody speak Turkish?" I swear to God, like this. Nobody knew Turkish. Then a Greek man jumped in and asked me where I want to go in Greek.

I said, "Haringey."

"I have taken three or four people there already. I will put you on the train and you go one stop to Manor House. You can go to Haringey from there," he said in Greek.

"OK," I said. They offered to pay for my ticket as well. But I said, "No, I have money." I took my money out and gave it to him to buy me my ticket. So I went one stop on the underground but I'm still scared. There was a black lady near me on the tube. "Excuse me," I said.

"Yes," she said.

"Is this Manor House station?"

"Yes," she said and I got off. I swear to God, it may seem like a lie to you, but I went up the stairs to look outside. It was pitch black! I turned and went back down the stairs. "I'm going to stay here till morning," I said to myself. I sat there. Believe it or not, I looked up and saw the Greek woman that I see on the bus every day. She was slightly crippled. She was with her husband and I told her, "I don't know the way, so I'm going with you. It's dark and I can't find my way."

"Where do you live? I'll take you home," she said. I swear to God, believe it or not, I was on one of her arms and her husband on the other. She took me right to my door. I was living at 73 Kimberley Gardens then.

I didn't trust the first Greek woman but I had no choice, otherwise I would have had to stay in the station. I didn't know the first Greek woman, but this one I used to see on the same bus every day. We used to go and come on the same bus. I didn't know where she lived, but I used to see her on the bus every day. We went and knocked on the door. They opened the door for us. I thanked the Greek woman. It took me three hours to get to my home. I didn't go work for three days.

13. THE TROUBLES

For the political context of these stories, see the chronology on page 13. For biographies of some of the major figures, see key to names on page 237.

FEZILE AHMET: The situation in Cyprus in 1962-63 affected us a lot. We used to run home at night to sit in front of the television to watch what was happening. I can't say how other Turks felt because there wasn't many here. We didn't meet many other Turks here. We stayed amongst ourselves, me, my brother and the housekeeper. There just wasn't many other Turks.

ŞABAN LEFKARIDI: I joined the marches of course. There used to be marches in Trafalgar Square. Our big leaders, Kenan Evren, came here. Other people came here. We used to go everywhere. At that time we used to go, we didn't have many Turks. It used to start from Trafalgar Square and we used to go wherever we were going to go we went in London.

Let's say what they were gonna do, we saw in the newspapers that would come here. Turks used to meet each other at the cafés. So we used to hear from each other. When there was the Troubles in 1963 I was worried, of course. Because my family, my mother was in Taşkent.

There used to be so much turmoil in Cyprus, yet we used to mix, in truth. That is to say, my barber has always been a Greek man.

We knew some wanted to take advantage of this conflict. Somebody else used to cause trouble, and they would take advantage or benefit from it. Now, let's say some caused this turmoil in Cyprus for their own benefit, to take advantage of it. But in fact, they did harm to both sides.

We didn't use to talk about Cyprus issue here. We were still neighbours in 1963, but we never spoke about Cyprus issue. No. Politics. Like here now, we come here now [Southwark Cypriot Centre], but we don't speak politics. It was the same then. In the cafés, in the clubs, we used to mix and there was nothing. No one looked for an opportunity to talk about it. From respect, not fear. Why should there be fear! We were not afraid of each other, because we live in a different country. For all of us this country is the same, isn't it?

IBRAHIM MUSTAFA: We used to see what was going on in Cyprus in 1963 on the news. The problems. We used to go out to the Turkish houses and collect some money. This is for our village to make a hospital there. We used to collect money from the village people, we used to send the money to the village, and they made a hospital in Cyprus. In Akıncılar.

Later on organisations started collecting money for all the Cypriots, all the Turkish Cypriot people. It was people from my village. Even that thing still goes on, you know. They have, this organisation for our village which they do, they support the football team and everything. This organisation existed in 1963. I don't know where it was based, I can't remember.

We would hear what they needed in the village and then start collecting money.

There was a lot of people from Akıncılar here. A really large group of us. I have never involved in politics at all. I wasn't interested in politics at all. I don't know their politics, it doesn't bother me. But I kept in with my villagers. They used to get together. They used to decide we need to help the village. The hospital is still there now. Because the doctor goes there once a week. It is still there and is still being used.

EMINE AHMED: We use to hear the news about the events in 1963 from television. My mother and father were there. Nothing happened to our village because our village was all Turkish. Nothing happened. Bayar my son was eight, nine years old.

In 1963. The year I gave birth to Şensal, they didn't tell me [that her brother was missing]. They heard that my brother was lost, Cypriots held him with my aunt's son while going from one village to another village by van, they lost them, they didn't tell me. After a long time, suddenly someone blurted out and told me. They warned most of them, even the corner shops, in order not to tell me that my brother was missing. I was here when my brother went missing. My brother went missing in 1963. My brother went missing the year Şensal was born. Those Greeks, Greek Cypriots, held him, so that neither dead, nor alive. With my aunt's son.

I learned that he was missing after three, four months. Because I used to go to work, I used to work with Greek people. There were a couple of Turks there but most of them were *Rum*. There was a corner shop in Newington Green. Then I was staying in Newington Green. They warned owner of the shop, his wife was from Sinde. They warned them so that they wouldn't mention that my brother was missing while I am in there. Then they didn't tell me, suddenly somebody else told me. "Mercy, I felt pity to him, aren't there any news?" she said. I say "What?" The wife of the shop owner indicated to the woman to stop talking, so she wouldn't tell me. I insisted. The shop owner's wife said to me, "You are going to hear it anyway, so and so," she said. I couldn't do nothing. What can I do? It is not within your power. Following year we left and went, no, I couldn't go the following year either. I went to Cyprus after him but that is to say we used to get the news from the people going and returning.

I wrote a letter to them, that is to say we wrote a letter. At that time we couldn't send news either, I wrote letter saying, "I am sad, if you hear any news, let us know." Later on we went for holiday. My mother said to me, "If your brother comes back," she said to me, "If your elder one comes, are you gonna leave and come?" she said to me. I said, "I would come, why shouldn't I come?" She says to me, "I cannot believe what happened to your brother. I believe that he is going to knock on the door and come in, that is what I know," she used to say. She never accepted that my brother was lost, they killed him. She never accepted until she died. "He doesn't have a grave," she said, "so I can't go and visit." They took him, captured him as prisoner. "One day, they are going to knock on the door and come in, that is how I know," she said. After the war we gave up hope of him. He was younger than me. After 1974 because we thought if he was a prisoner, they might hand him over him, but I said, "Which one did they send out of all the prisoners?"

IBRAHIM AHMET: 95% of the people who were here used to go to those marches with flags. Young and old people. How many of the present youth go now days but we were patriotics then. Today's youngsters are not patriotics. Sin.

EMINE MEHMET: I used to see what was going on in Cyprus on the television. It was all in front of our eyes. When they were all running. I used to see it all on the television. I was young then, I had a nervous breakdown. I didn't go to work for six months I think. I stayed home and would be running to the doctors from worry.

We had letters from them, dear, but infrequently. Very infrequently. My mum left Anafodia and went to Köfünye. She stayed there. They gave them one room. They left everything.

There were Turkish organisations back then. We used to go on marches with them all. First demonstration. We moved to start walking, and there was this young girl holding the flag, the Turkish Flag – she was walking with the people. My deceased brother, God rest his soul, who died of a heart attack, this English girl Margaret took my brother's arm, and the two of them walked and the police stared. They realised that Margaret was English. She held out the flag in front of her, and walked with my brother in the crowd. They were looking at her. In that period of time. The first demonstration happened in that Association. Very important. There were lots of young people then.

I went to the club at that period of time. We used to all go together. Families would go on the marches. The whole community would be called. All the Turks, as many as there were, would go out on the street. The police would wait as the community marched.

The Association would arrange the march. The Directors of the Association would plan the march. The Turks were very united then. They had come to the country recently. They would run to support each other. There's nothing like that now. They used to get news to each other, probably by telephone. They use to let each other know that there will be a demonstration here, and so and so. There was my deceased husband, my brother was there, I mean there was lots of people. I used to bring my eldest child in her pram. When I gave birth again five-and-a-half years later, there were no demonstrations. The big one was there in a small pram. I would push her. They used to shout things about Cyprus on the marches. They had marches three or four times, but I was unable to go to them, but I was there on that first one. I couldn't go after that because I was working. I was helping my husband. I had a child, then the other one was born. It was a little difficult.

Political Rally, London, 1950s. Image courtesy of Cyprus Turkish Association Archive

ALI GASBAR: As we couldn't be there in the war, we would frequently collect and send amongst us aid in the form of clothing and finance. A lot of our friends went first to Turkey, then Cyprus to Eren Köy, to join and fight for the cause. Of course the most help had come from the Turkish public.

MEHMET ALI BEKIR: We wanted to go to Cyprus in 1963, when the wars started. And of course I was married at that time, I just got married then. We wanted to fight in Cyprus too. They didn't accept us. They only asked for money aid from us. Because they informed us that they couldn't enlist us in the army, that is why we used to give money aid.

In those days for example, money was collected from everyone. I didn't become a member of the Association here. But I was aware of it. I don't remember any marches because of the conflict over there, but of course, we were affected a lot here. Why were we affected? Of course there are two things. With the two religions, we were affected a lot because for example Cypriots and Turks couldn't live together. For instance in our time as we lived together with the Cypriots, we were together in our weddings, on the new year, over Christmas time we were together, so suddenly when such things erupted it made us really sad.

And also, of course, because of people's ignorance. Allah gave you brain for you to be able to think, this soul comes to this world only once, not twice. If I were to give you the whole London, would you give your life? That is it! I mean a human being doesn't have to think too much.

Until 1974 it didn't affect us that much because Cypriots mostly used to fight in their area. Of course it affected us because they used to kidnap us, waylay us. Before Turkey disembarked troops, they would have fights a lot amongst themselves, and for example here, my closest friends, when I was with my Cypriot friends, they were looking forward for Turkey to attack.

In '63 I went to Cyprus. After I got married there was an issue and I had to go to Cyprus. I went by plane. Those planes used to fly from Greece; we used to go to Cyprus from Athens. I went. Over there birth certificate was needed for my sister's children and when I went, Cypriots asked me where I came from. I told them that I was coming from England. And we started talking, and some of them ask when Turkey is going to hit, they would rescue us Cypriots. They were expecting to be rescued in 1963. In 1963, they say, whenever planes come and go and they wouldn't rescue us. Cypriots used to say these. In 1974, when Turkey hit, then the Cypriots here were very happy as the Cypriots were rescued. But they started to mix politics

EMINE AHMET: We listened to the radios to hear what was happening in Cyprus in 1963. How would you feel? You cry, shout, we used to wait by the radio before we went to bed.

I have never gone on the marches here. But I went in Cyprus a lot. I used carry a flag saying "Ya ölüm Ya Taksim" [Either Death or Partition] from 6 o'clock in the morning till 12 o'clock at night during Osman Ürek 's time.

HÜSEYIN HASSAN MEMOUR: I don't keep in touch with any of the people from Lurigina. It is very unusual, because I don't have any social things. I am not politically minded.

NIAZI OSMAN: I used to go to weddings. I used to go my relatives' weddings. I used to have a membership for the Turkish Association. I think it was called that, and I carried around a membership card. Not any more. No, I didn't go on marches. I didn't mix to those.

I don't like politics, I am not very into politics. I don't like those kind of problems, in fact I do worry when I hear something against us. I will do whatever I can do when they want help, but I didn't want to mix that much. I didn't used to want to mix.

ÇETIN KAYA MUSTAFA: In 1963. When was that, [that] a war [last] broke out there?*

OK, towards New Year's Day there was Hüseyin Russo. He was here, and I saw him. We heard it from him; we saw him in the cafés, he came a couple of times.

---

* 21 December 1963: intercommunal violence explodes.

He was here, and as soon as the conflicts occurred Hüseyin Russo went and he became a veteran there in Küçük Kaymaklı.

In those days many Turks prepared to go to Cyprus to help over there. Clothes were sent, they used to do a few things in those days. Well, we went there and took a photo, my brother went and I stayed.

I think I heard about the conflicts in 1963 on the radio, something like that. From radios I think. We used to hear, and letters. Not through letter, mostly from radios. We used to hear it in the cafés. It is true. It is heard, they say, "The bad news is heard quickly." I went once to one of the marches here, Kenan Evren was coming here. He came to Buckingham Palace, something like that. But I didn't join all the time. I don't like saying lies at all.

HÜSEYIN YUSUF: Oh, ye. I was aware of what was going on in Cyprus in the 60s, early 1963, when I was in the merchant navy. I was informed through the media. News. BBC things like that.

Well, to be honest with you I have been away all these years, I wasn't really an extreme while we are in the navy, I wasn't very interested in politics. All I was hoping was there was a settlement, and that everybody would be happy. But I wasn't a fanatic, anything like that. Because I had lots of Greek friends as well… who were working on the ship. There was a lot of Greek boys as well. And when I used to come home I had some Greek friends, we used to go around with. Even 1974, when the war was on, I used to work on the QE2 in 1974, '75 I finished. There was a lot of Greek boys on there. We came to a conclusion. We had a meeting, "Look, we have know each other for a long time, we are not politically involved, we are living in a different country."

I said, "In my opinion, the way I feel, we shouldn't get involved in politics. We should stay friends. We should sort of carry on the way we were." Neutral. There was a lot of them said, "No, Joe!". They used to call me Joe. Yusuf–Joseph. Don't worry about it. No problems with it. I didn't have any problems at all. I speak Greek as well as Turkish. A lot of people from Aytotoro can speak Greek.

GÜLSEN LARKINS: We used to see what is happening in Cyprus on the television. Of course, we used talk about what was going on as a family. God rest her soul, my mum used to talk about the Greeks. There was still fear. From that time they would kill some Turks.

HULUSI MAHMUD: I wanted to join the political group here, but I never get round to it. Because you get too much involved to you. At that time I didn't have power to do it. Because you need to work to look after your life, to live comfortably. If you join them, they might ask you to do some work voluntarily, and I can't afford to do that. I did go on the marches a couple of times. Long time ago. I don't go now. In the 60s I went a couple of times you know, just to join the march. They were all right. They have started from Trafalgar Square, Hyde Park.

When there was the troubles in 1963, having your mum and dad [in Cyprus], you were a bit sad about it. You can't help what happened. You are worried, but you know it was all right until last minute. They just took them away. After they moved the other side my dad only lived three years. He died, because like bird, a *bülbül*, you know, a nightingale. You caught them in the cage, he doesn't like it, he wants freedom. That is the way it happens to all people's life. I mean I went there in 1974, I have been there, the place where I have been born and bred and spend my youthful life, see what was going on, what was happening you know.

IBRAHIM DERVIŞ: When the events started in Cyprus in 1955 – 58, we of course were very concerned. We tried to help in every way we could. I was the seventh member. I still carry my rosette. We helped more after 1963. I would have to say that in reality, we didn't have much activity before then. We had meetings, 5,000 people, the "biggest demonstration ever seen in London," said the Evening News. Doctor Küçük came over, I think in 1956, '57 or '58.

 We passed by Fleet Street, where the newspapers were then: children in prams and all, we went through Holborn and to Trafalgar Square. It was the same situation as in India and Pakistan, a political partition by the English, and so on, they said. It was a very big crowd.

MUSTAFA HÜSEYIN: The marches started later on. In '58 when EOKA came about, for instance, we used to always go on a march, for example against the Greeks. Of course I went on them.

It was against them we used to go. Later on when the Republic was established all of us, altogether we protested that Enosis shouldn't happen. We Turks don't accept Enosis, 100%. Because when it was first established the intention of the English was to make Cyprus attached to Greece. If there wasn't any problem.

We used to always start from club and walk up to Hyde Park, or Whitehall. Quite a lot joined the march. In those days, people were more attached to each other. In those days, 200, 300, 400, 500 people used to march with Turkish flags. People were more nationalist then. Don't look at it now, they found everything lavishly and [with that] they have forgotten everything. Now for example in Cyprus they have started, "Peace, peace, peace!" Ya, there is peace. Do you want any other kind of peace? You sleep at home in comfort. The Army waits on duty. You have no fear. You are free. This is peace. Peace came in 1974.

People with kids used to go on the marches, with their kids, single ones with their friends. Of course all of the news about Cyprus was coming from this place. It used to always come to the Turkish embassy, that used to inform the Association. The Association used to inform us. I haven't gone for a long time. Since the 80s, I haven't gone there. It still continues in D'Arblay Street.

I stopped because I used to work in the City. I didn't have time to leave and go there. That is it, it didn't suit me. Later on television came about, we learned everything from the television. In 1963 I was married, I had a child. I got married in 1963, my big son was born right when I found out that Cengiz Topel became martyr.

CELAL HASSAN: The political situation when I came to England, it wasn't bad. It wasn't so much. Only a few bombs thrown in Nicosia, here and there, but not many in those days. After a couple of years they started this. '58, '59, they started to put, you know, in the village, this and that, and we hear the news from the radio you know. Some friends had a television, we used to go there and look at it.

SÜHA FAIZ: It was unstable, it was not a place you would like to bring up your children in. But as events showed, we were wrong and we learned this in 1974.

And the answer to your question is from 1960 to 1974 I am living in England, content with my selfishness if you like, with my personal life, my mother is safe and secure, she has lost everything, the house is now ruined but you get this episode of the 1974 and my feeling then, it is put in the book, was "Thank God."

Between 1963 – 64 my mother had actually lost her house, in January 1964, and we were in Canada. She came across with my brother, he was by then in England. It is a long story. She was then secure. During that period, between my mother coming to England and our return from Canada, and 1974, as far as I am concerned I am English, I am Mr Fair.

MEHMET ŞEREF ALI: I was in the army in this country. I had been in the army for five months. I was a foot soldier and telephone operator. Something came up. I heard something that they wanted a translator in Cyprus. That is to say, we can go to Cyprus as a translator. I went of course; I applied for it. They accepted it. Last decision had been given. We came back to camp of course. They would grant you 15 day leave. It is called embarkation leave. That is to say, when you go abroad they would grant you 15 days leave. They granted me that leave, as well the leave to go abroad. I forgot the exact date. We went to Kasra, a place where I do my army service. We boarded on a plane, came to Orly Airport in France. Foot soldiers, paratroops, RAFs gather over there, from left and right. There are two army planes. Maybe it can contain 350 people, soldiers.

They call full kit, I would stand, he would announce your name in alphabetic order, Albert, Almond... But as the Bs finished, there is no one who announces our name. The whole thing, how should I say, an airport, pitch, like a football pitch. All of them finished, they boarded inside, I stayed there. "I didn't hear my name," I said. I wonder if I didn't hear. "We didn't call you so that's why you didn't hear," he said to me. I asked him why. "You can't go to Cyprus," he said. I said, " What is the reason? Why can't I go?" "You can't go!" he said. I said again, "Why can't I go?" A newspaper in that pimp's hand, I wonder where he found it from. He said to me, "When you go to Cyprus, on which side are you gonna be?" I said, "I have been a soldier for a long time, how can you ask which side?" He said to me, "I wonder if you saw today's newspaper." "Which newspaper?" I said. Daily Mirror. I said, "But that is in England. Is there here as well?" He unfolded it and showed me the newspaper" 'British soldier had a clash with Turks.' At Kyrenia Gate. I think that was 28 December 1957.

Well, at that time, I don't know, that is how it is. Turks clashed with English soldiers and so on. Possibly he thought this boy might be in the Movement. "Anywhere in the world," he said to me, "but not to Cyprus." I shouted and argued angrily, but came back [to base].

There had been another situation. When we went back you had to have a duty. It had been five months, six months. I said, "I should learn morse, wireless." Now we should tell the truth, I improved my English that much. We got used to it, from one up to 10 in morse. I can receive them but I can't send, when it comes to giving an answer I can't do it. And also I had very little writing – and lots of girls! I'm not boasting. We shouldn't be proud, but why lie now? One, two, three... I said to the sergeant, "I am going to give up from this job."

He asked me why.

"I don't even understand that job," I said.

Tak, the doors had been opened. Three English people came inside. RP, that is to say, Regimental Police.

"Signal man?"

"Yes."

"Come with us." Good God! We went. *Tak tuk* he writes. I asked, "What have I done?".

"In a minute, in a minute!" Then they said, "We are giving you to the Court Martial." You know, the High Court.

I said, "What happened? What did I do? Why?"

"You are a bloody liar," one of them said to me.

I said, "Don't talk to me like that. What did I say it was a lie?"

"I'll tell you." This is someone with one star. That one had gone, another one came. Still I don't know what is going on. In the end, another person would come, that one is not one of the people I know. He is from our camp's men.

I said "Sir," I said, "What happened? What is going on?"

He said "Did you fill in this form?" I filled in the form so that I can work in morse department, asking about any imprisonment, how old you are, what you do, all family details. For security reasons. Well, in Cyprus I did something with my motor, I had been imprisoned there. In fact it was a fine, it was a three lira fine. As there wasn't money, imprisonment for 20 days.

Chief Inspector said, "He asked you, 'Have you been in prison?,' and you said no. But it is a lie, now."

I said "Look, I should say something to you. It is not written here whether I was imprisoned in England or not. How would I know?" I said, "I didn't know I was asked about my imprisonment in Cyprus."

"That is a good point," said the one with two stars.

We attended the court, well, military court, not the Court Martial but the one before. They had a conversation. I used to get on with the captains.

One said, "You should look at everything carefully," he said to me.

I said "How was I to know?" I told him the reason that I was fined and then I was imprisoned. Neither I stole anything, nor I spied on anyone.

"But," he said, "morse is a secret."

I said, "I already gave up, I don't want your morse either." I wouldn't be able to pass the examination, why should I tell a lie? If it was today maybe, at that time I wouldn't be able to pass.

There was an old man, he said, "Change your regiment, there's the Intelligence regiment, go there."

"They found my shit in morse, how are they gonna recruit me into Intelligence?"

"Apply," he said. So I applied. Of course in that regiment you need to know a language. Anyway, they called me. There was someone called Major Kos, they called us. A person sits next to me. I asked him, "What are you doing here?" We went for an interview of course.

"I will become a translator," he said.

"What languages do you know?" I asked.

"I know Greek," he said. I speak to him in Greek and he doesn't even know one word.

"But you don't know any Greek," I said. "Here you are", "Sit down", three words, five words, that was it all. He was called, he went in of course. I know Greek, Turkish, I worked in Egypt for seven, eight months, I learned some Arabic. By the way I had an Italian girlfriend, I'd learned five or ten words in Italian! Well, bachelorhood then! When they called me of course, they asked how many languages I knew. But when he came out I asked him, "What happened?"

"I passed," he said.

I said, "Good God!" That is to say, if he passed with that Greek then I should pass with my Italian and Arabic, as well. He called us, I went inside. He asked me "What do you know?"

I answered, "Six."

He asked, "What do you know?"

I said, "Good English, bad English." He laughed. But first I counted, "Turkish, Greek, Arabic, good English, bad English."

"I know good English, but I don't know bad English," he said.

"I know all swearing words, I know all of them."

There was an Association. It was in West End, we couldn't go many times. I had a job, inappropriate hours, there weren't many transports then like there is today. The weather wasn't appropriate. There were times, we couldn't go out for three days. It was snowy.

I didn't become a member of the Association. I did go on one of the marches in uniform – I didn't know that it wasn't allowed. Luckily I didn't get caught. They took picture as well. I don't know at all what happened to that picture.

ALI HASSAN: We used to hear what was going on in Cyprus because we was all involved in the walks, protests, now these days they don't even do protests. Now everyone, saying it might sound rude [...] has sat in the chair and stayed like that. They wait for someone to cook for them, and to bring the plate to them. Us in those days, when we did protests, we used to wake up the West End. When we started these protests we used to walk shouting. We used to go all the way to Downing Street and protest. There were more than a hundred people. There were thousands.

There was a Turkish Association. Of course we used to get everyone's news from there. The clubhouse in D'Arblay Street. Everything about Cyprus was first heard of from there. There was no radio, and because we used to act straight after hearing any news, if there was a protest, even on a work day we'd close up and go. Yes, women, children, everyone would go. Now, to be honest we can't really walk anymore, we've got old now. We can't take part in walks, the shouting and screaming. In fact even after 1974, when we did walks to protest, we used to shout. Shouting and shouting: "Turks in, Greeks out, Turks in, Greeks out," for the Turkish army. We went round shouting and screaming in the West End. In Trafalgar Square. Around there it would get crowded, and Trafalgar Square would get packed up. That many Turks would go. When you'd see that Trafalgar Square it was full.

The people from the association used to do the talks. There's a few people from *Galatya*, they used to talk. Of course I didn't even know them. But for me knowing them wasn't important. I wanted to show them some support. And towards them we used to show our support. Like, if there was protest and you didn't go, you might as well have changed your religion. Already from when we came, walks were happening anyway. We came in 1957 and there were walks often. Well, I'm not sure how many there were in a year, I'm not going to be able to be precise, but it wasn't just one or two times. The walks would happen five times a year. Everybody used to walk, everybody used to go. We used to start at the Association, we'd get our lines which we were to shout out, we'd get our signboards in our hands or whatever it was we needed. In 1958 the English army went to Famugusta, some Turks made fires in Famagusta, we got anxious, even for that we did a walk here. In Cyprus as soon as one Turk died, a walk would take place here.

We used to shout out the reasons for the walks of that time, for whatever reason it was happening, for example, "Stop Killing!" – stop it, don't kill the Turks – "Cyprus is ours," there was all sorts of things. Ask the nation, whoever you want, the people of that time will tell you. When there was a walk there was a walk. The streets used to get packed.

Political Rally, London, 1950s. Image courtesy of Cyprus Turkish Association Archive

Mostly everybody used to take part in the walks. There was hardly anybody who didn't take part in the walks in those times. The walks carried on after 1963 as well.

Volkan was an organised group before the TMT. Some tried to form the TMT, some tried to form the, the, I don't know what, and in Famagusta it was the Volkan. The members didn't know each other. We mustn't know the others [members] because if I was to get caught then I could burn [ruin] you and them.

We would join by, I know you, you know them, the other doesn't know me, the other would know someone else. In this way, in other words. You would swear on the Koran to become a member. You used to swear that under no circumstance would you burn/ruin others [members]. That if I get caught I would go to prison, and that's it. There was no "I know you." You didn't know.

Volkan was an organised group: if you gathered, the English would arrest you. For example I would carry out the work with you, and you would carry out work with someone else. It was a chain. We used to rule ourselves. Papers used to come to us. We didn't know who was really at the top. We used to get orders telling us what to do. "This and this is to be done today." The papers would be distributed. They used to be put under the door at night for us. There was no army in Cyprus at the time. The was a top person at that time. I'll say someone like *Denktaş* to you. He used to get the little papers sent out to everyone. Tomorrow there will be a march, the shops will close. We used go and knock on each door and close the shops. The had to close. If they don't close we would do dirty things. In any case, everyone listened when it was said. There was no need for that.

No, I don't know of any groups in London other than those in D'Arblay Street then. We didn't get involved with things like that here. We used to hear what was happening in Cyprus from them. They used to learn what was happening. We didn't used to ask, "Where did you learn this from?" of them.

And it was the truth. There wasn't nothing like "going to deceive you" at that time.

You could see it on the television anyway. When something happened in Cyprus at that time, you would let it be known that there was going to be a march that weekend. In other words if you heard that three Turks had been shot in Famagusta, then you would expect a march to happen.

We used to go on marches together with the children and all we had. Even to the youngest child, we would take with us. They used to look out for each other on the marches. Now they do marches and people walk over you. We have become wild, instead of becoming modern, we have become wilder. In that time everyone used to walk orderly on the marches. The police would by the side

And you would go in threes or fours. Is there anyone who walks with discipline now? Look now, they hold the flag as if they are holding a rag.

In 1960 when the Republic was established, I went back because the army was going. I stayed for three weeks. I went back again in 1966.

14. GOING BACK

EMINE MEHMET: I went back ten years after I came. My mother was still in the village. They had not left their home in Anafodia. When I went and the villagers heard, and they said Ibrahim's daughter has arrived. But which daughter? We were three sisters. They didn't know which one.

My mother's doors were open, because in Anafodia everywhere is open, the café, everything. The Greek Clubs, the Turkish clubs, the schools they were all there. Her doors opened and all the crowd from cafés came. I did not recognise any of those that came, I talk but don't recognise people – some talk in Greek and some talk in Turkish.

I stayed there for three weeks. I went there by plane, the *Olympia*, a small plane. I think we landed somewhere else first but I don't know where.

HULUSI MAHMUD: In 1969 I went [to Cyprus] the first time for a holiday. I was with the kids and everybody took on the rooftops with guns and so on. Gardens, roads, the tanks – it was kind of Civil War.

I didn't think of staying because you have to come back to London, because you are from there. You have got no home there any more in Cyprus. So that is how it was. You have got to go where your life is.

I felt like England was now my home. I live in the council place. When I go, I am going home because that's where you live. So that is your home.

NIAZI OSMAN: I didn't go back till 1988, I didn't. I used to think those Greeks were very rich, this is an untrue propaganda, very rich. They used to say, "North Cyprus has been occupied by the Turkish army." Until now I used to believe that, I used think I am going to find soldiers everywhere. They even made me believe it. I mean, believe they are that rich, it is an untrue propaganda. I went, of course, the time the plane was going to land, my eyes started to water. I look and see, all civilians. In everyone's house very nice life. I was baffled at the Greek propaganda. I went back in 1988. My family used to came before then. I lost my deceased mum in 1963. My family used to come.

ALI HASSAN: When I came here I was not intending to stay and live here. After that in fact, in 1960, I sold the house in order to go back. My brother-in-law Hüseyin is there, he was a policeman. He'd say, "Ali, Ali, this stuff hasn't been sorted out yet, it's not finished, don't come." We returned, we got the other house in 1960, I sold it out of independence, to be able to return. Because however much safer it could have been, I was still a tailor myself, and working under someone else's management was a bit difficult. That's why. Because of that in 1961, '62 I opened a factory and became a bit independent.

GÜLSEN LARKINS: I went back to Cyprus after my nan died, after my grandmother died. I did want to go, but my husband didn't take me. His sister wouldn't let him go. We got married and we were going to go. He wanted to go. My mother heard and called him, and asked him for an explanation. He gave an explanation.

"They are newly wed, so as they want to go on holiday, they should go," my mother said.

I wanted to go to Cyprus. His sister stopped it.

SÜHA FAIZ: I come back to Cyprus with a degree to do what. A degree in law. But I was never a lawyer. And this is the other thing, now I don't know any Turkish at all. Totally gone.

Was I regarded as English? No, I am a Turk. I am Süha Faiz. No other Turks at the school. But there were one or two Pakistanis, one or two Indians. And one Greek Cypriot – now I can't remember it, maybe in Greek […] something. But we were very small, it didn't count – I mean we were English people at an English school, of rather exotic background. Nobody sort of said, speak to me in Turkish. Even if they had, I couldn't have done it anyway. I am thoroughly English, by those who wish to regard me as such, friends and so on. Even though I had this name, which is obviously – I am Ahmet Süha Faiz, right through my English period and when I go back to Cyprus, and then I join the colonial service, not Cyprus, I get sent to Africa, Gold Coast [now Ghana].

I am Ahmet Süha Faiz. I came back to Cyprus in 1946 with my degree, my father had died during the war, so I have a widowed mother and Münir Bey is alive. Münir is in a sense the head of the extended family. So anyway my mother and me, very properly go and take his advice. What do we do now, he has got his degree, very good degree, I wanted to be in Cyprus. Münir advices against, "Don't get an appointment in Cyprus," he says. "You will merely be like any other local appointee."

MELEK KAZIM: I used to write to all my aunts [my mother's sisters], my grandmother. My youngest aunt is still in Cyprus. It's just her alone left in Cyprus from my mother's side of the family. Her sister, I would write to her. I use to write telling them that I did not like it here at all, that it smelt here. I use to say that it smelt. I use to say, "The streets smelt of dogs." They still do. Ah yes, I did want to go back. I use to ask my mother, "Why have we come here? Let's go back." Her response would be, "We are here now, what are we going to do back there?" My mother very much loved it here, because she did not like the heat. She would become ill because of the heat. It was also freedom for her here.

EMINE AHMET: I went to Cyprus after eight years. 13 years later I went with my husband and kids. I missed everything about Cyprus.

REŞAT NIAZI: I started swimming in the river in the village. The river in Nicosia and sea all the time. Cycle to the sea. I still love the sea. That is what I miss. I went to Cyprus in 62. I fly there. I got some money from the Legion Office to help. I went back, with one way ticket. I wasn't quite sure if I would come back. I went there, if I say there was no work I would have been wrong. Because I knew I can always get a job in Cyprus, because my father was in the army and I was governmental, and I used to be in the RAF.

EMINE AHMED: When I think about it now, I don't know if I should have stayed in Cyprus. How should I know? If only I hadn't sold that house in Turnpike Lane, I wish I had kept it. Now I am in Cyprus again. OK. My children wanted here, I brought them and they studied, graduated, settled down, and got married. I was again in Cyprus but I regret selling that house. Because I suffered a lot of pain until I bought that house. When I bought that house with the kids, I felt relieved, I said, "I would work until morning until I pay its mortgage." Otherwise I suffered a lot from being a tenant.

IBRAHIM DERVIŞ: I went back to Cyprus to stay, but I saw the economic state was not good – that's why I came back. I stayed in Cyprus for about six months and then returned by boat with my wife. That was in 1951.

ALI HASSAN: After 1966 I started think of London as home. I have, I still have the intention [of going back]. If I go, I'll to the area of Çatal Köy, towards Kyrenia. I don't have family there, most of them have gone. I have a sister in Lefke. My sister in Lefke is old like me. That is to say we miss our land.

After the child's school has finished we are going to go and buy land there. We'll stay there for a while. In case my wife will retire with in a year. I'm 70 and she 60. Here we take, we work. In other words we don't say no to work. It's not the money, but it is important to gain the blessings from the elderly. My they keep us more lively. You run from here to there – exercise. I look after three elderly Turkish Cypriots here, one in Wood Green, one in Edmonton and one in Tottenham.

As I was leaving there [Cyprus], some members of authority, authority from the Union, said, "Come back in a year," but I saw that this problem was not going to be solved in a year or two. I said, "I will start my life here [London]. When the Cyprus problem has straightened out and strong foundations are laid, then I can return.'

HULUS IBRAHIM: I still have that intention. I went there and bought land in Cyprus. I researched about building a house there. I wasn't satisfied. I went to the ready-made houses. There was a newly built house. There were very nice newly built houses, and I liked them, so did my wife. We bought it for   £40, 000 in '95. We thought that when there is a solution to the Cyprus situation and dust will settle, we can retire there. I am retired and my wife is retired, well, she is unwell and still young, and we thought we could live there. But as the situation there hasn't straightened out we only go there twice a year, once for six weeks and once for seven weeks. We have an empty house there. Three bedrooms.

ÇETIN KAYA MUSTAFA: *Vallahi*, I tell the truth, I have never thought about anything like that [going back]. I came in 1961 and went back in 1963 my mum said to me that they found a nice girl and come, stay. No, before that they wanted me to be there, to go back; I mean for example my family didn't want me stay away from home. They would say to me, "Come, your dad needs someone in the shop to work," for example. I believed, in fact they wanted me to go there. When I went there, my deceased mum says, "I don't think we need someone in the shop, because we can barely making a living from."

"You wrote me in your letter," I say "That you want me. I have come, how am I going to work somewhere else now?" I didn't want to work somewhere else, either. I couldn't come all the way from London to work somewhere else. Because when you come from London, everyone says, "Look, he came from London." So you don't like to look for a job everywhere; you don't like that kind of thing. I said "I'd rather stay in London."

That was in 1963*. I came, didn't stay too long. I think for a couple of months, something like that. I didn't stay more than that. I booked my ticket from the beginning and went to London. I think when we came back with my mum in 1963, after a month, let's say. We came to London with my mum. We came to London and when we came to London my mum told me that she found a girl for me in Cyprus, and that I should go and get married to her, for example. In Cyprus. We came, my mum stayed for quite a while, for a month, something like that, I think. After that with my mum, we came to Cyprus by boat, yes, I remember. After that, then the Bayram† was close. I keep waiting to see the girl, who is this girl I am going to get marry? I don't know, they don't show her to me. I am waiting in front of the shop. Then I take a look, in those days, the people coming from London were very popular amongst the young generation. I have special shoes, nice, modern, they are different. Trousers are fashionable, something different. And when I put them on, when I went out, everyone used to look at me as if I was an artist, famous. Everyone comes to me, asks, "How is London?" I don't know. There was something which seemed strange to me. I saw, a friend came, but no, when I stood, when I went to Cyprus I found people backwards a lot. When you come here, you would speak, you would go and avoid from saying, "See you" I don't know why. This time, when people pass by, you call to speak to them. It was very different.

"Hey Ahmet, Hey Mehmet, come here, hey my good fellow, where are you?" Maybe they didn't see me, I don't know. They come, you talk and talk for example, when they are about to leave, they buried their head down and go. That is to say, he doesn't say, "Come on, see you later." We got used to it here, we say "See you", or "See you later" – this thing seemed strange to us. I mean here is a bit more awake, more advanced. I saw so many different things. But it is our place, we liked it, of course, and during the first days I kept looking. Who is this woman I am going to marry. I couldn't see her until Bayram finished. I could see her after that and I liked my wife. We went, got engaged, got married.

I stayed [in London] from '61 till '68. First we would come, for example, I mean when you go to Cyprus from here, if the friends over there, in Cyprus see you quite a lot for example, they ask what are you doing?

---

* He later corrects himself and says it was in 1967 or 1968.

† A religious festival

"I came for a holiday, I will go back." If they see you after a month, they start saying, "Aren't you still going back?" They start make fun of you. "You won't be able go to London, you are left as a Cypriot! Hey Londoner, you were gonna go back!" They used to say. I mean you get embarrassed this time.

"I am gonna go, it doesn't suit me, I am not ready yet."

"No, no, you can't go," they say. They make jokes. My morale would be affected. What should I do, I wanted to come back. I will tell you, when you first go back to Cyprus you would see your friends, your family. But then when I first went back, well, I went, for example London is a big place, as I said, and when I came to my mum's house, when I got up everywhere used to seem to me small and short. Houses, roads, everything.

IBRAHIM AHMET: In fact we have been taken as hostages here, first by our children and now by our grandchildren. We came here with an aim. I came here with an aim. I was going to save money and go. I came with seven-and-a-half lira in my pocket. They found a job for us in the basement floor and I used to wash the dishes. The wages was £5.

HÜSEYIN YUSUF: Actually I went back to Cyprus when I was working on a ship in 1969. We did a Mediterranean cruise and, we went to Famagusta with a ship I was working on. I took a day off. I applied to the captain; he gave me the day off. By the time we arrived, I went to the village, Aytotoro, and spent the day with the family, you know, and I then went back to the ship. It was nearly midnight.

I left Cyprus in 1949 and I went back 20 years later. I was, tell you like, I cannot explain it, but you know. I am always the same, when I do things, when I get reminded of them, I get goose pimples. I get funny feelings inside. I took a taxi from Famagusta to the village. As soon as I entered near the village I was dreaming all the times which passed and looking at the place, very little changed. I was really excited.

I was ashamed of myself because I wasn't a very good communicator with my family. I don't know for what reason, negligence, I used to write to them say I am all right. Not to worry, that was it. My mother used to be very upset. When I went there, in 1969, I went to the village to my house, she sort of, she was so excited she passed out. She didn't know I was coming. Ye, it was a real shock.

After that, we did keep in touch more often, I went back to London and I went to Brighton. I tried to help a little bit, I used to put a standing order and a couple of pounds to my dad, my mum. It was something for them. They were happy.

HATICE FETTI: I have never gone to any other country. Lots of years ago we used to go to Cyprus by bus, we went through Turkey and things. I haven't been since. My husband won't go to Turkey. He is too scared to go. I say, "Look, we have been in this foreign country for years, amongst these foreign people, why shouldn't we go to our place, familiar people, to drink our coffee, have our chats?" What would we understand from a foreign country? That's why I haven't made the desire to go anywhere else. If it was left to me, I would go to Turkey, but my husband won't go.

I am very happy with my husband. Thanks to God. I hope that everyone can be as happy as I am. I hope Allah would give everyone my last day. I am very comfortable very. With my husband we have been married for 60 years. We get on, we loved each other and married.

My husband used to work in a bottle factory here. He used to work with leather as well. He continued to do his quilt-making.

No, I never wanted to go back. But I did want to go on holiday every year. No, my husband didn't want either.

My husband made quilts here was well. He used to make a lot of quilts very nice, he used to work in leather factory as well. There were so many customers, Greeks, Turks, many of them. He used to do it with somebody else as partners. It wasn't a shop. Everyone knew where to go, they got used to them. Continuously. That man used to find the work, my husband used to sew it. He used to sew in everybody's house. There was a place with the man that they were partners. In his place there was a space, in his house. They used to go and bring the quilts; they used to sew them there. It was very nice. He made quilts in Cyprus, and continued here. I'm telling you, we didn't struggle at all.

My husband doesn't like the readymade quilts here, because he says they go lumpy, so I bought a stitched one from Cyprus. That's what he likes on the bed.

He did it for many years. Then he gave up. His partner gave up. When his partner gave up, he gave up as well. He started doing quilt-making when we came to this house, in 1963. He used to do quilt-making on many Saturdays and Sundays.

DUDU HAKKI: When I went back to Cyprus in 1963, I went with Emel my daughter, who was young. My sister's husband had died, and I thought I would go and see my sister's children.

GÖKMEN MEHMET: I have no regrets about coming here. I never been back. I went back in 1989. I went to the Dome hotel, and everything to me was different. I have not been back since. I got a flat in Kyrenia, but I never bother to go. I used to go to other countries. When my children was young.

CELAL HASSAN: My brother came in 1953. He wrote an invitation. There was no telephone in those days. It only took a few days to arrive. Because it used to be on a plane. To travel yourself it was very expensive. My brother didn't mention it if he liked it [England] or he didn't like it very much. Every time when I went back to Cyprus, I found the life better here. Because people were more polite, there was trouble all the time since 1960, we were waiting to get better, and last 30 years it never got better. And you can't go and settle down where the place is not settled down. That is the reason you know.

MEHMET ALI BEKIR: I am thinking of going back to Cyprus. Of course not for good. As we are becoming weaker in terms of health, of course because of the job I am doing as well. And as I don't know what the situation is like over there, for example medicine charges, doctor's fees. But suppose if the Cyprus problem were solved, if there was peace, if both groups go into EU, we'd be more comfortable, there wouldn't be a doctor or a medicine problem. Because we will be the same standards [as England].

HÜSEYIN HASSAN MEMOUR: I went back [to Cyprus] in 1955. That is the time the EOKA people began. Greeks wanted to unite Cyprus to Greece. I didn't want to go back because those who know me in this place [London] said, "Don't go back, don't be mad. Stay here!" Because I used down to go to Hyde Park and preach there. "You don't go. Or if you go you'd better behave."

I was teaching when I went back [to Cyprus]. Teaching Bible in three languages at this American School in Larnaka. One of the best schools in the Middle East there. My students were Greek and Turkish, Armenians, some Arabs. Quite a few nationalities, because back in those days we had all sorts of nationalities, from Lebanon, from Ethiopia, Middle East, even from Turkey. I was teaching bible studies in the school. Because it was very, very obvious why I was teaching, how I loved it. But then there was such hatred.

In 1958 I lost my dad, and I couldn't stop [in Cyprus] any more, and I also used to get threatening letters from anonymous persons. Because I was saying that by God's health and love we can live together, and all that, some didn't like my teaching. I left Cyprus in 1958.

SÜHA FAIZ: I had decided in fact in 1960, that I shall never come back, my mother stayed and she lost her house in 1964.

Cyprus has finished for me. What have I got in Cyprus? I was wrong, it wasn't but –

Particularly when after my mother lost her house and she came and lived with us in this big house in Kensington I made the basement a flat and she lived there. Family is here, what else is there, I mean I have got people. Necati is still in Cyprus. What's gonna happen? I didn't think that the Greeks would be so, the Greeks had it all. Bloody idiots. They really are their own worst enemies. Even now, I say this deliberately, there are nice Greeks, like this taxi driver Andreas, there are plenty of others, I am sure. But the people who operate what is going on I am afraid –

As far as my mental state was, I am finished with Cyprus, *Allah a Şükür*, and we shall see, what we shall see and we saw it pretty quickly. Because pretty soon we then get, we are hearing all this, Turks being, this hope here which is a blank with English, what happened between 1963 and 1974, those 11 years. People don't know, and let's be honest we also, I am sure that I would do the same. We use it to our advantage. We did things which I think we should have regretted afterwards, nevertheless we did it, in the light of the circumstances, but still Makarios held the trump hand and they, these idiots and it was the *Junta* particularly who is responsible for this, decided using Samson, similar people but they did it before, that this chap tried to kill Makarios.

EMINE AHMET: First our work kept us here, and now children and grandchildren. We were going to go back after five years. Those five years still didn't come. Our lives had been wasted and those five years still didn't come.

MUSTAFA HÜSEYIN: Some went as substitute, to Cyprus, in 1963. I gave my passport as well at that time but they said enough people from here had gone and soldiers from Turkey went as well, so they said it is not necessary. Then I had two kids, little kids. I didn't go after that. It wasn't our destiny.

Yes, I did want to go. They wanted me as well because I did my national service for the English, I had some knowledge. I had some knowledge about guns and things. As I know English, I could communicate with United Nations.

In the first times I used to keep in contact Cyprus with letters. Or when some went again with letters. I went back in 1969. I went for the first time in 1969, by plane. Then it was with Olympic Airline. There wasn't that much that had changed. In the past, there was only farmers with animals, for example, later on when we went there were tractors, machines. The difference was that. Farmers, shepherds used to chat in the same place, in the same thing, in the same villages. I stayed there I think for four weeks. My wife stayed here with the kids. I went for four weeks.

HATICE IBRAHIM: There was this husband and wife in our house. They were very nice. One day she said, "Look Hatice my girl, have you never been back to Cyprus?" I had been here for 15 years and I had not been.

I had sisters to see in Cyprus. "No," I said. "I will not go" – but I used to work and get £10 10 shillings. I used to work in Elephant and Castle. I used to say I'll save £5 and spend £5 on shopping.

My husband was at the table. "You can't go," he said. "I will go, I will go, I will go," I said. A big fight. He got up and got me by my hair. A big beating, a big beating, I can't explain it.

There was no possibility of going back once the children increased. I went back to Cyprus 25 years later, because I divorced in 1972. I had a young child – don't forget the one that happened by force. The others were at school. The council gave me a three-bedroom flat, and I lived in that and paid rent. I did not receive any payment from the government [social security benefits]. I used to sew clothes, I worked.

Velhasi, after 25, years when I got off the aeroplane, I started to cry and cry and cry. For that land.

15. REFLECTIONS

HATICE FETTI: My dreams came true. I used to want to have a nice house, a comfortable lifestyle. I used to want to go on holiday when I long for, own a car. What else? I would marry my children. I didn't waste them. I brought my children here. Five boys, four, then I gave birth to one here as well. I never wasted them. My children don't have any bad habits. All of them have their business, their job.

I supported them. I used to sometimes speak to my children like a mum and sometimes like a friend. But I used to say, "I brought you here, but I don't want you to be neither a hashish addict nor alcoholic, or a thief." Thanks to God, neither they went into prison. They didn't have bad habits. When it was six o'clock, their table was set. I used to cook their food, their table was set, they would come to eat, and then they would go upstairs, to their rooms, to their television sets.

My life was as I expected. Thanks to God, it was.

KEMAL AHMET DAVRANDI: *Velhasil,* we lived through those days. I started to get used to it after I got married, made money, I had work, a little money. That's when I said, "We'll stay from now on."

I learnt some English. I didn't keep in touch with Cyprus at all, no, no, not at all. No letters, no nothing. We used to hear what was going on in Cyprus in 1963 in cafés. I learned all what was going on in the cafés. I had Turkish and Greek friends. The English used to come in the cafés as well. There were black people too, But only a few would come in there. Life here was very hard. Work things, it won't do not to go to work here. Compulsory.

EMINE AHMED: I have no successes. Nothing, nothing, I am left with disability. Success, there is nothing. That is to say, my children got married – one of them is like this, one is like that. How should I know? I have become disabled. My shoulder is stiff. I had no choice but to go back there. Here the weather doesn't do us good any more. I prefer Cyprus more. That is to say, I prefer my motherland Cyprus more, I have a reservation here. My children. If I didn't have any reservation, I prefer Cyprus more. Because it is person's motherland. Whatever you say, its weather is also better. It is not like here, its weather is better. If I didn't have the kids, sometimes I come, from time to time they come. I miss them as well. I will handle with it, what shall I do. The weather in Cyprus is really nice. It is good for my health.

IBRAHIM DERVIŞ: I am now 78 years old. I can say I was successful, until this very day I help friends with language, with hospital visits. A respectfulness. My most biggest richness is respectfulness from people, from society.

HULUSI MAHMUD: My expectations of London? If they say, "You go along", then you don't expect nothing. You felt more secure kind of thing when you are here, but in Cyprus you felt like you are here now, you are gone tomorrow. All the troubles, which is still there, but not as bad as before. In London if you work you live, if you don't you have got no money.

NIAZI OSMAN: My intentions for here was a future, a good life. There wasn't any in Cyprus. When a person thinks open-mindedly in Cyprus, he would live on very little, and I used to feel that it wasn't a living. Organisations, everything belongs to them. They used to give very little opportunity to us, Turkish people. It is a normal life here, yes. Here, you can buy everything you want, legally for example.

In my opinion yes I have a better life. Thanks to God, we are fine, we make our living well. A holiday in Cyprus.

No, I knew what to expect in London. I found it like I expected. It was advanced, that is how I found it here. My success is honesty, punctuality, if you keep your promise your honesty would be your advertisement. You come for example, a promise is given to you. As you are promised your job is done. You of course will go and tell somebody else, "He is a good person." Through this way I made so many friends. I mean customers. My professional life was like that. Yes, honesty is the biggest success. You should note down your promise, that is to say somebody's called you, it was written, you take the name, telephone number, what is that person's aim. I used to ask my secretaries to do so. Whatever you promised you will do that. I used to ask a lot for example, I used to employ two secretaries there, I used to check them. This honesty has continued, thanks to God.

EMINE AHMET: How can I tell you, I am very happy with my marriage. My husband, God bless him, looks after me, I look after him. My children, God bless them as well, are good. I can't do one day without talking on the phone to them. They call me, I call them. I am very lucky on life's road.

MEHMET MUSTAFA: I had three sons. Can is the eldest one. I think 35, 32.

Now, how shall I say to you. Maybe if we think about the thing that happened in Cyprus I am very happy with my migrant life. I have everything, my kids are at school. I am well off. I made some money, it is not a problem. But when I see these donkeys in Cyprus, they are dying to give Cyprus away, I wish I stayed there. All of my friends are from the members of the parliament. All of them are the same. I mean, most of them. One of them died.

My intentions were like every young people. Now when I see them I feel I shouldn't say anything. All these youngsters would like to come. They say, "But you went to Europe." I say, I make it up, "I came for girls. Why do you want to go?" As a matter of fact, now if they say, "Yes, I am gonna go for girls," maybe I can forgive them. Do you think they should sell Cyprus? Cyprus is living its golden period. In our time, we used to go underneath the bed, because they used to bomb us. It is not the same. When they give a cloth in your hand and say to you have finished college but you're a technical cleaner, it's not on. But now, when I go on holiday, when I go to bed and wake up, I wake up with the call to prayer. I thank to God 100,000 thousand times. There weren't people saying this. There weren't people thinking of this. These would give their everything for Europe.

By God, my achievements, I went to school during my whole life, here as well. Here I have three or four diplomas to do with my trade. I am a good citizen, I went to Old Bailey as a juror, in murder cases. In every sense I am all right. I have no failure, I am happy with my wife. We have three successful sons, one of them still at college and the other two take exams continuously. They earn £120,000 a year, soon the other one is going to earn £120,000 a year. Every week, he pays £1,000 for repayment charges. I went to see his house yesterday, there were two Polish, they continuously do building work for himself. He bought a new house. Both of them bought houses. Both of them, the youngest one didn't buy. He stayed with a Bosnian girl. We look for a Muslim family, he went and said to me, "I am gonna get a Muslim." He found a Bosnian.

Before this I used to do management for Vision Hire. I run the whole Vision Hire company for many years. I had my own staff, I used to cover the North London. All of these Greeks, they have shops here, all of them are businessmen here, ones that work with televisions, and so on, were my former apprentices. I was the manager there. A Mercedes underneath me, I used to come and go like a king.

I can't stay there continuously. Can't be stayed. We were brought up like an English here. As a matter of fact, that is my world. Here is not changing either. I don't like, when somebody breaks the law I get angry.

Now, there is a saying amongst the Turks. "You have eaten this place's fish and chips." They say. You have drunk London's water, it is the same. It is not only that, when I go back, not only when Turkish people, but also Greeks go back they don't feel at home they say.

I brought up my children strict even though they are boys. The one 35-year-old sits down when I say so and stands up when I ask him to stand up. Out of respect. There isn't any respect left now. No respect.

Whoever comes says to me, "Well done! You control your sons." The people at present go to the bad, use hashish and so on. One son only smokes cigarette, I get angry with him "You shouldn't smoke cigarette." "You are lucky, everyone takes hashish, drugs," he says to me.

HATICE IBRAHIM: I have raised my children well, they are married. I have not other happiness other than that. My son-in-laws are very nice. I am very happy.

My experience is that if people are honest and kind-hearted, then you don't slip into bad places. My lodgers supported me in difficult times. I had really kind lodgers. There were families and married couples as lodgers. It has been lots of years since we have seen each other.

I mean, I don't why I didn't like London. I didn't really see London and I didn't really want London. I suppose that because I grew up alone, I wanted to settle down in one place. In that sense.

MELEK KAZIM: When I finally think back to whether it was a good thing coming here, or whether my life would have been different in Cyprus – it was a big mistake in me coming here. I say that. In other words if it was in my hands [if I had a choice] I would not have come here. If you now look around, however many Turkish-speaking people, whatever many mothers and fathers say, children born here are different. Especially these days, mothers, nor fathers know. In other words there is freedom. They go where they want to, do what they want to. I have seen what happens to Turkish girls a lot. That's why it's a mistake to come here [London]. I have never been happy here. I have never liked it here.

I still go to Cyprus regularly. Because my father's family still lives there. Within this negative life, the most beautiful thing for me was my children. My three children. They are all business men. My two sons were musicians. They had albums, they went on TV, but they are now doing business. My son is a millionaire. He is rich. He lived in a penthouse in Epping and he regularly visits different countries due to his work. My oldest son was a little unwell; in March it's been one year since he had an accident. In Switzerland. Whilst skiing. My daughter is a manager in Great Ormond Street. A franchise. A charity thing. I had seven grandchildren. There are six remaining.

In other words, it was very difficult for me. It is still difficult for me. Fifty years in this country and I am still struggling. It has not been good for me here at all. I think it is a big mistake to leave and go to another country, there is this constant longing, a pain, you constantly miss that place, there is this emptiness, and the emptiness is always there. Also you can lose your culture. Like me. I lost my culture. In the end. My children are not going to carry their culture. They don't consider themselves Turkish. They only know about my mum and dad. Only my mum and dad. My youngest son recently went to Turkey due to work.

I am just mum. To me it is important to show love and respect. I don't want anything else from them. Love and respect. In our area now there are many Turks and I can see many. I see how parents speak. Even at this age, I still cannot speak in this way. I cannot speak to an elder in this way. Because I remember what my parents would tell me when I was little.

Now as my parents are not alive, I do miss them. I have Turkish friends that I mix with. I am slowly getting back into the Turkish way of living.

Since my mother died. Three years ago. Yes, for three years I am getting back into it. Yes I attend religious [Muslim] readings, I try to read them, to read the Koran. I am very happy that I am re finding my roots again.

I say that I wish that I listened to my parents when I was older. Yes, I wish, I made a mistake. Both my children married English. That's why I say now I have regrets. Because my children lost their culture.

HÜSEYIN YUSUF: In my opinion, financially, if you work hard enough, you can make what ever you want. But also, my two kids still studying, I spend most of my money on my kids. They all studied. All three of them. In the meantime we went on holidays like everybody else.

Oh, yes, I like travelling. Even when I go to Cyprus I get excited on a plane, things like that. This is something in you and you can't lose it. If you like travelling, if you like where you are going, you get excited. Even I get excited thinking about it sometimes.

I had good times in the Merchant Navy. At first, the beginning was hard when we started first. Because we used to work very hard, cleaning the floor and everything, you know. Serve people food, two seatings at a time. It was really hard the first two years, and I changed companies. I went to a different shipping line. More experienced. It became easier. In the end I became wine butler, which was very cushy. I was my own boss. Money was good. We used to go to Brazil during carnival time, we used to go to a lot of places, you know. To the Far East, to Japan.

Well, it is 30 years since I left. Actually the last time I was talking to one of the captains on the QE2, Captain Jackson his name is. It was when they had the Falkland War. He was still on the QE2 and I rang him up once. He recognised my voice. And this Captain Jackson was an officer when I was in the QE2, we used to trek to together. It is quite interesting you know.

IBRAHIM MUSTAFA: When I came over, in the first few years, The thought never crossed my mind that I would stay forever. Never. I took every day as it came. One day at a time. I must like it [London]. I have been here for 44 years.

How do you say it? It is a different life here than it would have been in Cyprus. In Cyprus, most probably we would have got married; I would be working in the fields. Waiting for the God to make rain so we can produce, you know. That is why it is different. At least here we work, we get the money, we spend it. That is the difference. The quality of life.

I consider my successes and achievements as normal I suppose. If someone asked me what is the best thing that I have done in England, I would say buying a house. Producing two kids. Ye, children. Children, and my grandchildren. All I got is a boy and a girl. Reyhan and Mustafa. I have four grandchildren. Two from Mustafa, and two from Reyhan.

GÜLSEN LARKINS: I raised my children by myself, with my family. Such respect, the whole world talks about my children. My greatest success is my children. My children very educated. One is a painter. My daughter works in Boots. She works in the chemist, all this things. I am very happy, they look after me. My children's names are Ayşen and Mehmet. One my mother-in-law's name, and one my dad's.

ALI HASSAN: We have done successful things. We have live a good life. Some have known this and some haven't. Good work things, house things. We have established all our things comfortably. I have two sons from my latest wife. I have three grandchildren. I now live in Hackney. Now we have bought that place. That is ours too. I have been married to my wife since 1978. We have a 25-year-old son and one 23, he goes to college. He is going to be a an IT 'doctor'.

MERYEM SHEREFETTIN: I'm glad I came to London because of the freedom. It's freedom. Yes, because in our days the Greeks and Turks they start fighting. They just started fighting you know in '55, and we left and we came here. And after we was here, after we left that, they were killing each other and this and that, and we were so glad that we came here. No trouble and up to now. In the beginning we suffered too much. I mean when we came no house, nothing to, how am I going to say? No family, just my brothers here, no mother, no father, no family and we have very difficult times, but now I'm glad I'm here. I'm glad.

You know we work hard, we have good life when we was young, we been holiday and we enjoyed ourselves you know. And I'm still happy, any time I'm not well I can call ambulance and coming and take me to hospital. I don't know about my country very much if they can do that, what I have here. But I'm glad because anytime that I'm ill they are here for me, that is important for me.

I have never thought about going back, no. This is my country, this is my country. Not even in the beginning. In the beginning it was too difficult, I was crying every day and night you know, when you come you feel lonely, you miss your parents, I mean you miss even your neighbours, and when we came here – no Turkish people, only a few here, and I was feeling lonely. Every lunch time I was quickly finishing the lunch and start to write letter, every day letters. Go and come back letters [to and from Cyprus] but now, you know, I'm glad, after we settled down.

MEHMET ALI BEKIR: I only thought about coming to England. I had no other expectations. I mean, it wasn't money that came to my mind, of course in those days life was very different. In the 60s, life was very different from the present time.

If I stayed in Cyprus I might have died, because of events, because I was active [for the Turkish combat].

Today when I look back, my life has passed nice. Even if I didn't make money, my life, without any fear, not afraid of the future, that is to say, even if I was walking on the road, I wouldn't look behind me. Because, how should I say to you, I did all the things I did with these two hands? I've never gone to the bad. Because in our time, it was very easy to go to the bad. We, all of our friends, have never gone to the bad.

At that time, drugs were easier. The rich, for example, at that time to bring drugs to England was easy, because in those days the English weren't shrewd. To manipulate girls was easier. How should I say to you, everything, lawless things were more.

There was no one to take care of me, but there was this [indicates his head]. If I hadn't my intelligence, I would have gone that way very, very easily. I was only three years single in this country. After three years I got married. I never gamble, my only problem was drinking, and smoking. Never gamble, I used to watch gambling, I've never done it, dogs or horses or cars, I have never done them.

When I was single I worked 10 hours a day. After I got married, 60 hours a week, 70 hours a week. Because married, mortgage, we bought a new car, three kids. I didn't make money, it is nothing to do with wealth, being successful is my kids, raising my kids, they are healthy kids, my son, they are getting close to Cyprus now, they wanna move, they wanna live in Cyprus. They had an English mum, but they love Cyprus a lot, by themselves.

My son got married on Cypriot side in Paphos, his wife, is English. After the Cypriot side, he visited Turkish side for a holiday and he liked Turkish side. Now he bought a house there and twice a year they go. This is Turhan, he was a mechanic but now he works in Fort[Ford]Garage. Meral used to work in a bank, she got married. Her husband is in bank. Aydin works for the council. I have three, five, seven grandchildren. Plus two from my step-daughter.

In this country, today, for young people, there isn't, there hasn't been left any love for one's country. How should I tell you, you don't feel homesick, how do they say in Turkish, you don't long for your country any more. That kind of longing for one's country has gone, finished. Because the world has become smaller. I mean if you want go somewhere and come back on Monday, or tomorrow if you want. The distances have become closer. That longing for one's country has gone. When we came it took us seven days. Six nights, seven days. Coming from Cyprus to here. Now, wherever you go, whichever part of England you go to, you can find someone who can speak your language. That longing for one's country has finished.

It took 18 months, two years, for me to learn English. In Pergama in Cyprus, I went to farm school. I never experienced anything here that surprised me. When I came to England, I tried to adapt myself to the English lifestyle. In those times, for example, they used to come and leave the milk bottle outside your door. Nobody would touch your milk. You wouldn't lock the door. Doors were open, your friend, family would come in straight away. Your car is open, the key are on its door, nobody touches, no alarm, no nothing. In those years we wouldn't know thievery. People were more, how should I say, more honourable, more trustworthy. Whether English, or whoever you want.

But at present, how should I say to you, is it because unemployment, or did people's manners go out of order, or people are doing one thousand kinds of things to earn money? Because of excessive drugs, excessive hashish, people started going into thievery. The old lifestyle is not left in England. Of course it is not left in Cyprus either, but we don't know that. We know what we lived in this country. Old lifestyle in England is not left at all.

How should I say to you, as I said to you, I never liked England and still I don't like it, its weather or its people. Let's not go into politics now. I can't say this is my country. But my country is not Cyprus. Because when I go there I feel myself a stranger over there, and a stranger here.

Of course I got used to here more because how should I say to you? I lived 20 years in Cyprus, 45 years in England. This is my place. Stranger over there, stranger here too. But you would feel better here.

I have a son for example, 17 years old. He would like to go Cyprus as well. Look, I should tell you something. We human beings are like birds, when those birds are free, what do they do? Those birds would go, work to feed, nourish their kids. We are the same. How would I say how we feel stranger in Cyprus? I would say something to you; people, friendship is dead there as well. Friendships have gone. Environment has changed. That is to say, we Turks are more attached to each other here. They greet me as a stranger there. Yes. Love is not left there either. That is why, whatever we do, for example here we Turks are together more. There is more love amongst us. In Cyprus that has gone, finished, died.

One reason young people go to Cyprus might be hearing things about Cyprus from their parents. Longing, like English people would like to go to Australia, New Zealand, for a new life. They feel exactly the same thing when we come to this country. But they try to do best they can in that country. Because the same thing when we came to this country, we try to easy our life. Improve our quality. When they run away, wherever they go.. Which is interesting. The things we were looking for here, they are looking for there.

I always said there were three lives in Cyprus, we have got two lives here. Work and sleep. In Cyprus they have got three lives: sleep, work, and enjoy themselves. No social life here. At all. They have it. Probably when our kids go and see, they can see different kind of life, completely different than us.

The reason for me not to be able to go back was because of getting married. Marriage stopped me. Both she was a foreigner, and of course we bought a house. You will pay for the mortgage. You can't run away, either. Because of the system. That is to say, losing everything and running away. The reason for not being able to go there is mostly your attachment here; you set up a family here, bought a house, now you can't run away and lose everything… Because you have a settled family here, the mortgage has to be paid. You can't take the risk of going by destroying this. But for example now I can do that. Because now another life is beginning for me. The children don't need me. Because of my age, that is to say staying in this country doesn't have any thing left for me. For example, no one knows how long he is going to live for. That is why we would like to live in our country.

CELAL HASSAN: My biggest success is to get to England, you know, but I tried very hard. To get married, to settle down, make a family and then when I go home I have some hot food to eat, you know anything like that, wash your clothes by your wife, work together.

SÜHA FAIZ: The answer to your question is I don't think I am successful by the normal standards of success, it doesn't matter to me anyway. But to be reasonably satisfied with your life, I think I am reasonably satisfied. For one thing I think and I hope I have a family which I think one can be proud of, whether they are successful in inverted commas is another matter again.

SADIYE BAYRAM: My dear my life is like a novel, it's like a novel.

FEZILE AHMET: I came here but was never ever with my husband. Never ever, I tell you.

Of course it was very hard. You're closed in one room, you have to sleep in the same room. You sleep, get up go to work, come back late, it was hard. There was no one to talk to about your problems. My brother used to go into their room, and I would sit in the other. We used to live together. When they got married, they had one room and we all shared the other room. There was only one [bed]room. There was a gas cooker in the hallway that we all used to use to cook. It was very, very, very hard.

When I first worked in Kentish Town, I had no friends. In the first 12 years there was a Pembe Hanım, Ilkay and Sema, we used to chat but only at work. I used to go to work everyday, and we would talk there, but there was no chatting when I got home. I have been here for 42 years, and I don't know the way to the West End. I did not go sightseeing when I first came here. My brother used to bring me a plate of food that I would eat in the morning, afternoon and in the evening. I swear to God it was like this. Believe it or not, I cannot lie. My brother was working hard, he didn't have a car or a horse, so where could he take me? We didn't really go out. My brother used to take me to an aunt and a cousin who lived in Finsbury Park.

Later on I had a friend called Pembe, she has passed away now, and there was her husband Mustafa Abi. He used to take us out. I'm not lying, There's a God. We went to Southend, Brighton and Devon. We went twice to Devon. I met them about three years after I came here. I had never been to central London, I swear to God, but even if I wanted to see other places, what would they be? Look, my brother did take me once to see the Queen's house and park. This was a long time after I came. One day I came home, and he said, "Let me take you to see the Queen's park." I remember him taking me there.

When I first came here, I wanted to go back to Cyprus. Because I had no one here, no one to chat to. I would go to work all day, then come home at night, with bras to clean the cotton from until the morning. At first I used to cry a lot. Night and day I would cry.

There weren't telephones around like there are now in everyone's hands. You used to have to wait for letters to arrive in order to get news. I couldn't read or write, so I had to wait and listen to others while they read them for me. What could I do? It was very hard. How can I tell you this? For someone who cannot read and write, it was very very hard. Work helped me get used to living in London.

I used to say to myself, "As I have come all this way, I should try and save enough money to buy a house in Cyprus, so that I can lay my head down when I retire."

That was my intention: "I don't want them to laugh at me," I used to say to myself. I didn't want others to say, "Look, she has come to London, has been here for years, and has returned without achieving a thing!" Because of that I was very tight with my money and very economical.

Thank God I have somewhat achieved something. I haven't achieved anything here. I worked. What have I achieved? All these years I have worked, and have built a smallish house. When I go [back] there, no one can say that I am out in the open.

There's nothing that I can think of that I would still like to achieve or do. After all this time, what am I capable of?

Of course I am pleased now. To tell the truth, I wasn't happy back then because there was no one to have chats with, all we did was work and sleep. I'm happy now but it's too late because we are old now. Thank God I am comfortable now.

I go back and forth to there.

GÖKMEN MEHMET: I was a good mother, good friend, so far so good. Everybody love me, everybody respect me. I have lots of English friends. My customers still come round to see me.

I have done everything that I wanted to do. Thanks to God. I got good children and grandchildren. The older daughter has a very good job and Tina is very educated.

ŞABAN LEFKARIDI: When I was in Cyprus, it may sound like I'm boasting, people who know me, the lifestyle I had in Cyprus, I have been unable to have. When I was in Cyprus, not everyone had a suit, I had seven suits and each suit's shoes were different. Because we had a vineyard, our income was quite a lot. Everyone thought that when I came here, I came with a great deal of money. In fact when I came here I had £8. I used to like eating, drinking, going out. In our village let's say, after finishing the olives, vineyard, grapes, if I went to Lefkosa, I would for a month. If I went to Larnaca I go for a month. To Limassol it is the same.

I even used to say, "If one day the people run away from Cyprus, I will be the last one to run away." I used to say it like that, I swear it is so. I now say, "Look how it happened later [turned out], I left and came before everyone else!" That is to say, thanks to my Allah one thousand times, I am happy with my life.

Vallahi, until now many thanks to my Allah, until now I have had no problems. Only on these women issues, we have become separated from kids.

People must be clean-hearted, lying, mischievous behaviour, cheating somebody, those are idle things. You should be honest, not deceive anyone, not eat somebody else's money. That is my belief. Many thanks to my Allah, one thousand times thanks, until now I have never remained deprived of anything by God. Many thanks again, I am making my living as I wish.

MUSTAFA HÜSEYIN: Wouldn't a person miss the place he was born in; wouldn't a person miss the place he has grown up? Wouldn't a person miss his family? Of course you miss it. You miss everything. You miss its soil, weather, you miss it.

You can never get used to being here. You never say, "OK, this is my place, my country." It can never be. Of course. I sometimes go three times a year. Sometimes when I get fed up, I would get my ticket and go with my wife, together. Thanks to God, the money we receive from the government is enough. The kids have grown up, all of them have a job. They don't have any needs. There is no change. When I stay here I pay more than £40 for the petrol for the car anyway. It is better to stay there. I can live on £40 per week comfortably.

We go to café and talk about the old days. Why shouldn't we? But not about longing or sufferings, no. Thanks to Allah we didn't suffer. We didn't become rich but our life was average. Neither poor, nor richness. We lived on the money we earned.

I succeeded, I succeeded. The biggest thing is to become a grandfather. I would see the grandchildren, become happy; what else should I wish for. Do I have any other success? Richness is that. Whatever the richness is, it is love and respect.

NEVCIVAN JEVAN: I got used to it now, because everything is easier now. I don't work now, my house is well equipped. Everything is proper. Central heating. I don't have to go to public bath anymore.

We used to phone and send letters to our family. Well now, we got used to here when we had children.

DUDU HAKKI: I have been here for 45 years. Since 1960. I came here for a holiday. I still have not done what I came here to do, sight-see! We once went to Windsor. Someone visited from Cyprus; I think it was my nephew Şakir.

London! London! London! It wasn't how I hoped it would be. You thought that you would find an ease of life. But we met with lots of difficulties, because there was no ease of life. Firstly you have no acquaintances, no relatives; secondly you have to go to work. Nobody would even donate you a halfpenny if you want to buy bread here. Then there was the fog, the snow, the buses, the trams.

Vallaha, I'll tell you, I haven't achieved anything. I have lived with ill health. Worries, worries, worry for this person, worry for that person, worry for this and that. I have had lots of problems and illnesses. I have not been successful at all.

Sometimes I say maybe it would have been better if I had never come here. I would like to go back, but my husband has passed away, and what would I do alone there? He really wanted to go back. But there were the Troubles. Somehow we were unable to return. I worked a lot here. I always worked, always on the machine. Thank God my children are healthy, they have studied, they are independent. I am happy from that point.

I came here, thinking I was going to be going back but then I got married and wanted to stay in this country. I wanted to open a business, run a business. I bought three shops but was unable to run them with my husband. He didn't want them anyway. He would shout and then we would sell up the following year.

I used to work on the machine day and night, and was bored and wanted to open a business and he didn't. So we would buy and sell, buy and sell. This is what I have been unable to achieve. That's what I wanted.

ALI GASBAR: I have become a good businessman in this country. A man who is respected in every job he has done, loved, given importance and value to his thoughts, is a helpful person who is proud.

I have a 45-year love marriage, and I am still in love with my partner like the first day. We are like the halves of one apple. She is my everything. I have three children. One son is a businessman and is occupied with trading; my middle son is a policeman and my little daughter a hairdresser. I have two granddaughters and four grandsons. I think I have everything a person could have in life. A successful work life, a magnificent soulmate, decent, intelligent children and six magnificent grandchildren.

Friendships and relationships continue with remaining friends, and when possible we come together speak of the old days and be happy.

REŞAT NIAZI: Anyway when I came the Turks were very few. Cypriot Turks came after the 60s. They started to come after the 60s. Turks from Turkey after the 70s.

SEYIT MEHMET: I have two daughters. I have got, my granddaughter she is a nurse in Kings College Hospital. She went to university for three years. she is a Staff Nurse. She is 23 now. My grandson is only 17. He goes to university next year I think. She [my first daughter] was born in 1958 and the other one was born in 1960.

I have to help my wife with the children. I used to, I remember, both were born in Guy's Hospital. I bought plastic bath and I use to bath them myself sometimes. My wife, we got married, three months later she become pregnant, she never worked until my children were 14, 15 years old. Housewife.

My successes and achievements couldn't have been better. When I look back, I worked hard in my life. I got married, I raised children, I educated them and they married and settled down. I give them a nice wedding party. I am living now with my wife. I am getting old. If I look back I am a very happy and content man. If I come back again, I would do the same thing. Nothing I regret.

I honestly say that, I have been married 49 years, and she has been a good mother and a good wife. We precise and very clean. My children where young, three months, and she used to bath them everyday and when they started to go to school in Ilkerton Road, she used to change the older one in the morning and come back from school and change her in the afternoon. Even the Head Teacher, Mrs Howard was her name, she was saying, "What a lovely mother she is!" And they used to call her the Lady of Bermondsey. She was really very very clean, good wife and good mother. You couldn't have any more.

ÇETIN KAYA MUSTAFA: After I got married I used to get depressed [in Cyprus], the one who got used to London can't stay in Cyprus easily. When you get old it changes. But when you are young, how should I say to you, everything is slower in Cyprus. It is not like here. Here if you have wisdom you can make money. You buzz about, you do it, that is to say the jobs to do are a lot. Opportunity. Whatever you look for you find it easily. It is exactly the opposite there. I mean, there it is like, it is something like a stillness.

I like my place a lot. I don't see myself like a tourist. I go there to see my family, and every time when we go to Cyprus, I long for to stay there. Because people are all over you, for example they treat you nice.

When you get old here, you say "I am gonna go to Cyprus and stay there." I told photographer Hassan. Nureccin Abi. I said, "Oh, you have grown old now, Simsak. You will stay there."

"Why am I gonna stay there? I am forced to come here for my medicine," he said. Because when you grow old this time you are OK, but this time you are under the care of your doctor. You will go and come back. That is the easiest one. Sometimes here, they always do that. Wise people do that. Three months there, three months there. Time passes, you wouldn't know. As long as your health is fine. The important thing is that.

But there isn't a place like our place, tell the truth. That is to say, no matter how much you love London, in the end you say my country, my country. I won't forget Cyprus. I am now a Turkish. Turkish Cypriot. But I've spent most of my time in London, tell the truth. I would be considered as an English but I don't want to accept it. I am a British citizen but I will never forget my Turkishness. I would say, even if you forced me, I would say that I am a Turkish Cypriot. I don't like that. We many Turks here always talk with a Cypriot accent. We made our children used to it as well. When our children speak for example, the youth here, they speak like us that they like it a lot. I mean, you want to remember your home, talking and everything. Home sweet home. No place could ever be like our own place. What is it here, we live on, eat, drink, easy.

EMINE MEHMET: I came back here and I felt like I had returned home because my husband was here, we had friends, work friends and so and so. I mean I got a book from the Post Office and started to save a little money. In other words, I mean I began to warm to [London]. We bought a radio, gramophone. I helped to save £3 to buy one. We used to always play records. We always played Turkish records. There used to be a record. [The words were something like] 'No brother, no nothing,' it was a sad record. I would put in on and cry in that period of time.

Now here has become ours. Now we prefer it here. Now wherever I go I miss this place. Because my home, my place is here. Most of my life has been here. I was 22 when I came. Most of my life has passed here. My children are here, my grandchildren are here. The corpses of my mother and father are here, my husband's, my brother's corpses are here, my nephew's corpse is here, my uncle is here, all dead.

One by one, they all died here.

Has it been as I expected? I suppose it has been as I expected.

v. KEY TO MAJOR POLITICAL FIGURES

MUSTAFA KEMAL ATATÜRK

As the first President of Turkey, Atatürk was responsible for the cultural reforms that followed his appointment (e.g. the fez was banned and Turkish men were encouraged to wear European attire). The hijab (scarf which covers the head) for women, while never formally banned, was strongly discouraged and women were encouraged to wear western apparel and enter the country's workforce. From 1926 the Islamic calendar was replaced with the Gregorian calendar. In 1928 the government decreed that the Arabic script be replaced by a modified Latin alphabet.

(1881 – 10 November 1938)

GLAFKOS CLERIDES

Clerides participated in the 1959 London Conference on Cyprus, and during the transitional period from colonial administration to independence (1959-1960) he served as Minister of Justice. During the same period he was Head of the Greek Cypriot delegation in the Joint Constitutional Committee. In July 1960 he was elected to the House of Representatives which, in turn, elected him as its first President. He held this position until July 1976. In the first presidential elections Clerides backed Makarios III, the other candidate being his father Ioannis Clerides.

(24 April 1919 –)

RAUF RAIF DENKTAŞ

Denktaş was the first president of the Turkish Republic of Northern Cyprus (TRNC) until 2005, having served four five-year terms in that office. In 1957, Denktaş helped found the Turkish Resistance Organisation (TMT), an organisation that was formed to resist EOKA's struggle to proclaim Enosis (Union With Greece). In 1960 Cyprus won independence from Britain, and the Republic of Cyprus was established. Denktaş was elected as the President of the Turkish Communal Chamber. In 1976 he was elected President of the Turkish Federated State of Cyprus, condemned by the United Nations. and only recognised by

Turkey. He played a key role in the 1983 proclamation of the Turkish Republic of Northern Cyprus (TRNC). Denktaş was the chief negotiator in the UN sponsored peace talks from 1968 till 2005, when Mehmet Ali Talat succeeded him as President.

(27 January 1924 −)

KENAN EVREN

Evren led the 12 September 1980 military coup in Turkey against the elected civilian government. After the coup, he became President of Turkey on 7 November with the approval of the new constitution that was submitted to a public referendum. He is considered to have ruled the country with an iron fist until 9 November, 1989. He seemed to have great admiration for the founder of Turkey, Kemal Atatürk, but he shut down some institutions founded by him, and is often accused of deforming the country's legal system against Atatürk's principles. It was also during the power of Evren that TRNC was declared in 1983.

(1918 −)

NIHAT ERIM

A Turkish political figure and jurist, in 1956 Erim participated in the negotiations on Cyprus in London. The same year, he was selected as the Turkish member of the European Commission on Human Rights and served in this position until 1962. He lead the Turkish committee on the preparation of the Cyprus constitution in 1959, following Zurich and London Agreements. He continued legally advising the Turkish committees at further negotiations on Cyprus at the United Nations. He served as the prime minister of Turkey from 1971 until 1972, for about five months. He was assassinated on 19 July, 1980 in Istanbul.

(1912 - 1980)

HUGH FOOT

Foot was the Colonial Secretary of Cyprus, 1943-1945, and then became the last colonial Governor and Commander in Chief of Cyprus 1957 to 1960.

(8 October 1907 − 5 September 1990)

GEORGE GRIVAS

Also known as Digenis by Greeks, a name he adopted while in EOKA. Between 1955 – 59 he led the Cypriot liberational anti-colonial struggle against the British, EOKA. He was given the leadership of EOKA by Archbishop Makarios, and found great support, especially among the youth of the island. He left Cyprus in 1967 after a crisis which seriously escalated when the Cyprus National Guard under Grivas attacked TMT forces in the Turkish Cypriot village of Kofinou. He once more returned to Cyprus from Greece secretly in August 1971, to form and lead the underground organisation EOKA B, again with the rallying cry of Enosis. The official cause of his death was heart failure, but some of his supporters still claim that he was murdered.

(1898 – 27 January 1974)

DR FAZIL KÜÇÜK

The first and only Turkish Cypriot Vice President of the 1960 Republic of Cyprus. In 1941 Küçük founded the newspaper *Halkın Sesi (The Voice of the People)* and became managing editor. Owing to his campaign against the British colonial administration, his paper was not given a permit for publication until 1942; the paper exists to this day. In 1943 he was one of the founders of KATAK but following disagreements with other members he later formed *Kıbrıs Türk Milli Birlik Partisi* (Turkish Cypriot National Union Party). On 3 December 1959 Küçük was elected Vice President of the new Republic, unopposed until its breakdown in 1963. Küçük continued representing the Turkish Cypriot community until 1973, when he was succeeded by Rauf Denktaş.

(1906 – 1984)

MAKARIOS

Born Mihalis Christodoulou Mouskos, Makarios was archbishop and primate of the autocephalous Cypriot Orthodox Church (1950 – 1977) and first President of the Republic of Cyprus (1960 – 1977). He became a leading advocate for Enosis, and during the early part of the 1950s he maintained close links with the Greek government. Makarios, characterised in the British press as a crooked Greek priest and viewed with suspicion by the British authorities, was exiled to the Seychelles on 9 March 1956. Released after a year he went to Athens and continued to work for Enosis. On 1 March 1959 the archbishop returned to Cyprus to an unprecedented reception in Nicosia, where almost two-thirds of the adult Greek Cypriot population turned out to welcome him.

(13 August 1913 – 3 August 1977)

GEORGIOS PAPADOPOULOS

Papadopoulos was the head of the military coup d'état that took place in Greece on 21 April, 1967 and leader of the military government that ruled the country during the period 1967 – 1974.

(5 May 1919 – 27 June 1999)

JOHN REDDAWAY

Reddaway was a diplomat who served as Deputy Commissioner-General of the United Nations Relief and Works Agency, 1960 – 1968 Served in the Colonial Administrative Service, Cyprus, 1938; Imperial Defence College, 1954; Administrative Secretary, Cyprus, 1957-60. Director-General, Arab-British Centre, London, 1970 – 1980.

(12 April 1916 – 25 June 1990)

For further information and detail on any of these figures, see www.wikipedia.org

vi. GLOSSARY

Aba or Abla	Turkish Cypriot version of the word *Abla*. Added to the name of an older male. A respectful term of address to a female.
Abi	Added to the name of an older male. A respectful term of address to a male.
AKEL	Anorthotikon Komma Ergazomenou Laou (Progressive Party of the Working People). A communist party in Cyprus, taking into account current international political and economic developments. It supports an independent, demilitarised and non-aligned Cyprus and a federal solution for the internal aspect of the Cyprus problem. It places particular emphasis on rapprochement with the Turkish Cypriots.
Allaha ısmarladık	Good-bye said by person leaving, to which the response is *Güle Güle*.
Allah inandırsın seni	May God help you believe this (said if the speaker thinks something is unbelievable).
Allah Rahmet Eylesin	May God have Mercy on him.
Allah a Şükür	Thank God!
Bacanak	The husband of one's wife's sister.
Bey	Gentleman, Sir. Sometimes used by women referring to their husbands.
Boylu poslu	Used to describe someone tall and well developed, handsome (male or female).
Ciras / Ciracık	Term used most by first-generation Turkish Cypriots when referring to a Greek Cypriot woman. (Is considered a derogatory term by some but also used colloquially.)
Dayı	Maternal uncle, mother's brother.
Davul Zurna	A type of drum and reed instrument.
Delikanlı	Youth, young man.

Dünür	The mother-law or father-in-law of one's child. Frequently used to describe relative-in-laws.
Efendi	Gentleman, a well-bred, polite, courteous person. Sometimes used by women referring to their husbands.
Enosis	Greek for Union. Primarily used to refer to the unification of Cyprus and Greece, it became a political issue and a goal of Greek foreign policy, during the years of British colonial rule in Cyprus (1878-1960).
EOKA	Ethnike Organosis Kyprion Agoniston (National Organisation of Cypriot Fighters). A nationalist organisation formed by Archbishop Makarios and headed by George Grivas (see list of Key to Major Figures) with ambitions for Enosis. (Active 1953-1959).
EOKA-B	A Greek Cypriot right-wing pro-*enosis* paramilitary organisation formed in 1971 supported by the ruling Greek junta which came to power in 1967 overthrowing the legitimate Greek government of George Papandreou. When George Grivas returned to Cyprus in 1971 he created EOKA-B in response to President Archbishop Makarios's deviation from the policy of Enosis.
Eyvah	My God! How awful!
Gavelle	Word used mostly by first-generation Cypriots meaning oh dear me!
Git Işine	Go on your way!
Gözün arkada kalır	Going forward with your heart casting a backward glance.
Gonga	Also known as kongen, A card game.
Hanım	The female equivalent of bey.
Hellim	Turkish Cypriot word for a cheese made in Cyprus, also known as Helloum.
Helva	A sweet dessert.
Hoş Bulduk	A welcoming greeting said by the guest in response to *Hoş Geldin,* which is said by the host.
Junta	"The Regime of the Colonels", or in Greece "The Junta" is a collective term to refer to a series of military governments that ruled modern Greece during 1967-1974. Nicos Sampson was the Junta leader in Nicosia, Cyprus.
Kabile reisi	Chieftain.
Kollakas	Root vegetable cooked by Cypriots.

Lakab	Cypriot word for nickname.
Lefkara işi	Embroidery from the Village of Lefkara.
Maşallah	May God preserve him/her from evil.
Molohiya	Type of leaves that are cooked by Cypriots.
Muhtar	Village Elder, Head of a village or neighbourhood.
Nene	Turkish Cypriot word for Grandmother.
Neşber/Neşbercilik	Farmer/Farming.
PEON	Pankyprios Enotike Omospondia Neoleas, a Greek Cypriot youth movement in the early 1950s. Its registration was withdrawn in 1953 owing to its subversive activities. Members from this movement were later recruited to EOKA by Grivas.
Pilavuna	Cypriot pastry made with cheese, raisons, aniseed and sesame seeds.
Rahmetlik	The late…(strictly speaking applies only to Muslims)
Sizlere ömür	He or she has passed away. He or she is dead.
TMT	Türk Mukavemet Teşilatı (Turkish Defence Organisation). A Turkish Cypriot resistance group formed by Rauf Denktaş to counter the Greek Cypriot Fighter's Organisation EOKA, in response to the growing demand for Enosis. The TMT was active mainly between 1957 and 1974, promoting partition (in Turkish: Takism) for Cyprus. The TMT's motto was Ya Ölum Ya Taksim. (Death or Partition)
Usta	Master. Used by Turkish Cypriots when referring to a boss or someone who they work for.
Uşak	Boy or youth.
Uyuz Oldum	I have become unkempt or ratty-looking
Vallahi/Valla	I swear.
Velahsi/Velahasil	In short.
Zeytinli Bitda	Cypriot olive bread that can also be made with Hellim.

vii. MAP

The following map appears courtesy of the Royal Geographical Society.

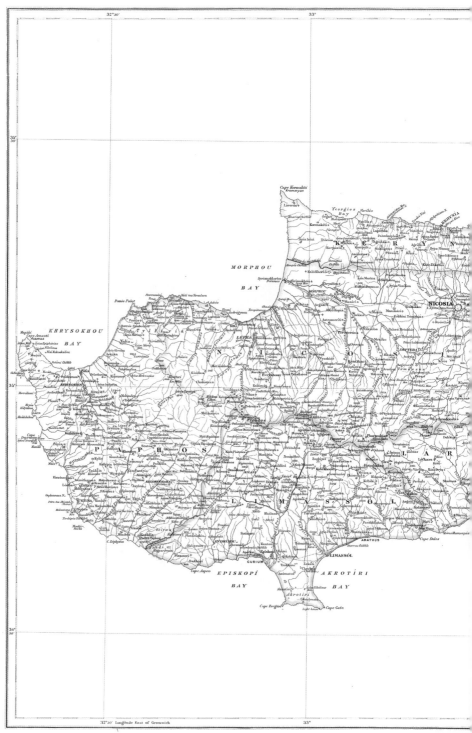

CYPRUS

Scale 1: 506.800; 5 English Miles to 1 Inch

EXPLANATION

Roads	———	Chief Town of District **FAMAGUSTA**
Roads in Construction	....	·· Subdistrict *MÓRPHOU*
Telegraph Lines	-·-·-·-	
Boundaries of Districts	———	Ancient Places **SALAMIS**
·· Subdistricts	··	

Mon.	—	Monastery
(R.)	—	Rais
Pano	—	Upper
Kato	—	Lower
Ayia	—	Saint
Ayioi		

Heights in English feet 6406

Ancient villages are distinguished thus +

Modern ·

55 Charing Cross.   1905.

viii. NOTE FROM THE EDITORS

Hatice Abdullah and Mark Sinker, Editors

Where are you from?

One of the most interesting things noted while interviewing contributors for this book, first-generation Turkish Cypriots, was how often interviewees asked the question "Where are you from?" Many other questions were asked, but every interviewee asked this particular one, at the start of each interview. It soon became apparent that it was commonly asked, by most of these first-generation Turkish Cypriots, of all other unfamiliar Turkish Cypriots. But why, exactly?

This collection of interviews and photographs from old family albums is intended to give insight into the social history of the Turkish Cypriot migrant community in England between 1935 and 1963, in other words, from the earliest arrival date we knew of until the time of the constitutional crisis and the eve of the Troubles. We drew up a list of potential interviewees and contributors from names put forward by colleagues, family members, friends, as well as responses to an advertisement in the Turkish paper [*Toplum Postası*] The personal and intimate family histories documented were to be from Turkish Cypriots who relocated to England during these years. We made a conscious effort to include Turkish Cypriots from all across London, making contact with community organisations in Haringey, Hackney and Southwark.

The interviews took place in informal environments – the people's homes, local cafés, the Turkish Cypriot Community Association – with participants often enjoying such traditional home-made foods as *zeytinli bitdtas* and *pilavuna*. Those selected were asked a standard set of questions, to help structure and guide the interviews. Most interviews were conducted in Turkish, a few in English, the language determined by the interviewee's preference. As so often with oral history projects, the interviews developed in a conversational manner, with interviewees given the option to respond to as many of the questions as they wished. The interviews were then transcribed, translated if need be, and edited for cogency and clarity.

When turning the results into this book, we decided to break the interviews up into 15 sections, reflecting both the original questions asked, and the shared themes and areas that had emerged. This allowed us to highlight subtle differences within the wide range of detailed variation in perception, response and feeling to what might – to outsiders – seem a broad similarity of experience. The edited transcriptions and translations are not verbatim, generally containing question and answer – but apart from this we have tried to conform to the individual speech characteristics of each contributor. Maintaining strict official correctness of English grammar would have imposed an unrepresentative tonal sameness on these many voices. Better, we felt, to retain some of the flavour and vividness of an interviewee's personal style of speaking, in Turkish or English. Importantly, no attempt has been made to verify or validate accounts through other sources. We have tried to ensure all names are spelled correctly, but given the vagaries of memory across the decades, and the number of languages involved – certainly Greek, Italian and Hebrew as well as Turkish and English – we have sometimes had to approximate (especially with the names of ships). A glossary of Turkish words – in particular words used in Cyprus but not in Turkey – is included, as is a biographical key to some of the major historical figures mentioned.

This publication presents an account of the integration of the first generation of Turkish Cypriots into their new home, through their own memories, and their own understanding and interpretation of their experiences during the period under examination. Their first sense of London, their view of themselves and their identity as members of a migrant community as well as their subsequent integration into British society, were significantly shaped by their earlier experiences in Cyprus. With the help of these invaluable personal contributions, we feel this publication gives the reader an insight into Cyprus itself, and its cultural climate and politics during these decades.

So, "Where are you from?" It turned out what interviewees wanted to know, when asking this question of a second-generation Turkish Cypriot, was actually which villages the parents come from. Why is it of such interest to know where someone's parents come from? What may it mean to each of these first-generation Turkish Cypriots now resident in London? Is it a means of identification? If so, of who? Relatives within their own generation? Or did it help identify common links – via Cyprus – between themselves and a younger generation? For some migrants the relationship between their place of origin and where they now live – in terms of defining their cultural own identity – appears straightforward and resolved; for others it leads to confusion and contradiction. First-generation Turkish Cypriots may or may not maintain strong links with Cyprus since leaving it, but it still seems deeply to inform their sense of identity, even when they have lived in London for the majority of their lives.

Even the wealth of invaluable information gathered since interviewing began in October 2004 merely touches the surface of the astonishingly rich history of this community. No conclusion about or extensive evaluation of the contents of this publication can be offered here – any such attempt would conflict with the purpose of this project. But the doors have been opened, we sincerely hope, for further investigation and enquiry into the Turkish Cypriot Heritage in England.